To the Reader

Over the past 15 years, financial optimists have encouraged all kinds of risky behavior, such as: investing in stocks ("for the long run"), real estate ("it never goes down"), oil ("the world has run out"), commodities ("China must have them"), precious metals ("gold is going to $10,000"), hedge funds ("quants have it all figured out") and even PIK junk bonds ("the economy is just beginning to recover"). Despite setbacks and bloat in these markets, everyone still agrees that deflation is impossible–central banks won't allow it. If you read *Conquer the Crash*, you'll get a different story.

If you were fortunate enough to have read the first edition of Robert Prechter's *Conquer the Crash*, your money was safe and sound during the first phases of meltdown in all these markets. If the author is right, the most intense portion of the financial crisis is yet to come, and those who are properly positioned will not just survive but prosper. So you can still benefit from this book, in fact more now than ever.

This brand-new third edition is being published near another peak in social optimism, with the Dow and S&P stock indexes at all-time highs, bears calling for hyperinflation, economists calling for 4% growth and officials content that they have saved the financial system. If you think all is well and your finances are safe, read this book before it's too late. If you act soon, it could save your financial life. If you put your money to work at the coming bottom, it could make your fortune.

About the Author

Robert Prechter, Jr., is a social theorist and market analyst. He is President of Elliott Wave International (elliottwave.com), a publishing firm serving investors around the world. Prechter has authored 14 books. His *Elliott Wave Principle* (1978) with A.J. Frost predicted the great bull market. *Conquer the Crash* (first edition, 2002) forecasted the unprecedented financial meltdowns that followed in 2002 and 2008. He thinks there is one more meltdown to go, by far the biggest yet.

Prechter's two-book set *Socionomics* (1999/2003) presents his seminal hypothesis that endogenously regulated waves of social mood determine the character of social actions. His Socionomics Institute (socionomics.net) is dedicated to explaining and applying socionomic theory.

For more information, please visit RobertPrechter.com

Reviews Appearing after CTC was Published

"*Conquer the Crash* woke me up to the realizations of long term changes in the economy and how they affect everyone, regardless of what news or goverments try to do. Before we had read the book, we had some money in savings and a house, car payment, some debt but no real direction of how to use money or avoid the mistakes with money....Since *Conquer the Crash*, we are now 95% liquid, sold our house at what I believe is the top of the housing market, and are living well below our means with almost 10 times what we started with in savings....I just wanted to give you my heartfelt thanks BEFORE the crash and your predictions come true (which I believe they will)."
—Kevin McGlothan, email

"I can understand the deflationist warnings of Robert Prechter, the Dean of the Deflationist School. His book, *Conquer the Crash,* is the ultimate reference book on deflation—The Deflationist Bible. The general importance of the inflation-deflation debate lies in its investment implications—inflation means investing in one set of assets, and deflation in a different set of assets. Assets appropriate for an inflationary environment can lose dramatically in a deflationary environment. The opposite is also true—assets appropriate for a deflationary environment can lose value dramatically in a inflationary environment. Whether one believes in a coming deflationary depression or not, one must nevertheless read the book and understand its arguments."
—Krassimir Petrov, PhD (blog)

"Most of what we read about in the financial columns today was brilliantly explained by Robert Prechter in his best seller of 2004 [paperback edition], *Conquer the Crash*....His explanation then of the likely unfolding of events is closer to what is happening right now than any other commentator present or past."

—Bill Bonner, quoting a reader from Australia, *Bits of News*

"The chapter on real estate was particularly prescient [in explaining] the games played by banks, mortgage brokers and property appraisers—the no-money down loans, the juiced up home valuations, the home equity withdrawals that were bigger than properties were worth—that made the credit binge possible. And there was this warning: Financial institutions that invest in mortgage-backed securities will 'surely regret' it....

"The good news—if you can call it that—is that when the economy, the stock market and real estate finally hit bottom, there's going to be one heck of a buying opportunity. Even Mr. Prechter agrees on that. So it wouldn't hurt to keep some cash on hand, just in case he turns out to be right."

—John Heinzl, *Globe and Mail*

"Prechter is a stock market technician who analyzes historical stock prices and patterns using the Elliott Wave Theory....In 2002 he wrote a book titled *Conquer the Crash: You Can Survive and Prosper in a Deflationary Depression*. In it he correctly forecast a huge credit contraction, brought on by all the mortgage debt issues that we're now facing.

"Reading this book today, it seems as if Prechter had a crystal ball. That's why his current view of the market is so compelling....He says the 'credit implosion' is not finished. Much like Japan, he predicts, we'll have to live through a long period of declining assets, summed up in one word: deflation."

—Terry Savage, *Chicago Sun Times*

"I looked into Robert Prechter's forecasts once I learned that early 2007 is when he positioned his subscribers for a stock market top. I read *Conquer the Crash*, and I have never been so riveted with a non-fiction book in my entire life. He describes things that had already begun to happen, and he wrote this book in 2002! *Conquer the Crash* describes how we get to, what will happen, and how to survive a deflationary depression."

—David Brown (blog)

"I have to shut my mouth around people who have lost 50% while I have gained 100% in one account. Do yourself a favor and read *Conquer the Crash* without delay."

—Biotechmgr (blog)

"Call him the ultimate contrarian. He is one man who did not flinch in the face of overwhelming majority of market commentators who predicted soaring inflation following the credit-awash policy central banks chose to drown the world in. Instead, he was steadfast in his belief that the outcome would be far more dangerous, i.e. deflation. The script he laid out in his book *Conquer the Crash* in 2002 has vividly played out since August 2007 as the credit implosion finally reared its ugly head."

—*Outlook PROFIT*

"I like the book *Conquer the Crash* by Bob Prechter and have been recommending it to people for years. Rooted in decades of serious research, published in 2002, this book was a frighteningly accurate predictor of the 2008 crash. It explains the 'big picture' of how economic conditions ebb and flow over time, how to profit from them and how to avoid getting caught in the inevitable squeezes that wipe out the unwary (i.e. 99% of the world.)"

—Ken McCarthy, *Independence Day Blueprint*

"Six years from his being a voice in the wilderness on deflation, most has come to pass now. It is frightening, even for the 'prepared.'"

—Tom McGraw, email

"I recently had the good fortune to attend a lecture given by Bob Prechter—his purpose was to update his 2002 book, *Conquer the Crash*....Prechter's brilliant insight is to note that the laws of supply and demand cannot be properly applied to the financial markets because there are no producers to provide the supply curve required for establishing price equilibrium.

"Neither prophets nor intellectual iconoclasts are often honored in their own time....Fortunately, as befits a man focused upon the future, Prechter has responded to this challenge by laying a solid, methodological foundation which can readily be built upon by others interested in following in his footsteps."

—Vox Day, *WorldNetDaily*

"Robert Prechter of Elliott Wave International and the leading proponent of socionomics (social mood determines events, rather than the other way around) has been, in my mind, one of the only analysts/pundits/economists out there who has legitimately called both the deflationary credit crisis and the ensuing rally that we are in now. His unique method tracks the stock market as a barometer of social mood which patterns itself in distinct formations representing fear and greed. The reason I believe that Prechter has been nailing the tops and bottoms of the last few years is because of his contrary position as to the causal nature of social and economic events."

—Matt Stiles, *Futronomics*

book lays one of the essential cornerstones of capital preservation. If you argue with its premises or dismiss its conclusions, the price could well be your permanent loss of wealth."

—Jean-Pierre Louvet
Founder & CEO, The SafeWealth Group

"This book outlines brilliantly and simply the rationale for how and why the bubble developed. Prechter will go down in history as a legend for having predicted the secular bull market and now having provided a lucid description of the economic cataclysm that unfortunately lies ahead. I urge you to read this book and give it to your loved ones, as it provides great tactical advice on how to prepare yourself financially. Reading this book could make the difference between agony and comfort over the next twenty years."

—David Tice
Prudent Bear Fund

2014: Last Chance to
CONQUER *the* CRASH

2014: LAST CHANCE TO
CONQUER THE CRASH
YOU CAN SURVIVE AND PROSPER IN THE DEFLATIONARY DEPRESSION

Robert R. Prechter, Jr.

New Classics Library

2014: Last Chance to
Conquer the Crash
You Can Survive and Prosper
in the Deflationary Depression

Third Edition published by New Classics Library

Printed in the United States of America

For information, address the publishers:
New Classics Library
Post Office Box 1618
Gainesville, Georgia 30503 USA
Phone: 800-336-1618, 770-536-0309
Fax: 770-536-2514
E-mail address for products: customercare@elliottwave.com
E-mail address for comments: feedback@elliottwave.com
Web site: www.elliottwave.com

New Classics Library is the book publishing division of
Elliott Wave International, Inc.

ISBN: 978-1-61604-067-3

Dedication

This book is dedicated to all my friends and colleagues at Elliott Wave International, who put up with months of my single-mindedness in producing this book.

Acknowledgments

In putting together this volume, I had invaluable help from Robert Prechter Sr., Lou Crandall, Pete Kendall and Jean-Pierre Louvet, who provided expert information that enhanced certain chapters in this book. Rachel Webb, Sally Webb and Angela Hall did the charts and formatting, and Robin Machcinski and Darrell King designed the jacket.

Contents

Book One: WHY A STOCK MARKET CRASH, MONETARY DEFLATION AND ECONOMIC DEPRESSION ARE LIKELY TO OCCUR SOON

Part I: The Case for Crash and Depression

Part II: The Case for Deflation

Book Two: HOW TO PROTECT YOURSELF AND PROFIT FROM DEFLATION AND DEPRESSION

UPDATE for 2014 Edition

Preface
to the 2014 Edition

The stock market began crashing in real terms in 1999. That's when the purchasing power of stocks, as measured in real money (gold), began a plunge that took values down by 86%, as shown in Figure 1. I call it the Silent Crash.

Record inflating by the Federal Reserve has fooled investors into thinking that stock prices have held up. But stocks haven't been rising; the value of the measuring unit has been falling.

Figure 1

Incredibly, the Fed's record $4 trillion credit expansion since mid-2008 hasn't stopped real estate, commodities or precious metals from losing value even in *nominal*-dollar terms. The Fed's stupendous inflating is having a limited effect.

The new wave of optimism beginning in 2009 has prompted banks and hedge funds to leverage the Fed's new credits primarily toward the purchase of stocks. But that game is about to end. Many measures of investor sentiment (see Section D) show more optimism and more risk today than at any time in stock market history—even more than in 1929, 1987, 2000 or 2007. Optimism has also propelled the total amount of dollar-denominated debt to its highest in history and the quality of the debt to the lowest in history (see Section F). Every financial crash has had the same setup. This one is the biggest yet.

Now it's time for the *nominal* value of stocks to fall, too. That's why I'm issuing this 2014 edition of *Conquer the Crash*.

If you didn't convert to cash at the all-time highs for real estate in 2006, commodities in 2008, gold and silver in 2011, and the bond market in 2012, you have one last opportunity to exit a market at an all-time high, this one in stocks. Aggressive speculators should benefit from a once-in-a-century ride on the short side.

Book One of this volume (the analytical portion) is republished exactly as it appeared in the original edition. Book Two (the strategy section) is also the same, except that printings in 2003-2005 added some bits of new material, which are retained here. The 2014 Update begins on page 269 and includes amended recommendations and bank ratings.

Investors who survive and prosper by following the advice in this book will be alone in having ample funds to invest at the final bottom. It should prove to be one of the greatest buying opportunities of all time.

—*Robert Prechter, June 2014*

Foreword

"Look out! Look out! Look out! Look out!"
— Barry, Greenwich and Morton,
via The Shangri-Las

My first book, *Elliott Wave Principle*, which I wrote with A.J. Frost, was very bullish. It came out in November 1978, with the Dow at 790. Today the outlook is much different. Now is not the time to take financial risks. It's time to batten the hatches so you can emerge safe from the storm.

As you can see by this book's title, I am once again calling for events that few expect. But this time, I feel more trepidation about doing so. Deflation and depression are exceedingly rare. Sustained deflation hasn't occurred for 70 years, and the last one was so brief that it lasted less than 3 years. During the past two centuries, there have been just two periods that historians unanimously identify as depressions. The 19th century had one, and the 20th century had one. Predicting such extraordinary events is a complex and challenging task. Everyone who has tried it in the past fifty years has failed. Amidst today's social psychology, merely addressing the ideas of deflation and depression is considered something akin to heresy or lunacy. Survey after survey shows that most economists believe that depression and deflation, considered together or separately, are utterly impossible now if not *ever*. Most believe that the U.S. economy is in a rising trend of perpetual prosperity with moderate inflation and that if any interruptions do happen along the way, they will be mild and brief.

Despite this overwhelming consensus, I am resolute. Book One tells you why, and Book Two tells you what to do if you agree with my conclusions.

If by some bizarre circumstance you are already convinced that preparing for deflation and depression is your desired course of action, you can turn to Book Two right now. If not, then you need Book One. Before you can take steps to protect yourself against a deflationary crash and depression, you have to understand what they are, believe that they are possible, and then agree that they are *likely*. Guiding you to that point is Book One's goal. After you assimilate those ideas, you will be primed to act confidently to insure your survival and prosperity, as outlined in Book Two.

Warning

I've been wrong before. The biggest mistake of my career was in the stock market. After identifying the start of the great bull market and later forecasting, "Investor mass psychology should reach manic proportions," even I never imagined that the stock mania would last as long or go as high as it did. So I jumped off the train too early. Regardless, I think my *basic interpretation* of the long-term financial picture, which we will explore in Chapter 4, is correct. It has never been a matter of whether we would experience a tremendous bull market followed by a historic bear, only a matter of timing and extent.

The reason that I remain willing to express my unconventional view is that I believe that my ideas of finance and macroeconomics are correct and the conventional ones are wrong. True, wave analysts make mistakes, but they also make stunningly accurate long-term forecasts. In contrast, those who do not understand waves can't make any useful social predictions at all.

It may seem to you that the prospect of taking actions that are contrary to the beliefs of a vast array of experts is a big risk to take. But a practical point virtually eliminates that risk: If you follow the advice in this book and no financial crisis occurs, you cannot get hurt. In fact, you should profit nicely from most of these suggestions. Even if my outlook proves incorrect, the worst case is that your money will earn less than it otherwise may have. Compare these outcomes to the opposing scenario: If conventional economists, who in the aggregate have a perfect record of failing to predict economic contractions, are wrong again, you will lose everything that you have worked so hard to obtain. You will also blow the chance to make a fortune beginning at the next major bottom.

Here's a bonus: If you end up missing out on some of the investment profits that a decade of prosperity can provide, I hereby truly apologize; I know what it feels like to miss an opportunity, and I will regret that I influenced you to do so. By contrast, if you get destroyed financially by following the bullish advice of economists, money managers, brokers, media experts and the like, they will not apologize. They will claim that the future was unforeseeable, so *the rock-hard convictions and platitudes that they cavalierly expressed, the ones that you relied upon to plan your financial future*, were wrong through no fault of their own.

There is one catch: I refuse to offer you an excuse to disclaim all responsibility. If you lose your money, your house, your income and your pension in a deflation and depression, at least you can blame the experts for it. You can cry, "I did what they all told me to do!" If you take action after reading this book, I insist that you do so because you agree with my case, not because you are blindly following my conclusions. To be successful in life, or at least to learn something along the way, you have to think for yourself.

—Robert Prechter, March 2002

BOOK ONE

WHY A STOCK MARKET CRASH, MONETARY DEFLATION AND ECONOMIC DEPRESSION ARE LIKELY TO OCCUR SOON

PART I

THE CASE FOR CRASH AND DEPRESSION

Uncomfortable woman in car: "I'm sitting on something!"
W.C. Fields: "I lost mine in the stock market."
                                    —*International House* (1933)

Chapter 1:

A Myth Exposed

How many times over the past decade have you heard glowing reports about the "New Economy"? Hundreds, maybe thousands of times, right? Those of you who have been living on a desert island or who are reading this book fifty years from now can experience the same thing vicariously through Figure 1-1, which displays the accelerating frequency with which the global media have been referring to the "New Economy" year after year. It's been everywhere. Economists celebrate the broadening "service economy" and proclaim that economic growth in the new Information Age has been "unprecedented" in its vibrancy, resilience and scope. Rhetoric is cheap. Evidence is something else.

What would you say if you discovered that we have not had anything near a New Economy, that all that talk is a lie? This chapter is going to show you that the vaunted economic expansion of recent decades in the world's leading economic power, the United States — much less the rest of the world — is far less impressive than you are being led to believe.

First take a look at Figure 1-2, which depicts the U.S. stock market from its low in 1932 during the Great Depression all the way to the present. This graph delineates five phases — or "waves" — of rise and fall.

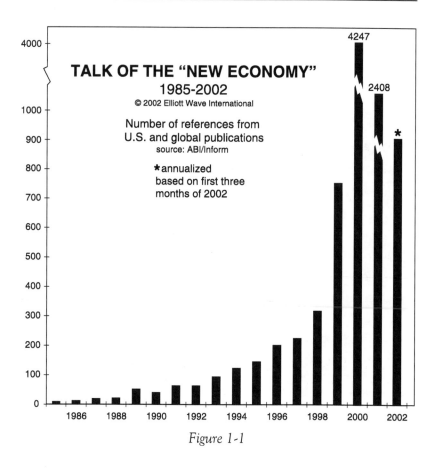

Figure 1-1

The notes on the chart summarize a shocking fact: The economic expansion during the latest phase, wave V, which lasted from 1974 to 2000, was demonstrably weaker than that during the preceding rising phase, wave III, which lasted from 1942 to 1966. Both periods sported a persistent bull market in stocks that lasted about a quarter century, so in that sense, they are quite similar. One noticeable difference is that the DJIA gained only 971 percent during wave III but a remarkable 1930 percent during wave V, twice the amount. This tremendous bull market in stocks in wave V is the great "boom" that people feel in their bones. Yet as you are about to see, the economic vigor

Figure 1-2

and financial health of wave V, the one that has received so much radiant press, failed to measure up to those of wave III by every meaningful comparison.

Please go through the following citations one by one. (Economists do not have all the data from the 1940s, so in some cases, our data for wave III begin later.) After you absorb this information, we will set to the task of finding out what it means.

Comparative Measures of Economic Health

(see Figure 1-3)

Gross Domestic Product

- In wave III, from 1942 to 1966, the average annual real GDP growth rate was **4.5** percent.

- In wave V, from 1975 through 1999, it was only **3.2** percent.

Industrial Production

- In wave III, the average annual gain in industrial production was **5.3** percent.

- In wave V, it was only **3.4** percent.

Figure 1-3

Combining GDP and industrial production figures, we may generalize from the reported data that the economic power of wave V was one-third less than that of wave III.

Capacity Utilization

Factories' capacity utilization depicts the energy of an economic expansion compared to the infrastructure's ability to handle it.

- In wave III from 1948 (when figures became available), capacity utilization rose 22 percent to **91.5** percent in June 1966 and stayed high through the late 1960s.

- In wave V, capacity utilization was net flat, peaking in January 1995 at **84.4** percent. U.S. plants were producing at only 82.7 percent of capacity at the ensuing peak in June 2000.

Unemployment Rate

This is an economic measure of *ill* health.
- In wave III from 1948 (when data became available), the monthly average of the unemployment rate was 4.9 percent.

- In wave V, it was 6.6 percent.

Comparative Measures of Debt, Deficits and Liquidity

(see Figure 1-4)

To grasp the full measure of the underlying weakness of wave V's "fundamentals," one must look beyond economic figures to the corporate, household and government balance sheets that underlie those results.

Balance Sheet Items at the End of Wave III vs. Wave V
(scales at left)

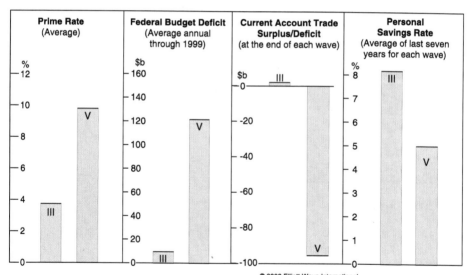

© 2002 Elliott Wave International
Data Courtesy of Ned Davis Research and Federal Reserve Board

Figure 1-4

Households' Liquid Assets

• At the end of wave III, households' liquid assets were **161** percent of liabilities.

• At the end of wave V, households' liquid assets were **93** percent of liabilities, meaning that they had *less cash on hand than they had liabilities.*

Federal Debt

• At the end of wave III, federal debt was **43.9** percent of GDP.

• At the end of wave V, it was **58.6** percent.

Consumer Debt

• At the end of wave III, consumer debt was **64** percent of annual disposable personal income.

• At the end of wave V, it was **97** percent.

Total Debt as a Percent of GDP

• During wave III, from 1949 to 1966, total credit market debt as a percentage of GDP slipped slightly from **151** percent to **148** percent.

• In wave V, it rose from **172** percent to **269** percent.

Prime Rate

• In wave III, the prime rate of interest, the cost of money for the highest quality corporate borrowers, averaged **3.74** percent.

• In wave V, it averaged 9.66 percent, nearly three times as high.

Federal Budget Deficit

- In wave III, federal budget deficits were not sustained. The only consecutive years of deficits were in the war years of 1942-1946. The average annual federal deficit was less than **$9** billion.

- In wave V, the annual federal deficit averaged **$127** billion, which is far greater even when adjusted for inflation.

Current Account Trade Figures

- At the end of wave III, the U.S. showed a net Current Account trade *surplus* of **$1.3** billion.

- At the end of wave V, the Current Account showed a record *deficit* of **$96.2** billion.

Personal Savings Rate

- In wave III, the personal savings rate followed a fairly flat trend, bottoming at **6.5** percent of disposable personal income in February 1969.

- In wave V, the personal savings rate dropped persistently, falling to a record low of **0.5** percent in March 2000.

U.S. Balance Sheet (not shown)

- At the end of wave III, the U.S. was a net **creditor**.

- At the end of wave V, the U.S. was a net **debtor**, owing a record $2 trillion more to foreigners than it is owed.

These figures, dramatic as they are, do not reveal the full extent of wave V's inferior relative performance because both the government's economic reports and corporate accounting methods changed during wave V in such a way as to overstate wave

V's economic vigor. If we adjusted for those cosmetic alterations, most of these figures would reveal an even greater dichotomy between the two periods. If we begin wave V's figures in 1982 to put the expansion in the best possible light, they change little and in a few cases are worse. If the Dow were to manage a new high in coming months, we would have to add the weak economic and financial figures of the past two years to wave V's average performance, which would drag it down even more. So you see, *it has not been a New Economy after all* but rather a comparatively lackluster one.

Economic Deterioration During the Final Decade of Wave V

The economic expansion waned not only on a long-term basis but also on a near-term basis, within wave V. While real GDP stayed fairly steady throughout the bull market, some measures showed a subtle but persistent slowdown in economic vibrancy. For example, average annual corporate profit growth fell from **10.8** percent in the first 15 years of the bull market to **8.8** percent in the 1990s, a decline of about **20** percent. From the stock market's low in September/October 1998 through the third quarter of 2000 (the peak of economic performance for that period), profit growth averaged only **4.6** percent, revealing further slowing as wave V crested.

Portent of Reversal?

Collectively, these statistics reveal that the economic advance in the United States has been slowing *at multiple degrees of scale*, a trend that is still manifest today. A continuation of this trend will mean that the expansion that resumed in October 2001 will be the briefest and weakest yet.

The persistent deceleration in the U.S. economy is vitally important because, in my opinion, it portends a major reversal from economic expansion to economic contraction. Chapter 5 will expand upon the reasons for this conclusion. As we are about to see, though, we need not rely on hypothesis alone. The 20th century provides two great precursors to the current situation.

The U.S. in the 1920s

If you recall your economic history, you know that a phrase in vogue in the 1920s was that the economy had entered a "New Era." Economists of the day, as President Hoover ruefully recalled in his memoirs, gushed over the wonderful economy, just as they are doing today. Were the Roaring 'Twenties truly a New Era, or was such talk a spate of hype spurred by the good feelings associated with a soaring stock market?

According to data from Professor Mark Siegler of Williams College (MA), from 1872 through 1880, the annual inflation-adjusted Gross National Product of the United States rose from $98 billion to $172 billion, a **68** percent gain. From 1898 to 1906, real GNP rose from $228.8 billion to $403.7 billion, a 56 percent gain. In contrast, from 1921 through 1929, during the Roaring 'Twenties, GNP in the supposed "New Era" rose from $554.8 billion to $822.2 billion, only a **48** percent gain. This latter performance was particularly poor given that the stock market enjoyed a greater percentage rise from 1921 to 1929 than it had done in any equivalent time in U.S. history.

Similarly to today, the economy of that time failed to keep pace with the advance in stock prices and under-performed the prior expansion. The aftermath was the Great Depression.

The Japanese Experience and Its Implications

If you are over 20 years old, you surely remember the "Japanese Miracle" of the 1980s. The country's products were the best in the world. Its corporate managers lectured and wrote books on how they did it, and the world's CEOs flocked to emulate their style. The Japanese Nikkei stock average soared, and foreign investors poured into the "sure thing." Was the Japanese economy truly miraculous, or once again were economists ignoring economic statistics and simply expressing the good feelings associated with its stampeding stock market?

Figure 1-5 shows real GDP growth in Japan from 1955 to the present. Notice that Japan's growth from 1955 through 1973 was extremely powerful, averaging **9.4** percent per year. But its economic growth from 1975 through 1989 averaged only **4.0**

Figure 1-5

percent per year. This relatively poor economic performance coincided with a record-breaking stock market boom. Just as in the U.S. in the 1920s, the economy in Japan's celebrated years failed to keep pace with the advance in its Nikkei stock index and under-performed the prior expansion. This double dichotomy signaled an approaching reversal of multi-decade importance in both stock prices and the economy. Since the top of its own "wave V," the Nikkei stock index has plunged 70 percent, the economy has had three recessions in a dozen years, and the banking system has become deeply stressed. As we will see in Chapter 8, this downtrend isn't over yet.

A Naked Emperor

The "New Era" of the 1920s ended in a bust. The "Japanese Miracle" of the 1980s ended in a bust. Is that what will happen to today's "New Economy"? We have already gotten a hint of the answer. The next seven chapters will provide a definitive reply to that question.

When historians return to this time, I suspect that they will discover the slow but persistent regression in both U.S. and worldwide growth over the decades in the latter half of the twentieth century and wonder why so few recognized it as a signal of the coming change.

Chapter 2:

When Do Depressions Occur?

Depressions are not just an academic matter. In the Great Depression of 1929-1933, many people lost their investments, their homes, their retirement plans, their bank balances, their businesses — in short, their fortunes. Revered financial professionals lost their reputations, and some businessmen and speculators even took their own lives. The next depression will have the same effects. To avoid any such experience, you need to be able to foresee depression. Let's see if such a thing is possible.

Defining Depression

An economic contraction begins with a deficiency of total demand for goods and services in relation to their total production, valued at current prices. When such a deficiency develops, prices for goods and services fall. Falling prices are a signal to producers to cut back production. In response, total production declines.

Economic contractions come in different sizes. Economists specify only two, which they label "recession" and "depression."

Based on how economists have applied these labels in the past, we may conclude that a recession is a moderate decline in total production lasting from a few months to two years. A depression is a decline in total production that is too deep or prolonged to be labeled merely a recession. As you can see, these terms are quantitative yet utterly imprecise. They cannot be made precise, either, despite misguided attempts to do so (more on that later).

For the purposes of this book, all you need to know is that the degree of the economic contraction that I anticipate is far too large to be labeled a "recession" such as our economy has experienced eleven times since 1933. If my outlook is correct, by the time the contraction is over, no economist will hesitate to call it a depression.

Depressions and the Stock Market

Our investigation into the question of forecasting begins with a key observation: Major stock market declines lead directly to depressions. Figure 2-1 displays the entire available history of aggregate English and American stock price records, which go back over 300 years. It shows that depression has accompanied every stock market decline that is deep enough to stand out on this long-term graph. There are three such declines, which occurred from 1720 to 1784, 1835 to 1842 and 1929 to 1932.

To begin to orient you to my way of thinking, I would like to explain Figure 2-1's title. The stock market is modern society's most sensitive meter of social mood. An increasingly optimistic populace buys stocks and increases its productive endeavors. An increasingly pessimistic populace sells stocks and reduces its productive endeavors. Economic trends lag stock market trends because the consequences of economic decisions made at the peaks and nadirs of social mood take some time to play out. The Great Depression, for example, bottomed in February 1933, seven months after the stock market low of July 1932. So psychological trends create economic trends. This causal relationship between psychology and the economy is the opposite of what virtually everyone presumes, so do not be alarmed if you find it counter-intuitive. Chapter 3 will elaborate on this theme.

If you study Figure 2-1, you will see that the largest stock-market collapses appear not after lengthy periods of market deterioration indicating a slow process of long-term change but quite suddenly after long periods of rising stock prices and eco-nomic expansion. A depression begins, then, with the seemingly unpredictable reversal of a persistently, indeed often rapidly, rising stock market. The abrupt change from increasing optimism to increasing pessimism initiates the economic contraction.

Figure 2-1

The graph shows that these reversals do not appear after every period of rising stock prices but only after some of them. If you are guessing that maybe one of the hints of reversal is a slowing economy in the face of such advances, you're right. We'll learn even more about this factor in Chapters 3 and 5.

Hierarchy in Finance and Economics

You might be interested to know that almost every smaller stock market decline observable in Figure 2-1 also led to an economic contraction. The severity of each contraction is related to the size of the associated stock market decline.

Unfortunately, this hierarchy in economic trends is difficult to display because conventional quantitative definitions of recession get in the way. Sometimes the economy just fails to breach the arbitrary definition of "official recession" that economists use, so their graphs show no recession when in fact the economy contracts, corporate earnings fall, and economic indicators weaken. In some cases of brief or small stock market declines, the economy simply slows down without actually having a "negative" month or quarter, but an effect occurs nevertheless.

Modern attempts to quantify the term "recession" by absolute size are flawed. It would be as if botanists decided to define "branch" or "twig" by length and width. The result may denote an "official" branch or twig, but the definition would obscure the actual continuum of sizes attending parts of trees. Likewise, attempted quantifications of the term "recession" derive from and foster misunderstanding with respect to the hierarchical nature of economic expansion and contraction. It would be far better for economists to adopt the perspective of the Wave Principle, a model of hierarchically patterned financial market change, which we are about to encounter in the next chapter.

All We Need

Such discussions aside, Figure 2-1 is all we need for our purposes. It shows that the biggest stock market declines follow long periods of advance of like degree. They lead to economic contractions so dramatic that nothing gets in the way of their being noticed and recorded as "depressions." Now let's see if we have the means to anticipate their arrival.

Chapter 3:

When Do Stock Markets Turn from Up to Down?

We see that depressions accompany major stock market declines. So if we can predict those rare and dramatic bear markets, we can predict depressions. Can we do that?

The Stock Market Is Patterned

In a series of books and articles published from 1938 to 1946 (available in *R.N. Elliott's Masterworks*, 1994), Ralph Nelson Elliott described the stock market as a fractal. A fractal is an object that is similarly shaped at different scales.

A classic example of a self-identical fractal is nested squares. One square is surrounded by eight squares of the same size, which forms a larger square, which is surrounded by eight squares of that larger size, and so on.

A classic example of an indefinite self-similar fractal is the line that delineates a seacoast. When viewed from space, a seacoast has certain irregularity of contour. If we were to drop to ten miles above the earth, we would see only a portion of the seacoast, but the irregularity of contour of that portion would resemble that of the whole. From a hundred feet up in a balloon, the same thing would be true. These ideas are elucidated in Benoit Mandelbrot's *The Fractal Geometry of Nature* (1982) and numerous publications since.

Scientists recognize financial markets' price records as fractals, but they presume them to be of the indefinite variety. Elliott undertook a meticulous investigation of financial market behavior and found something different. He described the record of stock market prices as a specifically patterned fractal yet with variances in its quantitative expression. I call this type of fractal — which has properties of both self-identical and indefinite fractals — a "robust fractal." Robust fractals permeate life forms. Trees, for example, are branching robust fractals, as are animals' circulatory systems, bronchial systems and nervous systems. The stock market record belongs in the category of life forms since it is a product of human social interaction.

How Is the Stock Market Patterned?

Figure 3-1 shows Elliott's idea of how the stock market is patterned. If you study this depiction, you will see that each component, or "wave," within the overall structure subdivides in a specific way. If the wave is heading in the same direction as the wave of one larger degree, then it subdivides into five waves. If the wave is heading in the *opposite* direction as the wave of one larger degree, then it subdivides into three waves (or a variation). Each of these waves adheres to specific traits and tendencies of construction, as described in *Elliott Wave Principle* (1978).

Waves subdivide this way down to the smallest observable scale, and the entire process continues to develop larger and larger waves as time progresses. Each wave's degree may be identified numerically by relative size on a sort of social Richter scale, but to keep things simple, this book's brief references to specific degrees use their traditional names.

Figure 3-2 shows a rising wave in a manner more consistent with Elliott's detailed observations about typical real-world development. Observe, for example, that waves 2 and 4 in each case take a slightly different shape.

Figure 3-1

Figure 3-2

Understanding how the market progresses at all degrees of trend gives you an invaluable perspective. No longer do you have to sift through the latest economic data as if they were tea leaves. You gain a condensed view of the whole panorama of essential trends in human social mood and activity, as far back as the data can take you.

Why Is the Stock Market Patterned?

For the most part, consumers judge prices for bread and shoes consciously and reasonably according to their needs and means. When human beings value financial assets, they must contend with a debilitating lack of knowledge and feelings of uncertainty. They contend with these obstacles to a great degree by forming judgments in sympathy with or in reaction to the opinions and behavior of others. This surrender of responsibility makes them participants in a collective, which is not a reasoning entity. The fact that price changes are patterned proves that the collective's net valuations are not reasoned, but it also shows that they are not random, either. The remaining option is that they are unconsciously determined. Indeed, shared mood trends and collective behavior appear to derive from a herding impulse governed by the phylogenetically ancient, pre-reasoning portions of the brain. This emotionally charged mental drive developed through evolution to help animals survive, but it is maladaptive to forming successful expectations concerning future financial valuation. The only way for an individual to temper the consequences of the herding impulse and to gain independence from it is to understand that it exists. For some evidence of these conclusions, please see *The Wave Principle of Human Social Behavior* (1999).

Examples of Real-World Waves

Figures 3-3 through 3-6 display advancing waves in various financial markets. As you can see, they all sport five waves up.

SAMPLE ELLIOTT WAVES

Figure 3-3

Figure 3-4

Figure 3-5

Figure 3-6

These five-wave patterns proceeded relentlessly, ignoring news of every imaginable variety, including Prohibition, a crash in Florida land values, Roosevelt's seizure of Americans' gold, Hitler's rise to power and the end of the Vietnam war.

I chose these examples because they display one of Elliott's guidelines, which is that bull market waves often end after reaching the upper parallel line of a trend channel. In most cases, the market creates channels in which the lower line touches the bottom of waves 2 and 4, while the upper line touches the top of wave 3 and, later, wave 5.

A Quiz

OK, now you try it. Figure 3-7 shows an actual price record. Does this record depict two, three, four or five completed waves? Based on your answer, what would you call for next?

Figure 3-7

"Surveying all the market's action over the past 200 years, it is
comforting to know exactly where you are in the wave count."
— *The Elliott Wave Theorist*, November 8, 1982

Figure 3-8

Let's compare your answer with mine. *The Elliott Wave
Theorist* in September 1982 called for the Dow to quintuple to
nearly 4000 and on October 6 announced, "Super bull market
underway!" The November 8 issue then graphed the forecast for
the expected fifth wave up, as you can see in Figure 3-8.

I have purposely kept this example as simple as possible. To
view the detailed labeling and real-time analysis that fully justified the prediction made in Figure 3-8, please see the discussions
attending the Appendix and Figure 5-5 and 8-3 in *Elliott Wave
Principle*.

As you can see, Elliott waves are clear not only in retrospect. They are often — particularly at turning points — quite clear in prospect. I could fill a book describing other triumphs (and failures) of applying the Wave Principle, but I hope this one example conveys its occasionally immense value for forecasting.

What Are the Signs of a Topping Stock Market?

Simply stated, a stock market uptrend ends when five waves of a specific construction are complete. The larger the degree of those five waves, the larger will be the ensuing partial retracement of their progress.

The real world is not as tidy as an idealized depiction of a wave, just as real trees are not as tidy as any single summary depiction of a tree in general. Often third waves are long, with distinct subdivisions. Sometimes first or fifth waves extend in the same manner. Using price patterns alone, there can often be some doubt as to whether one is accurately identifying a fifth wave or whether it might be part of another wave's extension.

To help overcome difficulty in real-world application, I recorded certain traits that waves seem always to display. Figure 3-9 illustrates some of these traits.

For the purposes of this book, the most crucial description is the one attending wave 5: "Market breadth and the economy improve, *but not to the levels of wave 3*. Optimism creates lofty valuation." These observations, which I formulated in 1980 after studying myriad fifth waves, tell us four things to look for any time we presume that the stock market is in a major *fifth* wave rather than a first or third wave:

(1) A fifth wave must have narrower "breadth" than the corresponding third wave, i.e., there must be fewer stocks advancing on the average day in a fifth wave than in the preceding third wave of the same degree.

Elliott Wave Characteristics
© 1980/2002 Elliott Wave International

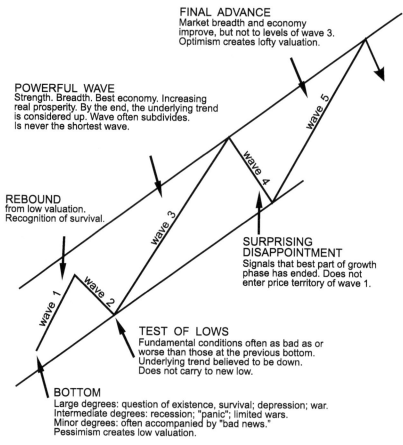

FINAL ADVANCE
Market breadth and economy
improve, but not to levels of wave 3.
Optimism creates lofty valuation.

POWERFUL WAVE
Strength. Breadth. Best economy. Increasing
real prosperity. By the end, the underlying trend
is considered up. Wave often subdivides.
Is never the shortest wave.

REBOUND
from low valuation.
Recognition of survival.

**SURPRISING
DISAPPOINTMENT**
Signals that best part of growth
phase has ended. Does not
enter price territory of wave 1.

TEST OF LOWS
Fundamental conditions often as bad as or
worse than those at the previous bottom.
Underlying trend believed to be down.
Does not carry to new low.

BOTTOM
Large degrees: question of existence, survival; depression; war.
Intermediate degrees: recession; "panic"; limited wars.
Minor degrees: often accompanied by "bad news."
Pessimism creates low valuation.

Figure 3-9

(2) In a fifth wave, there must be a lesser expansion in the economy and weaker financial conditions than occurred during the corresponding third wave.

(3) Stocks must attain high valuations based on their historic relationship to related data.

(4) There must be evidence of optimism among investors.

While we have already learned something along these lines in Chapter 1, Chapters 5 through 7 will discuss each of these aspects in detail, one at a time, with respect to today's stock market.

These distinctions, helpful though they are, do not eliminate uncertainty in interpretation. For example, sometimes fifth waves are quite brief, and other times they go on and on. Their own five-wave subdivisions will in turn display the proper characteristics of waves, of course, helping us to assess the picture. But because these wave characteristics are relative, there can always be more development that still reflects these guidelines even after the market has already met the minimum criteria.

That being said, we can often be certain of important things. For example, using the above criteria, we can *know* that a certain wave is — or is not — a fifth wave. The bigger it is, and the longer it has lasted, the more important that information becomes. Early in the process, we can anticipate the ultimate reversal; later in the process, we can begin to assert boldly that a downturn is imminent.

The reason that identifying the end of a fifth wave is so important is that when a fifth wave ends, a correspondingly large bear market ensues. That's what happened after each one of the bull markets shown in Figures 3-3 through 3-6. At this point, we have enough knowledge to figure out the position of the stock market in its wave pattern *right now*.

Chapter 4:

The Position of the Stock Market Today

Figures 4-1 through 4-3 display my interpretation of the stock market's wave position today at three degrees of trend. Once again, I am keeping these illustrations and explanations as simple as I can. Many fascinating nuances attend these structures, and you will be well rewarded for taking the time to study them via Elliott Wave International's publications if you are so inclined. Suffice it for now to say that the foregoing conclusions are consistent with the analysis of the main wave practitioners of the past century: R.N. Elliott (1871-1948), Charles J. Collins (1894-1982), A. Hamilton Bolton (1914-1967) and A.J. Frost (1908-1999). Their published works on the subject — along with my own — are available in their entirety (aside from a handful of Elliott's lost "market letters") for review at elliottwave.com/books.

Figure 4-1 shows the uptrend of a postulated "Grand Super-cycle" wave Ⅲ from 1784 (plus or minus a decade; records are sketchy) to the present. As you can see, its broad strokes seem to trace out a five-wave structure. I have left the preceding bear market of 64 years in British stock prices on the chart to show that the advance arose from the ashes of a bear market of corresponding degree, wave Ⅱ.

Figure 4-2 shows the detail of the fifth wave from Figure 4-1, "Supercycle" wave (V), which was born in 1932 at the bottom of the biggest bear market since the 1700s. As you can see, it is easily identified as a five-wave structure, which emerged from

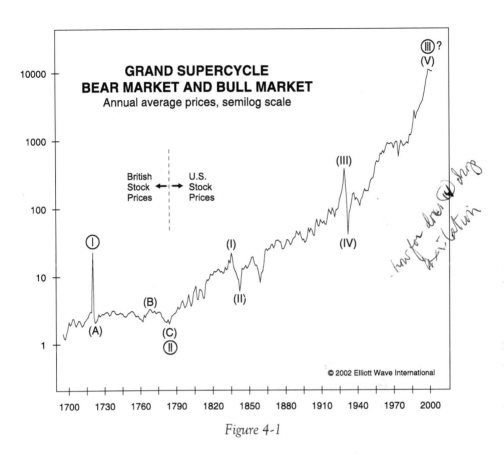

Figure 4-1

the ashes of a bear market of corresponding degree, wave (IV). As Chapters 5 through 7 will show, this labeling is definitive.

Figure 4-3 shows the detail of the fifth wave from Figure 4-2, "Cycle" wave V, which began in 1974 at the bottom of wave IV, the biggest bear market since the one that ended in 1942. As you can see, the rise can be labeled as five completed waves, and in this case, they form a trend channel. Although I would like to be able to assert that Figure 4-3 is definitive, certain nuances of wave identification allow a slight chance that the Dow could make another new high within Cycle wave V. In that case, the final rally, currently underway, will be brief and short.

Figure 4-2

My summary of these pictures, then, is that the uptrend from around 1784 is probably five waves, the uptrend from 1932 is definitely five waves, and the uptrend from 1974 is very probably a completed five waves. To conclude, then, here is what we have: A bull market that has endured since the time of the Great Depression is definitely ending, and its termination could well mark the end of an uptrend of one degree larger, which has endured since the founding of the Republic.

Figure 4-3

Specific Renditions of the Stock Market Fractal

The last time that the stock market formed a fifth wave of Cycle degree was in the 1920s. That's why Elliott wave forecasts from November 1978 and September 1982 specifically called for the emerging bull market to "parallel the 1920s." (See *Elliott Wave Principle*, Chapter 8 and Appendix.) Although the two waves in Figure 4-4 are quite different quantitatively in terms of both duration (8.05 vs. 25.1 years) and extent (596.5% vs. 1929.6%), you

Figure 4-4

can see that their forms are strikingly similar. If you apply your
calculator to the figures just quoted, you will also discover that
the lower graph rises 3.2 times the percentage gain of the upper
graph in 3.1 times the time. In other words, their overall rates
of ascent are essentially identical. If someone had showed you
these two data series — unmarked — under the guise that they
were concurrent, wouldn't you agree that they were correlated?
In my opinion, the similarities between the two advances are not
coincidental. This form is an expression of how mass psychology

progresses in Cycle degree fifth waves that contain extended fifth
sub-waves, apparently an ideal setting for an investment mania.

Worldwide Stock Values

The long-term Elliott wave position and outlook are hardly
confined to the United States. The World Stock Index, which
reflects the total value of stocks worldwide, also shows five waves
up from 1974 and portends a major decline. The wave labeling
in Figure 4-5 is slightly more detailed, showing Intermediate and
Primary degree subdivisions.

Figure 4-5

A Final Selling Opportunity in the Making

Immediately after the terrorist attack of September 11, 2001, the U.S. stock market was shut down. The entire country, not just the investment community, was in a panic. That day, my publication, *The Elliott Wave Theorist*, issued a forecast diagram of the Standard & Poor's 500 Composite Index. It called for the index to fall just a bit further and then begin the largest rally since it topped in March 2000. Six trading days later, the stock market bottomed and turned up.

You can see in Figure 4-6 why I made that forecast. In September 2001, the S&P Composite (along with the Wilshire 5000 and other indexes) was clearly finishing five waves down. If you re-examine Figure 3-1, you will see that a pattern of five waves down from a bull-market high always calls for a bear-market rally in an up-down-up pattern and then a resumption of the larger downtrend. The S&P's five waves down, then, called for a cor-

Figure 4-6

Figure 4-7

responding three-wave rally, which began on September 21, six days after the market re-opened.

Most segments of the market are still advancing here near the end of the first quarter of 2002 as I put the final touches on this book. The S&P and the Wilshire 5000 indexes have continued to follow the expected path, as you can see in the updated graph of the S&P in Figure 4-7, and the Dow has climbed back above 10,000.

This rally has been strong enough in selected secondary issues to propel two stock averages, which are constructed so as to reflect this bias, to new all-time highs, as you can see in Figure 4-8. While the first quarter of 2000 presented a whale of a selling opportunity for the S&P and the NASDAQ, the current rally is creating one just as good for many sectors of the market. Releasing this book into the heat of this rally should provide maximum benefit to you.

Figure 4-8

Further upside potential is nothing more than a near-term consideration. What you need to care about is the major reversal that is about to impact your financial health dramatically. The following three chapters demonstrate the extremely high probability that the larger advancing wave depicted in Figure 4-2 — the one that began seven decades ago — has run its course.

Chapter 5:

Evidence from Stock Participation and Economic Performance

Now let's conduct two key investigations to help answer the question of whether the advance from 1974 was truly a fifth wave. First we will examine the breadth of the market, and then we will confirm the value of our economic analysis in Chapter 1.

Stock Selectivity in Wave V

Elliott Wave Principle notes, "Fifth waves in stocks are always less dynamic than third waves in terms of breadth." In other words, if the advance from 1974 to 2000 is truly a fifth wave, then it must have been more selective than the third wave in terms of the number of stocks participating in the uptrend. Let's find out if wave V performed as expected compared to wave III.

Figure 5-1 shows the entire available history of what market analysts call the "advance-decline line." It is a cumulative sum of the daily ratio of the number of stocks advancing minus the number declining, the net then divided by the total number of changed issues. The resulting graph, for which the data begins in 1926, shows the tendency for all stocks traded to advance or decline on a daily basis. As you can see by the trend of this line, for most of waves I, III and V, when the overall trend of the Dow was up, more stocks advanced on the average day than declined,

Figure 5-1

and for most of waves II and IV, when the overall trend of the Dow was down or sideways, more stocks declined on the average day than advanced.

Look more closely at the details of the line. Notice that during the stock market advance from 1926 to 1929, which was a fifth wave within a fifth wave, the advance-decline line made almost no upside progress. Observe that near the end of wave III, when subwave ⑤ was in force, the advance-decline line was not rising as dynamically as it was during the earlier wave ③. This is the breadth guideline of Figure 3-9 in action.

Now look at the dramatic difference between the behavior of this line from 1974 to 2000 and how it performed from 1942 to 1966. Despite what pundits myopically call "the greatest bull market in history," the advance-decline line over 26 long years of bull market was so weak that it could not even retrace what it lost in the bear market of 1966-1974, a mere eight years!

Anecdotal evidence dramatizes the difference. Here is R.N. Elliott's 1946 description of one stunning consequence of the overwhelming breadth of wave ① of III:

> The first wave, from 1942 to 1945, disclosed inflationary characteristics. Low-priced stocks of questionable value surged ahead at the expense of the "blue chips." The New York Sun selected ninety-six stocks that advanced phenomenally. Every stock started at some figure below $2 per share. The highest rate of advance was 13,300 percent. The lowest rate of advance was 433 percent. The average for the group was 2,776 percent.

Contrast that performance with the briar patch of the 1990s. In *The Wall Street Journal*'s stock-picking contests, for example, the pros beat the Dow only a little over half the time. Here are sample reports from some of the rougher periods:

July 13, 1994: *Darts Beat Pros but Losses Are the Rule*

Four stocks chosen by a random throw of darts fell an average 8.7 percent between Jan. 10 and June 30, compared with an average loss of 13 percent for stocks selected by a team of four investment professionals. The Dow Jones Industrial Average, meanwhile, declined 6.2 percent.

July 10, 1996: *Pros Lose Out to Chance, Industrials*

The stocks chosen by the four pros declined an average 9.2 percent, while four stocks selected by flinging darts at the stock tables fell 5.3 percent. But the industrial average rose a tidy 10.2 percent.

February 11, 1997: *Investment Pros Defeat Darts, but Can't Top Surging Market*

Four investment professionals' stock picks posted an average gain of 7.7 percent in just under six months as of Jan. 31, 1997, a full three percentage points better than the Wall Street Journal staffers' dart board choices. However, the Dow's gain for the period was 19.6 percent.

April 9, 1997: *Pros Beat Darts, but in a Losing Contest*

Four stocks selected by the pros all lost money in the period from last Oct. 8 through March 31, declining an average 10 percent. They still did better than the forces of chance. Four stocks chosen by flinging darts at the stock tables dropped an average 16.9 percent. The Dow Jones Industrial Average, meanwhile, rose 9.6 percent during the same period.

May 13, 1998: *Pros Beat Darts, but Picks Trail Dow Jones Industrials*

Investment professionals walloped the [darts] but still couldn't keep up with the surging Dow Jones Industrial Average. The four pros racked up a 17.4 percent gain in the period from Nov. 12, 1997 to April 30, compared with an average loss of 10.5 percent for four stocks selected by Wall Street Journal staffers flinging darts at the stock tables. Meanwhile, the industrial average gained 22.5 percent.

November 5, 1998: *Darts Draw Blood as Pro Losses Far Exceed Those of Industrials*

If you have been having trouble picking winning stocks in recent months, you aren't alone. A team of four investment professionals posted an average investment loss of 23.6 percent in this column's latest stock-picking contest, from May 12 through Friday. A portfolio of four stocks chosen by Wall Street Journal staffers flinging darts at the stock tables did only slightly better, with an average loss of 21.5 percent in the period. The Dow Jones Industrial Average slid 6.2 percent.

Stock market investors in the early 1940s, rare though they were in the beginning years of the wave (V) uptrend, must have felt like geniuses. Whatever method they used to pick stocks would have worked. Fund managers and stockbrokers in the 1980s and 1990s had no such luxury. Every other month, their clients would demand to know why their selections were not keeping up with the Dow, S&P and NASDAQ indexes. As the averages were soaring skyward in 1998, one brokerage firm manager confided to me, "I'm more depressed than I have ever been in my whole life." The key to his misery is that aside from a breathtaking "Internet stock" frenzy in 1999, the blue-chip components of the Dow, S&P and NASDAQ were the heart of the mania. Few stock pickers, money managers or stockbrokers could outperform them because the number of other stocks participating in the bull market was relatively small.

The Wave Principle not only provides a basis for understanding this breadth dichotomy but also a model for predicting it. The observation in Figure 3-9 and the simple labels "IV" and "V" in Figure 3-8 portended relative selectivity in the forecasted bull market, which is exactly what we got.

It is crucial to observe that all fifth waves feature a sharp deterioration in breadth. At stock market tops, when the "fifth of the fifth" wave is in force, the advance/decline line is typically already heading down. For example, in wave V of the 1920s, the advance-decline line peaked in May 1928, 16 months before the final high in the Dow. It trended down while the Dow traced out its final wave (5) of ⑤. Similarly, in the latest wave V, the advance-decline line peaked in April 1998, 21 months before the Dow's high in January 2000. During wave (5) of ⑤, which began in late 1998, breadth was so weak that the advance-decline line went down not only as the Dow and S&P market averages went to a new high but also as the NASDAQ nearly quadrupled! This is one reason why I am fairly confident that the labeling of the sub-waves in Figures 4-3 and 4-5 is correct, which means that the time is right to undertake the safeguards outlined in the second half of this book.

Economic Weakness in Wave V

As noted in Figure 3-9, if the advance from 1974 is truly a fifth and final wave, then it must also display weaker economic performance and financial conditions than did the preceding third wave, the one that lasted from 1942 to 1966. As you saw in Chapter 1, that's exactly what it did, by every pertinent measure. Chapter 1 also described two precedents, the U.S. experience of the 1920s and the Japanese experience of 1974-1989, in which economic performance seriously lagged both the stock market and the economic expansion of the previous comparable period. Now we see that the Elliott wave model both supports the implication of these analogies to the current situation and explains them: All three cases involve a major fifth wave; in fact, they were all of Cycle degree, labeled wave V under the Wave Principle.

Observe the similarity between the trends of the economic data summarized in Figure 1-2 and the advance/decline line of Figure 5-1. Both sets of statistics show weakness in wave V relative to wave III as well as deterioration in the latter portion of wave V as compared to the earlier portion. These two sets of data reveal a parallelism between the "technical" and "fundamental" aspects of waves, i.e., the psychology of waves and their product.

The Value of Knowing the Difference

Economists do not even comment upon the blatant long-term deterioration in economic performance over the last half-century. Now you know that there is an approach to macro-economic forecasting that actually *predicted* it.

In fact, the idea that there is a difference between economic performance during a third wave and that during a fifth wave has been a part of the Wave Principle for over twenty years.

Frost's and my 1978 book *Elliott Wave Principle* describes third waves as "wonders to behold" as they bring about "increasingly favorable fundamentals." In contrast, "the fifth of the fifth [wave] will lack the dynamism that preceded it." By labeling the 1942 to 1966 bull market as "wave III," we established the economic growth rate of the 1950s and 1960s as a standard that the new bull market would not surpass. In an August 1983 report on the developing "Super Bull Market," *The Elliott Wave Theorist* reiterated the expected relationship between the two periods, adding, "This fifth wave will be built more on unfounded hopes than on soundly improving fundamentals such as the U.S. experienced in the 1950s and early 1960s."

These descriptions and forecasts were issued years before the data became available for wave V. Can you imagine any such perspective from conventional macroeconomics? I believe that wave analysts were able to anticipate the difference because we understand the dynamics that were set up to produce it.

Furthermore, we did not wait for recession to be in force before presenting this crucial data to business people who had to plan well ahead of the 2001 recession's arrival (which economists now date back to March 2001). In September 1998, five months after the top in the advance/decline line and 16 months before the top of wave V, we published "Wave V Fundamentals and Their Implications," which laid out the case (reprinted in *View from the Top of the Grand Supercycle* and recapped here in Chapter 1) for an approaching major reversal in the economy. Anyone who read that article was given the opportunity to begin positioning his business dealings for the approaching trend change while everyone else was becoming overly extended speculating on the New Economy. The good news is that there is still time to take advantage of the opportunity, well before anyone else knows what's happening.

The Reason for Narrowness and Deceleration

Why does stock participation narrow and why does the economy expand more slowly in fifth waves? The simple answer to this question is that stock market advances and economic cycles must get weaker before they reverse. The final rise is where that weakness must be evident. Advances come in five waves, so the fifth wave is where the relative weakness manifests.

The mechanism of that difference, I believe, is the immense optimism of major fifth waves, which encourages the populace to engage in financial speculation. Third waves are built upon muscle and brains. Fifth waves are built upon cleverness and dreams. During third waves, people focus on production to get rich. During fifth waves, they focus on finance to get rich. Manipulating money is not very productive. The entire enterprise costs a fortune in transaction costs, personnel and time. Extensive borrowing for speculation also requires extensive interest payments, and the rising cost of interest burdens the entire process of production. In a production-oriented economy, most enterprises benefit. In a finance-oriented economy, comparatively few entities benefit. These differences show up blatantly in the advance/decline line and more subtly in overall economic performance figures.

A prime symbol of the deterioration in wave (V) of ⑪ (for orientation, see Figure 4-1) is the Federal Reserve System. Its manipulation of money and credit for the past 89 years (see Chapter 10) has been so destabilizing that it has transformed America from a production powerhouse into a society obsessed with dodging inflation and manipulating money and credit. These preoccupations have so burdened the productive capacity of the United States that even the major expansion of the 20th century, wave (V), has experienced a slowing in the rate of real growth relative to the major expansion of the 19th century, wave (III).

A prime symbol of the deterioration in wave V of (V) is General Electric, the oldest name in the Dow Jones Industrial Average. Through wave III ending in 1966, GE was one of the finest engineering and manufacturing concerns in the world. Its goods lasted for decades. In wave V, accountants took over the company and transformed it from a manufacturing concern into a financial concern. Today, its manufactured goods are often mediocre and its vaunted company a cardboard edifice of credit services. It is the United States in microcosm.

It's a Fifth Wave

The latter half of the last sixty years has seen deterioration both in the breadth of stock participation in the market's advance and in the long-term rate of economic progress. The degree of slowing — covering decades — confirms that the advance since 1974 is a *fifth wave*, which supports the wave labeling of Figure 4-2.

Chapter 6:

The Significance of Historically High Stock Market Valuation

Recall that fifth waves produce "lofty valuation" for stocks. The evidence that wave V in the global bull market has produced historically high valuations for corporate shares could fill two books. Let's look at the primary data for U.S. valuations to verify this point.

Dividend Yield

The "yield" of the Dow Jones Industrial Average is the annual dividends that the 30 companies listed in the Dow pay out to shareholders as a percentage of their stock prices. If you study Figure 6-1, you will see that investors accept low dividends at market tops and demand high dividends at market bottoms. It is easy to understand why. At tops, they believe that stocks will go up much more, providing a huge capital gain, so who needs dividends? At bottoms, they believe that stocks will fall much more, providing a capital loss, so they demand high dividends to offset their perceived risk.

Of course, this thinking is backwards and makes investors lose money. It nevertheless must be this way because if they acted otherwise, markets would not be continually forming tops and bottoms.

Figure 6-1

Observe that the DJIA's dividend yield tends to be around 6.5 percent near moderate bear market bottoms. It went far higher at the bottom of the Great Depression. Conversely, the dividend yield has tended to be around 3 percent at major tops, including the historic top of 1929.

In 2000, the Dow's dividend yield did something that it had never done before. It reached 1.5 percent. A larger index of industrial stocks, the Standard & Poor's 400 Industrials, yielded only 1 percent. This is historically high valuation.

It takes about 1 percent of the value of a stock for an investor to buy and then sell it. The dividend payout in the year 2000, then, was enough to cover transactions costs *if* you were to buy and sell no more than once a year. If you own shares of a mutual fund, the managers take 1 percent annually for fees. At 1 percent, then, stocks effectively have no yield. What's more, the DJIA represents the best of the country's blue-chip stocks. Most companies listed on the NASDAQ exchange pay no dividends at all. Throw in transaction costs or management fees, and they have a negative yield.

Today, optimists argue that dividends "don't matter." They claim that "investors want companies to plow money back into the company" so that the company will be more profitable and the stock price will go up more. These are excuses and rationalizations. If no dividend is ever paid, of what value is a share of stock? Do you really want to own a share of a super-successful enterprise that handsomely pays everyone involved in it except you, an owner?

The few optimists who still think that dividends matter declare that stock prices need not fall because our "unprecedented economy" eventually will generate enough corporate income to pay those higher dividends. Yet after two decades of nearly uninterrupted economic growth, it hasn't happened. Given the evidence in this book, it isn't about to happen, either. The economy will be unprecedented, all right, but in the other direction.

The inevitable fluctuations of mass psychology assure that at some time in the future, the dividend yields on the Dow and other major stock indexes will be far higher than they are today. Unfortunately, the change is not going to come about with a simple adjustment downward in stock prices. The reason is that when stock prices fall substantially, the result is almost always a weaker economy. The degree of the currently developing downturn is so large that the economy will undoubtedly become extremely weak, and that trend in turn will put pressure on companies to *decrease* dividends. Falling dividends will follow falling stock prices, and falling stock prices will chase falling dividends, making it difficult for the stock market to return to an attractive yield typical of major bottoms. Stock indexes have a *long way down to go* before their yields return to levels that reflect investor pessimism.

Book Value

If a company has to value itself for liquidation, it does so on the basis of the market value of its assets. A company's "book value" comes close to reflecting that value.

As we are about to see, stock prices today reflect the most expensive valuation of corporate assets in recorded history. Today's stock prices are not just historically high compared to book values; they are amazingly, outrageously high.

How did they get that way? One of investors' requirements for buying expensive stock during the 1990s was that the associated company continually report higher earnings per share. Such an achievement is meaningless in isolation, because the real question is *what are the earnings relative to the size of the company* and *relative to the price of the stock*, questions no one has been asking. As you can see, we are not dealing with reason here but with rationalization. The last time investors adopted this guideline was the late 1920s. (For more on that point, see Graham & Dodd's comments in Chapter 14 of *Market Analysis for the New Millennium*, 2002.) Because investors adopted this guideline, "aggressive" accounting methods sprang up during wave V to help companies repeatedly perform the feat of reporting higher earnings per share. Achieving that goal often meant diluting the true underlying value of the company, for example by using company assets to buy back the company's own shares. As we will see in a moment, today's book values reflect this dilution.

A Composite Measure of Valuation

A low dividend yield might be acceptable if there were no other yields available, but there are. They come from bonds, and investors can choose between the two sources. To compare their valuations, we must ask, what is the relative yield between the best stocks and the best bonds?

Figure 6-2 combines two of our benchmarks. The vertical axis reports the price-to-book value of the S&P 400 Industrials index. The horizontal axis reports the yield from top-grade corporate bonds relative to the yield of these top-grade S&P 500 stocks. The rectangular box on the chart delineates the range of values that has held for most of the 20th century. Additional figures from prior years show that year-end bond yield/stock yield ratios were well to the left side of this box at least back to 1870.

Until 1987, only five years since 1927 (where our graph begins) ended with values outside that box, and only two of those were on the high-valuation side. These five readings indicated historic extremes of either pessimism or optimism and therefore a likely major turning point in the stock market.

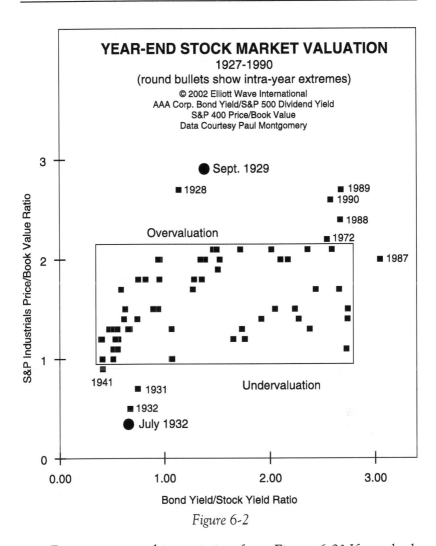

Figure 6-2

Do you see anything missing from Figure 6-2? If you look closely, you will see that it is lacking a crucial set of data points, namely, all of the year-end values for the past 11 years!

Now look at Figure 6-3, which includes the year-end valuations from 1991 to the present. The bullet denoting valuations in March 2000 looks like Pluto in a picture of our solar system, doesn't it?

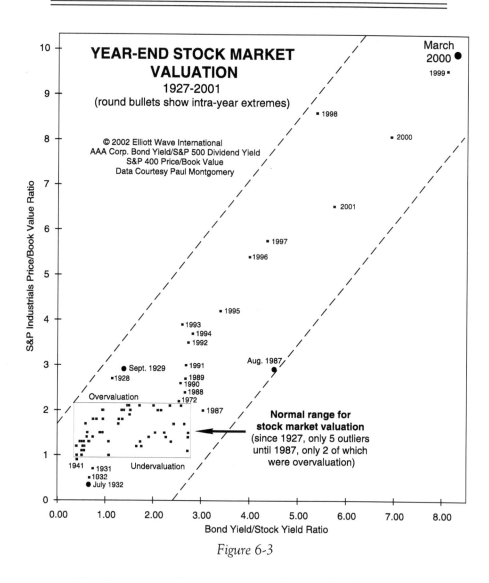

Figure 6-3

You do not need to investigate the worth of any argument that purports to justify these stock values. All you need is eyes.

The squares representing values at the end of 2000 and 2001 indicate that the trend has reversed. Rest assured that sometime soon, annual valuations will be back in that box. In fact, if investors follow their usual pattern, the decline will not end until there is at least one bullet below and/or to the left of the box.

The Price/Earnings Ratio

The price/earnings ratio is the only popular market valuation indicator on Wall Street. It is also the least valuable except in rare cases.

The P/E is the ratio between the price of stocks and the value of their associated companies' annual earnings per share. Sometimes the ratio's compilers use *projected* earnings, which is what brokerage house analysts think that earnings *will* be. Needless to say, earnings estimators are repeatedly too pessimistic at bottoms and too optimistic at tops, just when you most need the indicator to tell the truth. Therefore, our graph will compare stock prices to *actual* earnings for the preceding year.

Corporate earnings cycle with the stock market but with a 2-month to 2-year lag. Earnings do not begin to rise until well after stock prices have turned up from a bottom, and they do not begin to fall until well after stock prices turn down from a top. For this reason, the two trends often oppose each other. In contrast, book values and dividend payouts tend to be much steadier, cycling only on a very long-term basis with the largest economic trends, therefore providing a steady benchmark against which to compare stock prices to obtain a reliable relative valuation measure. There usually is little point in comparing stock prices to corporate earnings because the two opposing cycles push and pull on the ratio in such a way as to render most current readings nearly meaningless for market timing purposes. Most of the time, you could divide stock prices by the price of pickles and have a more reliable indicator.

There is one exception to this general objection. *After* the stock market has made a turn of *major* import, the earnings cycle comes into play with investor psychology in a most interesting way.

Usually, investors (erroneously) welcome rising earnings as bullish. There is one time that they don't, which (naturally) makes them wrong again.

MAJOR-TREND CONFIRMATION SIGNALS FROM THE P/E RATIO

Background Chart Courtesy Ned Davis Research
© 2002 Elliott Wave International

super bearish divergence

Standard & Poor's 500 Stock Index
Monthly Data 3/31/1926 - 12/31/2001 Log Scale
Dotted line is earnings

super bullish divergence

super bullish divergences

S&P 500 Price/Earnings Ratio
using actual trailing 12-month earnings

NOW

Figure 6-4

Go back to Figure 3-9 and note the characteristics of "wave 2." That's when people believe fervently that the larger trend is down, *even though it isn't.* An excellent example of this proclivity is the fact that a New York Stock Exchange survey conducted in 1952 found that a paltry 4 percent of eligible Americans owned stocks! The other 96 percent apparently believed that holding stock was foolish and risky. Of course, the market was in the early years of a multi-decade uptrend; that's when people think this way.

Figure 6-4 displays the P/E ratio for the S&P 500 Composite index from the mid-1920s to the present. Study the first set of arrows toward the left of the graph. Generally speaking, earnings were dutifully following the stock market upward after the major bottom of 1932. Nevertheless, in 1942 and again in 1949, investors' pessimism was so strong that it pushed the P/E ratio *below its level at the preceding lower stock market bottom.* These readings indicated *deep pessimism in the face of rising stock prices and an expanding economy* and therefore an immense psychological potential to drive stock prices higher. The middle set of arrows marks a second occurrence of this phenomenon in 1980, when stocks had a lower P/E ratio than they did at the preceding lower stock market bottom in 1974. In each of these cases, stocks had already launched a huge long-term advance, and most of it lay ahead.

Today, for the first time in the history of the figures, we have the opposite situation, with the opposite implication. When stock prices decline from a major top, commercial activity decreases, and lower earnings follow. Last year, earnings fell faster than the S&P did, so the P/E ratio rose despite lower stock prices. In fact, it rose so strongly that the P/E ratio at the end of December was 46, the highest ever. The P/E ratio on the S&P 400 Industrials was 53. P/E ratios for the S&P 500 have ranged from around 7 at bear

market bottoms to the low-to-mid 20s at bull market tops. So the
S&P's P/E ratio today is twice what it is at a typical bull-market
top and *six to seven times* what it is at a typical bear-market bottom. In other words, the S&P would have to fall about 85 percent
to get its P/E to normal bottom levels, *and that's if earnings fall
no further.* Earnings *will* fall in a bear market that size, so today's
P/E ratios portend the same stock price debacle that is implied
by the stock market's wave structure, the low dividend payout,
overpriced book values and the high bond yield/stock yield ratio.

Today's record P/E ratios alone are enough to command
attention (the stock/pickles price ratio is near the highest ever,
too), but what matters more is the P/E ratio *relative* to the action
of the market and the economy. Examine the third set of arrows,
toward the right of Figure 6-4. Although earnings have been dutifully following the stock market downward since shortly after
the top in the first quarter of 2000, investors' optimism remains
so strong that it has pushed the P/E ratio to *above its level at the
preceding higher stock market top.* This dramatic rise to an all-time
record indicates *entrenched optimism in the face of falling stock prices
and a weakening economy* and therefore an immense psychological potential to drive stock prices lower. The implication of this
divergence is that blue-chip stocks have already launched a bear
market with much more ahead of it than lies behind.

Why does this phenomenon occur? Early in major uptrends,
investors remain deeply scarred psychologically by their experi-
ences in the preceding bear market and economic contraction.
Though the downtrends and contractions are over, the fear of
them remains. The P/E ratio reaches an extreme low because
people believe that the rise in earnings is temporary and that
the economy will collapse back downward, justifying low stock
valuations. The second arrow in the final set (marked "NOW")
reflects investors' diametrically opposing attitudes today. Though
the trend of stocks has been sideways to down for two years and

the economy has receded, the presumption that the old uptrend and expansion are the natural order of things remains as firm as ever. Investors anticipate — directly opposing their counterparts of the 1940s — more glory days ahead. People think that earnings will begin rising again, and they want to own as much stock as they can before that happens.

The first problem with this idea is that investors have priced stocks so high that to get them bear-market cheap again, earnings would have to soar 600 percent, and that's if the S&P does not budge a single point higher than it is today! The second problem is that the extended economic expansion that so many expect almost certainly is not going to happen. If my interpretation of the P/E disparity is accurate, it has not been a stock market "correction" in the S&P; it's a bear market, which means that the economic contraction is not merely a "mild, brief recession," it's the first contraction in a developing depression.

Obfuscation and Rationalization

As I write this chapter, the "watchdog" of earnings, Standard & Poor's, has just bowed to pressure to change the basis of its earnings reports to "operating earnings" rather than total company earnings. As a result, the reported P/E ratio has suddenly changed to about half of what it really is. Analysts are expected to tack these ratios onto the old ratio's eighty-year history as if they are the same thing. Operating earnings omit several items, the main one being "non-recurring expenses." *Hello!* All expenses affect a company's performance. A creative accountant can drive a truck through that loophole and manipulate operating expenses to almost any desired level. Yet another proposal, to report only "core earnings," will exclude gains or losses due to companies' pension fund obligations. If my outlook is right, these obligations will soon be killing the profitability of industry. Leaving potentially massive drains on capital out of the earnings calculation is

like leaving torture equipment out of a description of a dungeon.
Real investors want real numbers, and these changes provide the
opposite. The desperation within the financial world to avoid
reporting "bad news" (i.e., the truth) is obviously immense.

How do so many public and professional investors justify
holding such expensive stocks today? The latest issue of Money
magazine (March 2002) quotes a manager at one of the largest
stock mutual funds in the world: "You have to trust them. To some
degree they become faith stocks." Money concurs, "Investors must
rely as much on gut instinct as on objective analysis. Sometimes
an extra-large helping of hope is required." One could hardly utter a worse guide to life, much less to the assumption of financial
risk. Those of us dedicated to objective financial analysis aren't
always right. But those who rely on extra-large helpings of trust,
faith, hope and "gut instinct" always regret it.

Chapter 7:

The Significance of Historically Optimistic Psychology

The engine of high stock market valuation is widely shared optimism. The greater the degree of the advance that is ending, the greater the optimism at its peak. Optimism also tends to remain strong in the early stages of a bear market (waves "A" down and "B" up, in wave parlance). Bull markets, they say, climb a "Wall of Worry." I like to add, "and bear markets slide down a Slope of Hope."

Today, are investors optimistic or pessimistic, and to what degree? The answer is that measures of optimism in early 2000 reached awesome, historic levels, and they remain just below — and in some cases even above — those levels today. As you are about to see, psychology is a long way from the shared deep pessimism that produces a buying opportunity.

Psychology of Academics

In about 1997, professors, PhDs and decorated economists at universities and think-tanks began peppering the media with articles that essentially put before the public the idea that macroeconomic science has lent its sanction to the historic extremes in stock values generated by the great asset mania of the 1980s and 1990s. In *The Wall Street Journal* alone, we have read bullish essays and learned of bullish studies by two Nobel laureates, a former Fed Governor and scholars at the American Enterprise Institute, the University of Pennsylvania, the Massachusetts Institute of Technology, the Brookings Institution, the Wharton School, the University of Rochester, Princeton University, New York University, Bear Stearns, Credit Suisse First Boston, the Federal Reserve Banks of Dallas and Philadelphia, the Hoover Institution, the Discovery Institute and the Graduate School of Business of the University of Chicago, to list just the ones with the most prominent credentials. These articles were most abundant between March 1998 and April 2000, though they still appear today. Not one bases its conclusions on an analytical method that has any forecasting history at all, and others contradict ones that do. During the period that the quotations below appeared, only one academic made a passionate case for investor caution in the WSJ, in two articles published in April 1999 and March 2000.

As you look at the dates of the following quotes from some of these professorial essays, keep in mind that the Value Line Geometric stock average and the advance/decline line peaked in April 1998, the Dow and S&P in gold and commodity terms topped in July 1999, and the nominal highs in the S&P and NASDAQ (and probably the Dow as well) took place in the first quarter of 2000. Here is what the experts have told us:

- March 30, 1998: "Pundits who claim the market is over-valued are foolish."

- July 30, 1998: "This expansion will run forever."

- February 3, 1999: "We have at last arrived in a new-era economy."

- March 19, 1999: "A perfectly reasonable level for the Dow would be 36,000 — tomorrow, not 10 or 20 years from now. The risk premium is headed for its proper level: zero."

- August 30, 1999: "The recent dramatic upswing represents a rosy estimate about growth in future profits for the economy."

- September 18, 1999: "Researchers have found compelling evidence that conventional accounting understates the earning power of today's companies."

- January 1, 2000: "In much the way Albert Einstein's theory of relativity transformed the time-space grid of classical physics at the beginning of the twentieth century, the Einsteins of Internet communications are now transforming the time-space grid of the global economy."

- April 18, 2000: "Don't be fooled. Historical forces continue to point toward a Great Prosperity that could carry the Dow Jones Industrial Average to 35,000 by the end of the decade and 100,000 by 2020."

If this one-sided outpouring of scholarly judgment proves to be anything other than a manifestation of the prevailing optimistic mass psychology that crystallized after 7 decades of mostly rising stock prices and 2½ decades of dramatically rising stock prices, I will be mightily surprised.

Psychology of Economists

Two years ago, as most major U.S. stock indexes reached their all-time highs, *The Wall Street Journal* observed, "Economists are downright euphoric." Of 54 economists surveyed, all but two were bullish for 2000. One year later, when the Dow, S&P and NASDAQ were down 8 percent, 15 percent and 51 percent from their respective highs and the onset of recession was just weeks away, the consensus for continued growth was even stronger. Only one economist out of 54 surveyed called for a recession in 2001. On New Year's Day, January 2002, although the economy had been slumping for nearly a year, economists managed to achieve an even greater optimistic consensus, thanks surely to the Dow's rally back above 10,000. Not one of the 55 economists surveyed for *The Wall Street Journal's* 2002 forecast expects the recent contraction to develop into a serious decline. All predict that the economy will expand this year if it hasn't begun to do so already. The recent stock-market rally — reflecting an improving social mood — has naturally led to an improvement in a number of economic indicators. These changes have induced economists to keep up the drumbeat. Here are just three excerpts out of hundreds:

The Atlanta Journal-Constitution, February 22, 2002: "Economists Optimistic: Survey Says Recession Likely Is Already Over"
> The U.S. recession has probably ended, according to a survey by the National Association for Business Economics that projects growth of at least 3.5 percent in the second half of 2002 and in 2003.

USA Today, February 28, 2002: "'Recessionette' Might Be at an End"
> Bank One's chief economist calls it a "recessionette," and the U.S. Chamber of Commerce's chief economist insists the current slump is no recession at all.

Fortune, March 18, 2002, adds that such is "the opinion of virtually every economic forecaster out there."

Obviously, economists of all stripes, from theoreticians to practitioners, have been bullish throughout the past two years, right past the top in most stocks, right past the onset of the 2001 recession (which may or may not be "officially" recognized) and right through today. You no longer need guess at the source of those "New Economy" quotes tallied in Figure 1-1.

Economists as a group have an unbroken record of failing to predict economic contraction. Most of the time, ill-timed optimism is harmless because most of the time, recessions are indeed mild and brief. The reason is that the fluctuations in the economy are a hierarchical fractal, as described in Chapter 3. Small, mild retrenchments occur more frequently than large ones, so forecasting errors are only mildly damaging. Yet rarity does not equate to impossibility. It is wrong to assume, after a long period of prosperity with only mild recessions, that the large economic contractions will never occur again. Yet that belief invariably materializes at such times. Why is that?

Economists' forecasts always seem to be little different from a description of the present, tempered or augmented by the forward-weighted trends of the past. That's how human nature works. People — including professionals who should know better — generally accept recent experience as "normal," no matter what it is. Economists would serve their clients much better if the trends and extremities of their opinions were the opposite of what they are.

Psychology of Brokerage Strategists

Professional brokerage-house equity-allocation strategists tend to recommend a heavy weighting in stocks just before

Figure 7-1

the market falls and a lighter weighting just before the market
advances. This is normal behavior, which itself helps to set the
market's highs and lows.

Figure 7-1 shows fifteen years of average weighting recommendations by brokers. Look at their current average opinion:
a *record* high weighting recommendation of 71 percent! This is
how advisors felt during the rally of early 1930, as well. Their
advice was not profitable. Nor should it have been. A consensus
this strong means that people are about as invested as they can
get. It is bearish.

Psychology of Money Managers

In the aggregate, money managers are always most invested
in stocks at tops and least invested at bottoms. Figure 7-2 shows
how pension funds and insurance companies increased their
percentage of stock holdings from 7 percent of total assets in
1952 to 53 percent on New Year's Day, 2000. Figure 7-3 shows
the percentage of cash that stock mutual funds hold in their
portfolios. Again, they usually hold lots of cash at bottoms and
little at tops. Needless to say, it would benefit their clients if they
did the opposite. Needless to say, it can be no different.

Managers' optimism today is stunningly one-sided not only
in the U.S. but throughout the Western world. Canadian poll-
ing firm Towers Perrin reports that among 48 Canadian and 23
foreign investment firms, *not a single one* expects negative returns
from their stock investments in 2002. Nor are they just mildly
optimistic. As Toronto's *Globe and Mail* (1/10/02) summarizes
the survey, "Money managers are looking for *double-digit returns*
from Canadian, U.S. and international equity markets this year."
Although the analysis in this book focuses primarily on the U.S.
equity market, similar conditions attend all stock markets around
the globe that have held near their highs.

Figure 7-2

Psychology of the Public

The public agrees with the experts. Figure 7-4 shows that investors' margin debt, a paltry $3 billion in late 1974, topped $250 billion in early 2000. In just 25 years, investors multiplied by over 80 times the amount of money that they borrowed from brokers to buy stocks. Figures 7-5 and 7-6 are long-term measures of the public's attitude toward stocks. It took decades, but in the 1990s, the public became, by these measures, more bullish than it was at the two biggest tops of the past century: 1968 and 1929.

AN INDICATOR OF PROFESSIONAL PSYCHOLOGY

Monthly Data 1/31/1960 - 3/31/2001 (Log Scale)

Standard & Poor's 500 Stock Index

Stock Mutual Funds Cash/Assets Ratio

Source: Investment Company Institute
Chart courtesy Ned Davis Research

Figure 7-3

Figure 7-5

Figure 7-4

Figure 7-6

In utter contrast to their underinvested counterparts of the early 1950s, over half of American families, which must mean most families that actually have money to invest, are invested in the stock market. These readings make investors' level of excitement during the Roaring Twenties look like ennui.

P/E ratios and brokerage strategists' allocations are not the only market psychology indicators at all-time highs. Here in the first quarter of 2002, the weekly survey of futures contract ownership shows that "small traders," i.e., the most naïve market players, have just reached an all-time record in their holdings of "long" futures contracts. The "commercials," i.e., the most sophisticated market players, have held record and near-record levels of *short* futures contracts since mid-2000. Figure 7-7 displays 13 years of history showing that commercials during that time were most bullish at the stock market bottoms of 1990 and 1994 and were most bearish recently; in other words, they tend to be right. Conversely, the public was most bearish in early 1995, as the market was blasting off for a record five-year run. As you can see, the public is generally wrong.

Figure 7-7

Becoming more bullish at lower prices is highly unusual behavior on the part of investors generally speaking, but, like the P/E phenomenon, *it is normal behavior shortly after a major top in stock prices.* As *Elliott Wave Principle* explained in 1978, "During the A wave of a bear market, the investment world is generally convinced that this reaction is just a pullback pursuant to the next leg of advance. The public surges to the buy side despite the first really technically damaging cracks in individual stock patterns." The B-wave rallies that follow exhibit "aggressive euphoria and denial." The past two years fit these descriptions. As with other indicators presented in this book, Figure 7-7 provides assurance that a major bear market is in force and that the bulk of it lies ahead.

The New York Times reports today (March 12) on a study of "newly optimistic" investor attitudes. It shows that an amazing *90 percent* of individuals polled say that the stock market will continue to advance over the next 12 months. This revival of optimism is emerging *six months after* the proper time to have been near-term optimistic, six months after *The Elliott Wave Theorist* forecasted the largest rally in the S&P since the all-time high, six months after the bottom of wave A. The article concludes, "The optimism of individuals…suggests that the coming year could be a good one for stocks." This claim reflects a bizarre incognizance of the multi-decade history of stock market sentiment indicators.

Psychology of the Media

As you can see by the graphs in this chapter, there is no question that optimism is entrenched horizontally throughout the nation and vertically through all strata of expertise. This overwhelming consensus has engendered an outpouring of elation from the nation's magazine covers and newspapers' front pages here in the first quarter of 2002. "Positive Reports Hint at Swift

Recovery," says *The New York Times*. "Better Times Coming," announces the Minneapolis *Star*. "Hope Soars in U.S." adds Denver's *Rocky Mountain News*. *The New York Post* enthuses, "Recovery at Last." *USA Today* announces, "Fed Chief Declares Recession at an End." *U.S. News and World Report* shows us "How to Cash In." The President himself assures us that 2002 will be a "Great Year."

The newspaper clippings on the following pages show that optimism permeates both local and national news reporting. (In case you can't see the one magazine cover clearly, that's Abraham Lincoln advising, "Buy!") Most of these headlines are from the cover of the magazine or page 1 of the newspaper in which they appeared, which means that editors deem the sentiments worthy of the strongest highlight. It's unfortunate, because such ideas expressed at the wrong time kill people financially and, in extreme cases, physically as well.

The Next Psychological Trend

When the stock market turns back down, academics, economists, advisors, money managers and media commentators will begin to turn bearish. Bad news will begin pouring out of the newspapers as a consequence of the emerging negative-mood trend. The more the market falls, the higher the number of bears will become, because enough time will go by that the trends not only of the present but also of the recent past will be down. The largest number of bears, public and professional, will be at the bottom.

Poll: Americans optimistic

President says 2002 will be 'a great year'

Positive Reports Hint at Swift Recovery
—New York Times, December 29, 2001

DECEMBER 31, 2001   BARRON'S

The Case for a "Super-V"

Three stimulating economic factors may come together in 2002

According to various surveys, strategists look for about a 9 percent gain by the Dow Jones industrial average next year, 12 percent for Standard & Poor's 500-stock index and 13 percent for the Nasdaq composite.

As 2001 bows out, economy looks up
—The Atlanta Journal-Constitution, December 29, 2001

American consumers are ending a frightening year in a cheery mood, more confident about the future.

Confidence in economy on the rise
—The Atlanta Journal-Constitution, December 29, 2001

Forecasters smell a recovery

Forecast For Growth: Even More

Consumer spending the key to forecasts for a rebound
—The Atlanta Journal-Constitution, December 29, 2001

A STRONG RECOVERY FOR STOCKS
—Financial Times, Jan 2, 2002

BANKS FORECAST

Economy shows signs of year-end comeback

Recession threatening North America is yesterday's story, chief economist says
—Globe and Mail, December 29, 2001

Smart Money
THE WALL STREET JOURNAL MAGAZINE OF PERSONAL BUSINESS

ANNUAL FORECAST ISSUE

THE Best Investments FOR 2002

Buy!

As our economy rebounds, these 10 stocks and 6 mutual funds will make you big money. Honest.

Hope Soars in U.S.

Consumer confidence hits unexpected high
—Rocky Mountain News, December 29, 2001

Yes, There Are Still Optimists in Japan
—New York Times, Dec 30, 2001

Market raises new year hopes

City optimistic after two year losing streak

Recession May Have Bottomed

Economy, consumer confidence, home sales and other indicators suggest early recovery.
—Los Angles Times, December 29, 2001

Factors see two in place to end market of sliding equities

"It's clear that we've started the next leg-up."

Economists Declare Recovery
—USA Today

The upbeat trend had economists revising their quarterly growth forecasts and fund managers enthusiastically reinvesting in the equity markets.

"Everything that could be going right for the recovery is going right." Indeed, from manufacturing and consumer spending to construction, almost every report for January and February has beaten expectations. Not only, in the words of one Federal Reserve insider, could the first half "be gangbusters," the momentum may well be sustainable.
—BusinessWeek, March 18, 2002

What Recession?
—Christian Science Monitor, Mar 12, 2002

Officials Question if Recession Was Real
—Reuters, March 4, 2002

Rallying Cry from the US
The US Economy Is Greeting the Arrival of Spring With a Host Of Golden Indicators
—Financial Times, Mar 9, 2002

...is not only on the mend, but that expectations are also rising for a more robust recovery than previously thought.

BusinessWeek

THE SURPRISE ECONOMY

GET READY FOR REBOUNDING PROFITS
—Business Week, March 25, 2002

Mood on Wall St. Is 'Euphoria'
—The Record, Mar 5, 2002

Traders say new buyers are stepping into the market because/no one wants to miss the next leg-up in the rally.

U.S.News & WORLD REPORT
TALIBAN HOLDOUTS •
2002 ECONOMIC REPORT
Business Bounces Back
Growing signs of a recovery
How to cash in

FOR MANY, RECESSION PROVED BARELY VISIBLE
—Boston Globe, Mar 11, 2002

With evidence now overwhelming that the recession has ended, some economists argue the decline in output was so mild it didn't qualify as a recession at all.
—The Wall Street Journal, March 11, 2002

Chapter 8:

Implications for the Stock Market and the Economy

If the analysis in the preceding chapters is correct, the U.S. stock market, and by extension most stock indexes worldwide, is rounding the cusp of a trend change of at least Supercycle degree. The DJIA has completed (or is completing) five waves up that will lead to a three-step partial retracement of corresponding degree. This means that the decline will not be a moderate setback such as the market has undergone from time to time since 1932. It will be at least large enough to complete the downside portion of Figure 3-1 if we label its start "1932" and its peak "2000." That is a large setback. We may even have to label its start "1784," in which case the bear market will be the largest since that of the 1700s. In other words, the stock market is embarking upon its biggest bear market assuredly since that of 1929-1932 and possibly since that of 1720-1784. If any such bear market occurs, then as we saw in Chapter 2, the economy will experience a depression.

How Far Will the Market Fall?

As implied in Figure 3-2, stock market corrections tend to bottom in the area of the fourth wave of the largest immediately preceding five-wave structure. Study the actual record, and you will see this guideline fulfilled often. Note, for example, in Figure

4-2, that wave II bottomed in the price area of the 1934 low, and wave IV bottomed in the price area of the 1962 low, which ended fourth waves within waves I and III respectively. Way back in 1978, *Elliott Wave Principle* said that when the great bull market expected for wave V was over, the DJIA would fall back to the area of the preceding fourth wave, which is at least to the 577 to 1051 range of wave IV (see Figure 4-2) and possibly down to the 41-381 range of wave (IV) (see Figure 4-1). To summarize, though my outlook may sound impossible, I am quite comfortable saying that the DJIA will fall from *quintuple* digits, where it is today, to *triple* digits, an unprecedented amount.

What I cannot say with quite as much conviction is which wave of the bear market will carry the Dow to that area. Odds are very strong that it will happen on the first major decline, a potential that the next section supports. Otherwise, it will do so on another decline decades hence.

Studies of Manias Bear Out This Downside Potential

In 1997, I undertook a study of financial manias. Manias are episodes of relentless financial speculation that involve substantial infusions of credit, wide public participation, and which drive values to unprecedented levels. For the full study, please see the first essay in *View from the Top*.

A pertinent observation with respect to our current concern is that a mania is always followed by a collapse so severe that it brings values to *below* where they were when the mania began. The apparent reason for this outcome is that so many ordinary people entrust their fortunes to the mania that its reversal brings widespread financial distress, which feeds on itself to force an immense liquidation of investment media.

Figures 8-1 through 8-7 show the record to date of seven manias. The first four of them are far enough in the past to show

Famous Market Manias
And Their Aftermaths, 1600-2001

Figure 8-1 through 8-4

Figure 8-5 through 8-7

the ultimate outcome in which values fell below what they were at the mania's start. The fifth graph is Japan's Nikkei stock index, which topped out on the last trading day of 1989. Its consequences have not fully played out yet, but the relentless fall has already wiped out 80 percent of the Nikkei's peak value and should, if the mania model holds, ultimately carry to or below the values of 1974. The sixth graph is the NASDAQ index, which topped in March 2000. It fell 75 percent into September 2001 and is recovering. Optimists believe that the bear market is over, but it has a long way down to go before erasing the entire mania. The final graph displays the U.S. blue-chip stock mania of the 1980s and 1990s as represented by the DJIA, which remains near its all-time high. If this index behaves like the others, the Dow should fall to below the starting point of its mania. That level is 777, the August 1982 low. So as you can see, the downside potential on this basis is compatible with that indicated by my interpretation of the market's position under the Wave Principle.

Implications for the Economy

If the stock market is going to fall far enough to retrace a substantial portion of the uptrend from at least 1932 and to retrace the price advance that it has undergone during its mania, then it will fall far enough to cause a significant contraction in the economy. How deep will the contraction ultimately become?

The termination of wave III in 1966/68 led to a string of four recessions between 1970 and 1982. Because wave V has had a weaker economic background, and because of the great imbalance between today's sky-high expectations and the decreasingly robust economy, the contraction resulting from this bear market will unquestionably be more severe than any of the contractions following wave III.

Re-examine Figures 2-1 and 4-1. Notice that the last two depressions marked on Figure 2-1 immediately followed the

Supercycle degree labels (I) and (III), as shown in Figure 4-1. As you can see in Figure 4-1, we have a new label, wave (V), in place. Notice that the first depression marked on Figure 2-1 immediately followed the Grand Supercycle degree label Ⓘ in 1720. In Figure 4-1, we also tentatively have a label Ⓘ in place. These labels, if they are correct, are precursors of a tremendous stock-market crash and a deep depression.

The proper models for the developing economic experience are those that accompanied the stock market setbacks of 1720-1722 in England, 1835-1842 and 1929-1932 in the United States and from 1990 forward in Japan. In two of those cases (1720-1722 and 1929-1932), the contraction was a relentless, acute, brief, all-out depression. In the other two cases (1835-1842 and 1990 to date), the economy contracted over a longer period in two or more steps, with recoveries in between. Either style of progression could happen now.

Japan's retrenchment has been long and slow because most of the rest of the world's economies continued their investment manias and economic growth, allowing vigorous trade to provide support during the first decade of its economic decline. When the rest of the world's economies falter, they will lack a group of healthy trading partners to mitigate the speed of their contractions. For this reason, the developing contraction in the U.S. and around the globe will likely be far swifter than Japan's experience to date.

For the purposes of this book, these observations are all the evidence we need to form at least a general idea of the downside potential in the stock market and the economy in the U.S., and by extension, the rest of the world as well.

No Alternative Scenarios

Given the evidence, I think it would be financially suicidal to bet on an extension of the bull market and a requirement of even moderate prudence to prepare for a major reversal. Aside from a near-term nuance allowed for the Dow in Chapter 4, I have no other long-term interpretations of the wave status and the economy and *no alternative scenarios* at the three illustrated degrees. The evidence as I see it is too one-sided for me to be anything now but a one-armed economist. If I turn out wrong, so be it.

PART II

THE CASE FOR DEFLATION

"Pay no attention to that man behind the curtain."

—*The Wizard of Oz*

Chapter 9:

When Does Deflation Occur?

Defining Inflation and Deflation

Webster's says, "Inflation is an increase in the volume of money and credit relative to available goods," and "Deflation is a contraction in the volume of money and credit relative to available goods." To understand inflation and deflation, we have to understand the terms money and credit.

Defining Money and Credit

Money is a socially accepted medium of exchange, value storage and final payment. A specified amount of that medium also serves as a unit of account.

According to its two financial definitions, *credit* may be summarized as *a right to access money*. Credit can be held by the owner of the money, in the form of a warehouse receipt for a money deposit, which today is a checking account at a bank. Credit can also be *transferred* by the owner or by the owner's custodial institution to a borrower in exchange for a fee or fees — called interest — as specified in a repayment contract called a bond, note, bill or just plain IOU, which is *debt*. In today's economy, most credit is lent, so people often use the terms "credit" and "debt" interchangeably, as money lent by one entity is simultaneously money borrowed by another.

Price Effects of Inflation and Deflation

When the volume of money and credit *rises* relative to the volume of goods available, the relative value of each unit of money falls, making prices for goods generally rise. When the volume of money and credit *falls* relative to the volume of goods available, the relative value of each unit of money rises, making prices of goods generally fall. Though many people find it difficult to do, the proper way to conceive of these changes is that the value of units of *money* are rising and falling, not the values of goods.

The most common misunderstanding about inflation and deflation — echoed even by some renowned economists — is the idea that inflation is rising prices and deflation is falling prices. General price changes, though, are simply *effects*.

The price effects of inflation can occur in goods, which most people recognize as relating to inflation, or in investment assets, which people do not generally recognize as relating to inflation. The inflation of the 1970s induced dramatic price rises in gold, silver and commodities. The inflation of the 1980s and 1990s induced dramatic price rises in stock certificates and real estate. This difference in effect is due to differences in the social psychology that accompanies inflation and disinflation, respectively, as we will discuss briefly in Chapter 12.

The price effects of deflation are simpler. They tend to occur across the board, in goods and investment assets simultaneously.

The Primary Precondition of Deflation

Deflation requires a precondition: a major societal buildup in the extension of credit (and its flip side, the assumption of debt). Austrian economists Ludwig von Mises and Friedrich Hayek warned of the consequences of credit expansion, as have a handful of other economists, who today are mostly ignored. Bank credit and Elliott wave expert Hamilton Bolton, in his February 11, 1957 letter, summarized his observations this way:

> In reading a history of major depressions in the U.S. from 1830 on, I was impressed with the following:
>
> (a) All were set off by a deflation of excess credit. This was the one factor in common.
>
> (b) Sometimes the excess-of-credit situation seemed to last years before the bubble broke.
>
> (c) Some outside event, such as a major failure, brought the thing to a head, but the signs were visible many months, and in some cases years, in advance.
>
> (d) None was ever quite like the last, so that the public was always fooled thereby.
>
> (e) Some panics occurred under great government surpluses of revenue (1837, for instance) and some under great government deficits.
>
> (f) Credit is credit, whether non-self-liquidating or self-liquidating.
>
> (g) Deflation of non-self-liquidating credit usually produces the greater slumps.

Self-liquidating credit is a loan that is paid back, with interest, in a moderately short time from production. Production facilitated by the loan—for business start-up or expansion, for example—generates the financial return that makes repayment possible. The full transaction adds value to the economy.

Non-self-liquidating credit is a loan that is not tied to production and tends to stay in the system. When financial institutions lend for consumer purchases such as cars, boats or homes, or for speculations such as the purchase of stock certificates, no production effort is tied to the loan. Interest payments on such loans stress some other source of income. Contrary to nearly ubiquitous belief, such lending is almost always counter-productive; it adds *costs* to the economy, *not value*. If someone needs a cheap car to get to work, then a loan to buy it adds value to the economy; if someone wants a new SUV to consume, then a loan to buy it does not add value to the economy. Advocates claim that such loans "stimulate production," but they ignore the cost of the required debt service, which burdens production. They also ignore the subtle deterioration in the quality of spending choices due to the shift of buying power from people who have demonstrated a superior ability to invest or produce (creditors) to those who have demonstrated primarily a superior ability to consume (debtors).

Near the end of a major expansion, few creditors expect default, which is why they lend freely to weak borrowers. Few borrowers expect their fortunes to change, which is why they borrow freely. Deflation involves a substantial amount of *involuntary* debt liquidation because almost no one expects deflation before it starts.

What Triggers the Change to Deflation

A trend of credit expansion has two components: the general willingness to lend and borrow and the general *ability* of borrowers to pay interest and principal. These components depend respectively upon (1) the trend of people's confidence, i.e., whether both creditors and debtors think that debtors will be able to pay, and (2) the trend of production, which makes it either easier or harder *in actuality* for debtors to pay. So as long as confidence and production increase, the supply of credit tends to expand. The expansion of credit ends when the desire or ability to sustain the trend can no longer be maintained. As confidence and production decrease, the supply of credit contracts.

The psychological aspect of deflation and depression cannot be overstated. When the social mood trend changes from optimism to pessimism, creditors, debtors, producers and consumers change their primary orientation from *expansion* to *conservation.* As creditors become more conservative, they slow their lending. As debtors and potential debtors become more conservative, they borrow less or not at all. As producers become more conservative, they reduce expansion plans. As consumers become more conservative, they save more and spend less. These behaviors reduce the "velocity" of money, i.e., the speed with which it circulates to make purchases, thus putting downside pressure on prices. These forces reverse the former trend.

The structural aspect of deflation and depression is also crucial. The ability of the financial system to sustain increasing levels of credit rests upon a vibrant economy. At some point, a rising debt level requires so much energy to sustain — in terms of meeting interest payments, monitoring credit ratings, chasing delinquent borrowers and writing off bad loans — that it slows overall economic performance. A high-debt situation becomes unsustainable when the rate of economic growth falls beneath the prevailing rate of interest on money owed and creditors refuse to underwrite the interest payments with more credit.

When the burden becomes too great for the economy to support and the trend reverses, reductions in lending, spending and production cause debtors to earn less money with which to pay off their debts, so defaults rise. Default and fear of default exacerbate the new trend in psychology, which in turn causes creditors to reduce lending further. A downward "spiral" begins, feeding on pessimism just as the previous boom fed on optimism. The resulting cascade of debt liquidation is a deflationary crash. Debts are retired by paying them off, "restructuring" or default. In the first case, no value is lost; in the second, some value; in the third, all value. In desperately trying to raise cash to pay off loans, borrowers bring all kinds of assets to market, including stocks, bonds, commodities and real estate, causing their prices to plummet. The process ends only after the supply of credit falls to a level at which it is collateralized acceptably to the surviving creditors.

Why Deflationary Crashes and Depressions Go Together

A deflationary crash is characterized in part by a persistent, sustained, deep, general decline in people's desire and ability to lend and borrow. A depression is characterized in part by a persistent, sustained, deep, general decline in production. Since a decline in production reduces debtors' means to repay and service debt, a depression supports deflation. Since a decline in credit reduces new investment in economic activity, deflation supports depression. Because both credit and production support prices for investment assets, their prices fall in a deflationary depression. As asset prices fall, people lose wealth, which reduces their ability to offer credit, service debt and support production. This mix of forces is self-reinforcing.

The U.S. has experienced two major deflationary depressions, which lasted from 1835 to 1842 and from 1929 to 1932 respectively. Each one followed a period of substantial credit expansion. Credit expansion schemes have always ended in bust. The credit expansion scheme fostered by worldwide central banking (see Chapter 10) is the greatest ever. The bust, however long it takes, will be commensurate. If my outlook is correct, the deflationary crash that lies ahead will be even bigger than the two largest such episodes of the past 200 years.

Financial Values Can Disappear

People seem to take for granted that financial values can be created endlessly seemingly out of nowhere and pile up to the moon. Turn the direction around and mention that financial values can disappear into nowhere, and they insist that it is not possible. "The money has to go *somewhere*...It just moves from stocks to bonds to money funds...It never goes away...For every buyer, there is a seller, so the money just changes hands." That is true of the money, just as it was all the way up, but it's not true of the *values*, which *changed* all the way up.

Asset prices rise not because of "buying" *per se*, because indeed for every buyer, there is a seller. They rise because those transacting agree that their prices should be higher. All that everyone else — including those who own some of that asset and those who do not — need do is *nothing*. Conversely, for prices of assets to fall, it takes only *one* seller and *one* buyer who agree that the former value of an asset was too high. If no other bids are competing with that buyer's, then the value of the asset falls, *and it falls for everyone who owns it*. If a million other people own it, then their net worth goes down even though they did nothing. Two investors made it happen by transacting, and the rest of the investors made it happen by choosing not to disagree with their price. Financial values can disappear through a decrease in prices for any type of investment asset, including bonds, stocks and land.

Anyone who watches the stock or commodity markets closely has seen this phenomenon on a small scale many times. Whenever a market "gaps" up or down on an opening, it simply registers a new value *on the first trade*, which can be conducted by as few as two people. It did not take everyone's action to make it happen, just most people's inaction on the other side. In financial market "explosions" and panics, there are prices at which assets do not trade at all as they cascade from one trade to the next in great leaps.

A similar dynamic holds in the creation and destruction of credit. Let's suppose that a lender starts with a million dollars and the borrower starts with zero. Upon extending the loan, the borrower possesses the million dollars, yet the lender feels that he still owns the million dollars that he lent out. If anyone asks the lender what he is worth, he says, "a million dollars," and shows the note to prove it. Because of this conviction, there is, in the minds of the debtor and the creditor combined, two million dollars worth of value where before there was only one. When the lender calls in the debt and the borrower pays it, he gets back his million dollars. If the borrower can't pay it, the value of the note goes to zero. Either way, the extra value disappears. If the original lender sold his note for cash, then someone else down the line loses. In an actively traded bond market, the result of a sudden default is like a game of "hot potato": whoever holds it last loses. When the volume of credit is large, investors can perceive vast sums of money and value where in fact there are only repayment contracts, which are financial assets dependent upon consensus valuation and the ability of debtors to pay. IOUs can be issued indefinitely, but they have value only as long as their debtors can live up to them and only to the extent that people believe that they will.

The dynamics of value expansion and contraction explain why a bear market can bankrupt millions of people. At the peak of a credit expansion or a bull market, assets have been valued upward, and all participants are wealthy — both the people who sold the assets and the people who hold the assets. The latter group is far larger than the former, because the total supply of money has been relatively stable while the total value of financial assets has ballooned. When the market turns down, the dynamic goes into reverse. Only a very few owners of a collapsing financial asset trade it for money at 90 percent of peak value. Some others may get out at 80 percent, 50 percent or 30 percent of peak value. In each case, sellers are simply transferring the remaining future value losses to someone else. In a bear market, the vast, vast majority does nothing and gets stuck holding assets with low or non-existent valuations. The "million dollars" that a wealthy investor might have thought he had in his bond portfolio or at a stock's peak value can quite rapidly become $50,000 or $5000 or $50. *The rest of it just disappears.* You see, he never really had a million dollars; all he had was IOUs or stock certificates. The idea that it had a certain *financial value* was in his head and the heads of others who agreed. When the point of agreement changed, so did the value. Poof! Gone in a flash of aggregated neurons. This is exactly what happens to most investment assets in a period of deflation.

A Global Story

The next four chapters present a discussion that will allow you to understand today's money and credit situation and why deflation is due. I have chosen to focus on the history and conditions of the United States because (1) I have more knowledge of them, (2) the U.S. provides the world's reserve currency, making its story the most important, (3) the U.S. has issued more credit than any other nation and is the world's biggest debtor, and (4) to discuss other countries' financial details would be superfluous. If you understand one country's currency, banking and credit history, to a significant degree you understand them all. Make no mistake about it: It's a global story. Wherever you live, you will benefit from this knowledge.

Chapter 10:

Money, Credit and the Federal Reserve Banking System

An argument for deflation is not to be offered lightly because, given the nature of today's money, certain aspects of money and credit creation cannot be forecast, only surmised. Before we can discuss these issues, we have to understand how money and credit come into being. This is a difficult chapter, but if you can assimilate what it says, you will have knowledge of the banking system that not one person in 10,000 has.

The Origin of Intangible Money

Originally, money was a *tangible good* freely chosen by society. For millennia, gold or silver provided this function, although sometimes other tangible goods (such as copper, brass and seashells) did. Originally, credit was the right to access that tangible money, whether by an ownership certificate or by borrowing.

Today, almost all money is *intangible*. It is not, nor does it even represent, a physical good. How it got that way is a long, complicated, disturbing story, which would take a full book to relate properly. It began about 300 years ago, when an English financier conceived the idea of a national central bank. Governments have often outlawed free-market determinations of what constitutes money and imposed their own versions upon society by law, but earlier schemes usually involved coinage. Under central banking, a government forces its citizens to accept its *debt* as the only form of legal tender. The Federal Reserve System assumed this monopoly role in the United States in 1913.

What Is a Dollar?

Originally, a dollar was defined as a certain amount of gold. Dollar bills and notes were promises to pay lawful money, which was gold. Anyone could present dollars to a bank and receive gold in exchange, and banks could get gold from the U.S. Treasury for dollar bills.

In 1933, President Roosevelt and Congress outlawed U.S. gold ownership and nullified and prohibited all domestic contracts denoted in gold, making Federal Reserve notes the legal tender of the land. In 1971, President Nixon halted gold payments from the U.S. Treasury to foreigners in exchange for dollars. Today, the Treasury will not give anyone anything tangible in exchange for a dollar. Even though Federal Reserve notes are defined as "obligations of the United States," they are not obligations to *do* anything. Although a dollar is labeled a "note," which means a debt contract, it is not a note *for* anything.

Congress claims that the dollar is "legally" 1/42.22 of an ounce of gold. Can you buy gold for $42.22 an ounce? No. This definition is bogus, and everyone knows it. If you bring a dollar to the U.S. Treasury, you will not collect any tangible good, much less 1/42.22 of an ounce of gold. You will be sent home.

Some authorities were quietly amazed that when the government progressively removed the tangible backing for the dollar, the currency continued to function. If you bring a dollar to the marketplace, you can still buy goods with it because the government says (by "fiat") that it is money and because its long history of use has lulled people into accepting it as such. The volume of goods you can buy with it fluctuates according to the total volume of dollars — in both cash and credit — and their holders' level of confidence that those values will remain intact.

Exactly what a dollar is and what *backs* it are difficult questions to answer because no official entity will provide a satisfying answer. It has *no simultaneous actuality and definition.* It may be defined as 1/42.22 of an ounce of gold, but it is not *actually* that. Whatever it actually is (if anything) may not be definable. To the extent that its physical backing, if any, may be officially definable in actuality, no one is talking.

Let's attempt to define what gives the dollar objective value. As we will see in the next section, the dollar is "backed" primarily by government bonds, which are promises to pay dollars. So today, *the dollar is a promise backed by a promise to pay an identical promise.* What is the nature of each promise? If the Treasury will not give you anything tangible for your dollar, then the dollar is a promise to pay *nothing.* The Treasury should have no trouble keeping this promise.

In Chapter 9, I called the dollar "money." By the definition given there, it is. I used that definition and explanation because it makes the whole picture comprehensible. But the truth is that since the dollar is backed by *debt,* it is actually a *credit,* not money. It is a credit against what the government owes, denoted in dollars and backed by nothing. So although we may use the term "money" in referring to dollars, there is no longer any real money in the U.S. financial system; there is nothing but credit and debt.

As you can see, defining the dollar, and therefore the terms money, credit, inflation and deflation, today is a challenge, to say the least. Despite that challenge, we can still use these terms because people's minds have conferred meaning and value upon these ethereal concepts. Understanding this fact, we will now proceed with a discussion of how money and credit expand in today's financial system.

How the Federal Reserve System Manufactures Money

Over the years, the Federal Reserve Bank has transferred purchasing power from all other dollar holders primarily to the U.S. Treasury by a complex series of machinations. The U.S. Treasury borrows money by selling bonds in the open market. The Fed is said to "buy" the Treasury's bonds from banks and other financial institutions, but in actuality, it is allowed by law simply to fabricate a new checking account for the seller in exchange for the bonds. It holds the Treasury's bonds as assets against — as "backing" for — that new money. Now the seller is whole (he was just a middleman), the Fed has the bonds, and the Treasury has the new money. This transactional train is a long route to a simple alchemy (called "monetizing" the debt) in which the Fed turns government bonds into money. The net result is as if the government had simply fabricated its own checking account, although it pays the Fed a portion of the bonds' interest for providing the service surreptitiously. To date, the Fed has monetized about $600 billion worth of Treasury obligations. This process expands the supply of *money*.

In 1980, Congress gave the Fed the legal authority to monetize any agency's debt. In other words, it can exchange the bonds of a government, bank or other institution for a checking account denominated in dollars. This mechanism gives the President, through the Treasury, a mechanism for "bailing out" debt-troubled governments, banks or other institutions that can no longer get financing anywhere else. Such decisions are made for political reasons, and the Fed can go along or refuse, at least as the relationship currently stands. Today, the Fed has about $36 billion worth of foreign debt on its books. The power to grant or refuse such largesse is unprecedented.

Each new Fed account denominated in dollars is new money, but contrary to common inference, it is not new value. The new account *has* value, but that value comes from a *reduction* in the value of all other outstanding accounts denominated in dollars. That reduction takes place as the favored institution spends the newly credited dollars, driving up the dollar-denominated demand for goods and thus their prices. All other dollar holders still hold the same *number* of dollars, but now there are more dollars in circulation, and each one purchases less in the way of goods and services. The old dollars *lose* value to the extent that the new account *gains* value. The net result is a transfer of value to the receiver's account from those of all other dollar holders. This fact is not readily obvious because the *unit of account* throughout the financial system does not change even though its *value* changes.

It is important to understand exactly what the Fed has the power to do in this context: It has legal permission to transfer wealth from dollar savers to certain debtors *without the permission of the savers*. The effect on the money supply is exactly the same as if the money had been counterfeited and slipped into circulation.

In the old days, governments would inflate the money supply by diluting their coins with base metal or printing notes directly. Now the same old game is much less obvious. On the other hand, there is also far more to it. This section has described the Fed's *secondary* role. The Fed's main occupation is not creating money but *facilitating credit*. This crucial difference will eventually bring us to why deflation is possible.

How the Federal Reserve Has Encouraged the Growth of Credit

Congress authorized the Fed not only to create money for the government but also to "smooth out" the economy by manipulating credit (which also happens to be a re-election tool for incumbents). Politics being what they are, this manipulation has been almost exclusively in the direction of making credit easy to obtain. The Fed used to make more credit available to the banking system by monetizing federal debt, that is, by creating money. Under the structure of our "fractional reserve" system, banks were authorized to employ that new money as "reserves" against which they could make new loans. Thus, new money meant new credit.

It meant a lot of new credit because banks were allowed by regulation to lend out 90 percent of their deposits, which meant that banks had to keep 10 percent of deposits on hand ("in reserve") to cover withdrawals. When the Fed increased a bank's reserves, that bank could lend 90 percent of *those* new dollars. Those dollars, in turn, would make their way to other banks as new deposits. Those other banks could lend 90 percent of *those* deposits, and so on. The expansion of reserves and deposits throughout the banking system this way is called the "multiplier effect." This process expanded the supply of *credit* well beyond the supply of money.

Because of competition from money market funds, banks began using fancy financial manipulation to get around reserve requirements. In the early 1990s, the Federal Reserve Board under Chairman Alan Greenspan took a controversial step and removed banks' reserve requirements almost entirely. To do so, it first lowered to zero the reserve requirement on all accounts other than checking accounts. Then it let banks pretend that they have almost no checking account balances by allowing them to "sweep" those deposits into various savings accounts and money market funds at the end of each business day. Magically, when monitors check the banks' balances at night, they find the value of checking accounts artificially understated by hundreds of billions of dollars. The net result is that banks today conveniently meet their nominally required reserves (currently about $45b.) with the cash in their vaults that they need to hold for everyday transactions anyway.

By this change in regulation, the Fed essentially removed itself from the businesses of requiring banks to hold reserves and of manipulating the level of those reserves. This move took place during a recession and while S&P earnings per share were undergoing their biggest drop since the 1940s. The temporary cure for that economic contraction was the ultimate in "easy money."

We still have a fractional reserve system on the books, but we do not have one in actuality. Now banks can lend out virtually all of their deposits. In fact, they can lend out *more* than all of their deposits, because banks' parent companies can issue stock, bonds, commercial paper or any financial instrument and lend the proceeds to their subsidiary banks, upon which assets the banks can make new loans. In other words, to a limited degree, banks can arrange to create their own new money for lending purposes. Today, U.S. banks have extended 25 percent more total credit than they have in total deposits ($5.4 trillion vs. $4.3 trillion). Since all banks do not engage in this practice, others must be quite aggressive at it. For more on this theme, see Chapter 19.

Recall that when banks lend money, it gets deposited in other banks, which can lend it out again. Without a reserve requirement, the multiplier effect is no longer restricted to ten times deposits; it is virtually unlimited. Every new dollar deposited can be lent over and over throughout the system: A deposit becomes a loan becomes a deposit becomes a loan, and so on.

As you can see, the fiat money system has encouraged inflation via both money creation and the expansion of credit. This dual growth has been the monetary engine of the historic uptrend of stock prices in wave (V) from 1932. The stupendous growth in bank credit since 1975 (see graphs in Chapter 11) has provided the monetary fuel for its final advance, wave V. The effective elimination of reserve requirements a decade ago extended that trend to one of historic proportion.

The Net Effect of Monetization

Although the Fed has almost wholly withdrawn from the role of holding book-entry reserves for banks, it has not retired its holdings of Treasury bonds. Because the Fed is legally bound to back its notes (greenback currency) with government securities, today almost all of the Fed's Treasury bond assets are held as reserves against a nearly equal dollar value of Federal Reserve notes in circulation around the world. Thus, the net result of the Fed's 89 years of money inflating is that the Fed has turned $600 billion worth of U.S. Treasury and foreign obligations into Federal Reserve notes.

Today the Fed's production of currency is passive, in response to orders from domestic and foreign banks, which in turn respond to demand from the public. Under current policy, banks must pay for that currency with any remaining reserve balances. If they don't have any, they borrow to cover the cost and pay back that loan as they collect interest on their own loans. Thus, as things stand, the Fed no longer considers itself in the business of "printing money" for the government. Rather, it facilitates the expansion of credit to satisfy the lending policies of government and banks.

If banks and the Treasury were to become strapped for cash in a monetary crisis, policies could change. The unencumbered production of banknotes could become deliberate Fed or government policy, as we have seen happen in other countries throughout history. At this point, there is no indication that the Fed has entertained any such policy. Nevertheless, Chapters 13 and 22 address this possibility.

For Information

There is much information available on the Fed's activities, but nowhere have I found a concise summary such as presented in this chapter. If you would like to learn more, I can start you

off on your search. For a positive spin on the Fed's value, contact
the Fed itself or any conventional economist. For a less rosy view,
contact the Foundation for the Advancement of Monetary Education or join the Ludwig von Mises Institute and order a copy of
their 150-page paperback, *The Case Against the Fed*, by Murray
N. Rothbard, which is just $5 plus shipping from www.mises.org/
catalog.asp. The most knowledgeable source that I have found
with respect to the workings of the Federal Reserve System is Lou
Crandall of Wrightson Associates, publisher of *The Money Market
Observer*, a service for traders. Contact information is as follows:

> *The Money Market Observer*
> Wrightson Associates
> Website: www.wrightson.com
> Email: sales@wrightson.com
> Address: 560 Washington St., New York, NY 10014
> Phone: 212-815-6540
> Fax: 212-341-9253
> Editor: Lou Crandall

> Federal Reserve
> Website: www.federalreserve.gov
> Phone: 202-452-3819

> Ludwig von Mises Institute
> Website: www.mises.org
> Email: mail@mises.org
> Address: 518 West Magnolia Avenue, Auburn, AL 36832
> Phone: 334-321-2100
> Fax: 334-321-2119
> Book catalog: www.mises.org/catalog.asp

> Foundation for the Advancement of Monetary Education
> Website: www.fame.org
> Email: info@fame.org
> Address: Box 625, FDR Station, New York, NY 10150
> Phone: (212)818-1206
> Fax: (212) 818-1197

Chapter 11:

What Makes Deflation Likely Today?

Following the Great Depression, the Fed and the U.S. government embarked on a program, sometimes consciously and sometimes not, both of increasing the creation of new money and credit and of fostering the confidence of lenders and borrowers so as to facilitate the expansion of credit. These policies both accommodated and encouraged the expansionary trend of the 'Teens and 1920s, which ended in bust, and the far larger expansionary trend that began in 1932 and which has accelerated over the past half-century.

Other governments and central banks have followed similar policies. The International Monetary Fund, the World Bank and similar institutions, funded mostly by the U.S. taxpayer, have extended immense credit around the globe. Their policies have supported nearly continuous worldwide inflation, particularly over the past thirty years. As a result, the global financial system is gorged with non-self-liquidating credit.

Conventional economists excuse and praise this system under the erroneous belief that expanding money and credit promotes economic growth, which is terribly false. It appears to do so for a while, but in the long run, the swollen mass of debt collapses of its own weight, which is deflation, and destroys the economy. Only the Austrian school understands this fact. A devastated economy, moreover, encourages radical politics, which is even worse. We will address this topic in Chapter 26.

A House of (Credit) Cards

The value of credit that has been extended worldwide is unprecedented. In 1995, United States entities of all types owed a total of $17.1 trillion dollars. I thought it was a big number. That figure has soared to $29.5 trillion at the end of 2001, so it should be $30 trillion by the time this book is printed. That figure represents three times the annual Gross Domestic Product, the highest ratio ever.

Worse, most of this debt is the non-self-liquidating type. Much of it comprises loans to governments, investment loans for buying stock and real estate, and loans for everyday consumer items and services, none of which has any production tied to it. Even a lot of corporate debt is non-self-liquidating, since so much of corporate activity these days is related to finance rather than production. The Fed's aggressive easy-money policy of recent months has cruelly enticed even more marginal borrowers into the ring, particularly in the area of mortgages.

This $30 trillion figure, moreover, does not include government guarantees such as bank deposit insurance, unfunded Social Security obligations, and so on, which could add another $20 trillion or so to that figure, depending upon what estimates we accept. It also does not take into account U.S. banks' holdings of $50 trillion worth of derivatives at representative value (equaling five full years' worth of U.S. GDP), which could turn into IOUs for more money than their issuers imagine. Then there is the problem of major coporations' unfunded pension plan liabilities. Companies have promised billions of dollars in fixed-income pensions, but their plan assets will fall so much in value that they will have to fund those pensions from their operating budgets. How much of those liabilities will turn into debt is unknown, but the risk is large and real. Is it not appropriate that you are now reading Chapter 11?

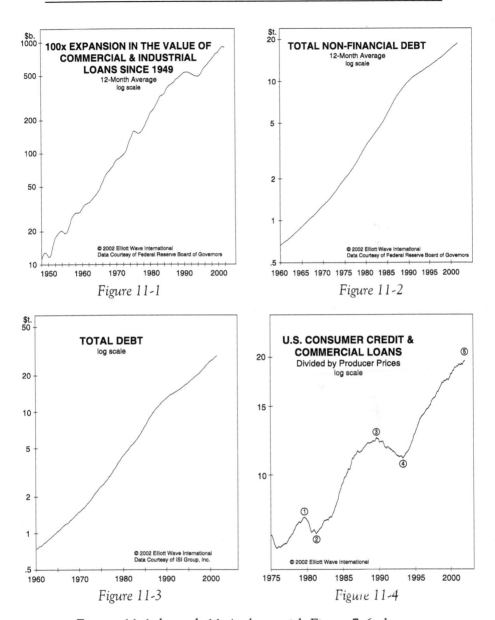

Figure 11-1

Figure 11-2

Figure 11-3

Figure 11-4

Figures 11-1 through 11-4, along with Figure 7-6, show some aspects of both the amazing *growth* in credit — as much as 100 fold since 1949 — and the astonishing *extent* of indebtedness today among corporations, governments and the public, both in terms of total dollars' worth and as a percent of GDP. There are

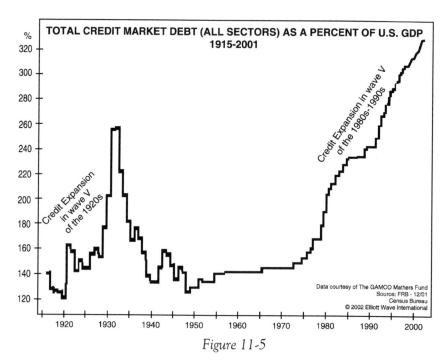

Figure 11-5

so many measures revealing how extended debtors have become that I could dedicate a whole book to that topic alone.

Runaway credit expansion is a characteristic of major fifth waves. Waxing optimism supports not only the investment boom but also a credit expansion, which in turn fuels the investment boom. Figure 11-5 is a stunning picture of the credit expansion of wave V of the 1920s (beginning the year that Congress authorized the Fed), which ended in a bust, and of wave V in the 1980s-1990s, which is even bigger.

I have heard economists understate the debt risk of the United States by focusing on the level of its net debt to foreigners, which is just above $2 trillion, as if all other debt we just "owe to ourselves." But every loan involves a creditor and a debtor, who are separate entities. No one owes a debt to himself. Creditors in other countries who have lent trillions to the U.S. and their own fellow citizens have added to the ocean of worldwide debt, not reduced it. So not only has there been an expansion of credit, but it has been the biggest credit expansion in history by a huge margin. Coextensively, not only is there a threat of deflation, but there is also the threat of the biggest deflation in history by a huge margin.

Broader Ideas of Money

It is a good thing that deflation is defined as a reduction in the relative volume of money and credit, so we are not forced to distinguish too specifically between the two things in today's world. Exactly what paper and which book entries should be designated as "money" in a fiat-enforced debt-based paper currency system with an overwhelming volume of credit is open to debate.

Many people believe that when they hold stock certificates or someone's IOUs (in the form of bills, notes and bonds), they still have money. "I have my money in the stock market" or "in municipal bonds" are common phrases. In truth, they own not money but financial assets, in the form of corporate shares or repayment contracts. As we will see in Chapter 19, even "money in the bank" in the modern system is nothing but a call on the bank's loans, which means that it is an IOU.

There is no universally accepted definition of what constitutes "the money supply," just an array of arguments over where to draw the line. The most conservative definition limits money to the value of circulating cash currency and checking accounts. As we have seen, though, even they have an origin in debt. Broader definitions of money include the short-term debt of strong issuers. They earn the description "money equivalents" and are often available in "money market funds." Today, there are several accepted definitions of the "money supply," each with its own designation, such as M1, M2 and M3.

The mental quality of modern money extends the limits of what people *think* is money. For example, a futures contract is an IOU for goods at a certain price. Is that money? Many companies use stock options as payment for services. Is that money? Over the past fifteen years, a vast portion of the population has come to believe the oft-repeated phrase, "Owning shares of a stock fund is just like having money in the bank, only better." They have put their life's savings into stock funds under the assumption that they have the equivalent of a money account *on deposit* there. But is it money? The answer to all these questions is no, but people have come to think of such things as money. They spend their actual money and take on debt in accordance with that belief. Because the idea of money is so highly psychological today, the line between what is money and what is not has become blurred, at least in people's minds, and that is where it matters when it comes to understanding the psychology of deflation. Today the vast volume of what people consider to be money has ballooned the psychological potential for deflation far beyond even the immense monetary potential for deflation implied in Figures 11-1 through 11-5.

A Reversal in the Making

No tree grows to the sky. No shared mental state, including confidence, holds forever. The exceptional volume of credit extended throughout the world has been precarious for some time. As Bolton observed, though, such conditions can maintain for years. If the trend toward increasing confidence were to reverse, the supply of credit, and therefore the supply of money, would shrink, producing deflation. Of course, that is a big "if," because for half a century, those wary of credit growth in the U.S. have sounded warnings of collapse, and it has not happened. This is where wave analysis comes in.

Recall that two things are required to produce an expansionary trend in credit. The first is expansionary psychology, and the second is the ability to pay interest. Chapter 4 of this book makes the case that after nearly seven decades of a positive trend, *confidence* has probably reached its limit. Chapter 1 demonstrates a multi-decade deceleration in the U.S. economy that will soon stress debtors' *ability to pay*. These dual forces should serve to usher in a credit contraction very soon.

Wave analysis can also be useful when applied directly to the realm of credit growth. Figure 11-4 is a plot of consumer credit and commercial loans divided by the Producer Price Index to reflect loan values in constant dollars. It shows that the uptrend in real credit value extended to consumers and businesses has traced out five waves since the major bottom of 1974. This is nearly the same picture that we see in stock market margin debt (Figure 7-4). Plots of the credit expansion's rate of change show that the growth in credit is running out of steam at multiple degrees of trend, which is what the analysis in Chapter 1 reveals about the economy. The downturn, it appears, is imminent if not already upon us.

If borrowers begin paying back enough of their debt relative to the amount of new loans issued, or if borrowers default on enough of their loans, or if the economy cannot support the aggregate cost of interest payments and the promise to return principal, or if enough banks and investors become sufficiently reluctant to lend, the "multiplier effect" will go into reverse. Total *credit* will contract, so bank deposits will contract, so the supply of *money* will contract, *all with the same degree of leverage with which they were initially expanded.* The immense reverse credit leverage of zero-reserve (actually *negative*-reserve) banking, then, is the primary fuel for a deflationary crash.

Japan's deflation and its march into depression began in 1990. Southeast Asia's began in 1997. Argentina's has just made headlines. The U.S. and the rest of the nations that have so far escaped are next in line. When the lines in Figures 11-1 through 11-5 turn down (the first one may already have done so), the game will be up.

How Big a Deflation?

Today, under what is left of bank reserves, there are $11 billion on reserve at the Fed plus $44 billion in cash on hand in banks' vaults. This $55 billion total covers the entire stock of bank credit issued in the United States. This amount equates to 1/100 of M2, valued today at $5.5 trillion, and 1/550 of all U.S. debt outstanding, valued today at $30 trillion. If we generously designate the U.S. money supply to include all Federal Reserve notes worldwide, totaling just under $600 billion, these ratios are 1/10 and 1/55.

Of course, since the dollar itself is just a credit, there is no tangible commodity backing the debt that is outstanding today. Real collateral underlies many loans, but its total value may be as little as a few cents on the dollar, euro or yen of total credit. I say "real" collateral because although one can borrow against the value of stocks, for example, they are just paper certificates, inflated well beyond the liquidating value of the underlying company's assets. One can also borrow against the value of bonds, which is an amazing trick: using debt to finance debt. As a result of widespread loans made on such bases, the discrepancy between the value of total debt outstanding and the value of its real underlying collateral is huge. It is anyone's guess how much of that gap ultimately will have to close to satisfy the credit markets in a deflationary depression. For our purposes, it is enough to say that the gap itself, and therefore the deflationary potential, is historically large.

Although the United States is the world leader in fiat money and credit creation, a version of the story told in this and the preceding chapter has happened in every country in the world with a central bank. As a result, we risk overwhelming deflation in every corner of the globe.

Chapter 12:

Timing Deflations: The Kondratieff Cycle

I believe I have a leg to stand on with respect to forecasting monetary trends. In November 1979, right in the culminating heat of a hard-money panic following 30 years of accelerating inflation, *The Elliott Wave Theorist* reasoned, "The incredible conjunction of 'fives' in different markets [gold, silver, interest rates, bonds and commodities] all seem to point to the same conclusion: *The world is about to begin a phase of general disinflation.*" That is exactly what began the following month and has been in force ever since.

As this example shows, Elliott waves provide an excellent tool for anticipating the nuances of inflation and deflation. However, a particular cycle of social activity has also proved useful in the effort.

Nikolai Kondratieff, a Russian economist, proposed in a 1926 paper that industrial economies followed a repeating cycle of change in prices and production. Actually, this cycle is primarily one of liquidity, not price, so rising and declining trends in prices for money, labor and goods are an effect of the cycle, not a cause. Although this cycle has averaged 54 years in duration, cyclic periodicities can expand and contract and are therefore inherently unreliable for precise timing. But the sequence of events within the Kondratieff cycle may be an immutable social process, regardless of how many decades it takes to play out. The presence of an inflating mechanism exacerbates the extremes of the cycle's manifestations.

Although the precise sequence and interplay of events can be different depending upon the position of the major Elliott waves, here is how recent Kondratieff cycles have played out: As liquidity expands in the initial phase of the cycle, commodity prices rise to reflect increasing business activity and (in most cases) inflation. As business activity and inflation accelerate, speculators begin to bid up commodity prices so as to reflect their increasing fear that inflation will *continue* to accelerate. After the *rate* of inflation peaks and begins to fall, the "acceleration premium" is removed from prices. Thus, commodity prices begin to fall despite continued but slowing inflation, a trend called disinflation. At the same time, a change in psychology away from fear and toward feelings of relief and hope induces people to channel the excess purchasing media created during disinflation into bidding up the prices of investment assets such as stocks. Because inflation continues, the wholesale prices that manufacturers charge for finished products, the retail prices that stores charge for goods and the level of wages that employers pay for labor all continue to rise but at a continuously lesser rate, following the rising but slowing trend of business activity and inflation.

Near the end of the cycle, the rates of change in business activity and inflation slip to zero. When they fall *below* zero, deflation is in force. As liquidity contracts, commodity prices fall more rapidly, and prices for stocks, wages and wholesale and retail goods join in the decline. When deflation ends and prices reach bottom, the cycle begins again.

The position of the current Kondratieff cycle supports the case for deflation directly ahead. In the previous cycle, wholesale prices of commodities generally bottomed in 1932-33. But many important prices, such as those for rent and corporate earnings

Figure 12-1

(see Figure 6-4), bottomed as late as 1949, 53 years after the preceding Kondratieff cycle bottom in 1896. You can see this influence in Figure 11-5, which shows that credit extension as a percent of GDP also bottomed in 1949. PPI-adjusted stock prices (not shown) ended an Elliott wave bear market pattern in 1949 as well.

The rise in liquidity after 1949 was the upside portion of a new cycle. Figure 12-1 shows that prices for monetary and agricultural commodities generally peaked in 1980-1981 and have been trending lower ever since. That top marked the transition to disinflation and the downside of the cycle.

You can also see evidence of the Kondratieff cycle in the price of money extended to reliable borrowers. Since total borrowing contracts during deflation, prime interest rates fall. Figure 12-2 shows most of four cycles. As you can see, long-term interest rates last bottomed in the 1940s as well. They topped again in 1981 at the peak of the current cycle and have been trending down ever since, as it heads into its low. This cycle is not to be taken as assurance that rates specifically on U.S. Treasury bonds will necessarily fall further. As we will see in Chapter 15, rates fall

Figure 12-2

Figure 12-3

only on the highest quality debt, which may or may not include long-term U.S. Treasuries in the current cycle.

The Position of the Kondratieff Cycle Today

Disinflation has been in force for over twenty years, since 1980-1981. During this time, wholesale and retail prices continued to rise but at a progressively lesser rate, following the slowing trend of disinflation. Today, the rate of upside change in both of these sets of prices combined has reached zero, as you can see in Figure 12-3.

In recent years, economists have been applauding the Fed for engineering a perfect world of economic growth with low inflation. We thus possess "the holy grail sought by most central bankers," as a national business magazine puts it. Are you shocked to learn that this is the same situation that economists applauded in 1929? In actuality, in both cases, the uptrend in goods prices that the Fed fostered for years through credit expansion slowed due to the drag of interest payments on the consumer's capacity to spend. As in 1930-1932, today's "perfect world" will soon be revealed as something quite different.

If the Kondratieff cycle performs normally, the combined rate of change for the PPI and CPI will soon go negative. Whatever the cycle's timing may be, its *sequence* calls for several more years of declining commodity prices, a few years of newly declining wholesale and retail prices and a sharp decline in industrial production. These trends will end when the deflation ends, at the bottom of the cycle.

If the duration of recent past cycles is to repeat, then the falling portion of the current economic cycle would last another two years, and the depression would reach bottom in 2004. If the cycle lasts as long as the longest cycle of the past three centuries, the depression would end in 2011. For our current purposes, these numbers are guides, not predictions, primarily indicating that we are talking a matter of years, not forever. As happened during the late 1700s and in 1835-1842 in the U.S., and as has been happening over the past twelve years in Japan, the economy could experience multiple contractions with intervening recoveries. In fact, since the initial stock market decline should take an A-B-C shape, I lean toward expecting two depressions with an intervening recovery. Regardless, as of today, the process of society-wide debt liquidation lies ahead. Given the long-term five-wave patterns in several debt series (see Figures 7-4 and 11-4), the near-term three-wave rallies in stock averages (see Figure 4-7), the CRB index (see Figure 21-10), gold and silver, the fall to a zero rate of change in the combined PPI and CPI (see Figure 12-3), the sharp drop in interest rates last year and the fact that house prices are scaling new heights all alone (a technical condition called a "bearish non-confirmation"), I conclude that deflation — a contraction in the total volume of money and credit — is probably due to begin just about now.

A Minority View

In the interest of full disclosure, I should warn you that most of today's economists dismiss the Kondratieff cycle as a fantasy. When markets and the economy oscillate violently, as they did for example during the 1840s-1850s, the 1930s-1940s, and the 1970s, cycles are a popular topic. Harvard professor Dr. Joseph Schumpeter wrote in the 1930s, "The Kondratieff Wave is the single-most important tool in economic forecasting." By contrast, when investment markets and the economic trend have been up for a long time, the very idea of cycles is generally dismissed out of hand. Here at the peak of a two-centuries-long uptrend, what more can cycles be other than a subject of derision? Ironically, this oscillating psychology toward the idea of cycles is exactly what allows cycles to exist.

More striking in my opinion is the fact that most of the rare believers in the Kondratieff cycle think it has already bottomed. Some say it bottomed in the early 1980s, an idea that is as contrary to Kondratieff's cycle as it could possibly be. Others were arguing that it bottomed in 1997 or 1998, which did not fit the degree of retrenchment required by the cycle at all. These interpreters have been calling for more decades of expansion, in fact an acceleration of growth.

I am convinced that the explanation for such opinions is that these analysts feel optimistic and have to rationalize why. I am aware of only two other writers who see the cycle performing in its typical way and with its normal timing. Ian Gordon, who in 1998 began publishing *The Long Wave Analyst*, is an astute historian and student of the subject. If you would like to pursue this subject further, you may request copies of his publication through the following means:

The Long Wave Analyst
Email: ian_gordon@canaccord.com
Address: Canaccord Capital, Suite 1200, 595 Burrard St.,
Vancouver, BC, V7X 1J1 Canada
Phone: 604-643-0280
Fax: 604-643-0152
Editor: Ian Gordon

The stock market and the economy weave around the Kondratieff cycle in interesting ways over the past 300 years. Generally speaking, when the Kondratieff cycle bottoms, stocks are at bargain levels.

Chapter 13:

Can the Fed Stop Deflation?

Consensus Opinion Concerning Deflation

Seventy years of nearly continuous inflation have made most people utterly confident of its permanence. If the majority of economists have any monetary fear at all, it is fear of inflation, which is the opposite of deflation. Two of the world's most renowned economists have reiterated this fear in recent months in *The Wall Street Journal*, predicting an immediate acceleration of inflation.

As for the very idea of deflation, one economist a few years ago told a national newspaper that deflation had a "1 in 10,000" chance of occurring. The Chairman of Carnegie Mellon's business school calls the notion of deflation "utter nonsense." A professor of economics at Pepperdine University states flatly, "Rising stock prices will inevitably lead to rising prices in the rest of the economy." The publication of an economic think-tank insists, "Anyone who asserts that deflation is imminent or already underway ignores the rationale for fiat currency — that is, to facilitate the manipulation of economic activity." A financial writer explains, "Deflation…is totally a function of the Federal Reserve's management of monetary policy. It has nothing to do with the business cycle, productivity, taxes, booms and busts or anything else." Concurring, an adviser writes in a national magazine, "U.S. deflation would be simple to stop today. The Federal Reserve

could just print more money, ending the price slide in its tracks."
Yet another sneers, "Get real," and likens anyone concerned
about deflation to "small children." One maverick economist
whose model accommodates deflation and who actually expects
a period of deflation is nevertheless convinced that it will be a
"good deflation" and "nothing to fear." On financial television,
another analyst (who apparently defines deflation as falling prices)
quips, "Don't worry about deflation. All it does is pad profits." A
banker calls any episode of falling oil prices "a positive catalyst
[that] will put more money in consumers' pockets. It will benefit
companies that are powered by energy and oil, and it will benefit the overall economy." Others excitedly welcome recently
falling commodity prices as an economic stimulus "equivalent
to a massive tax cut." A national business magazine guarantees,
"That's not deflation ahead, just slower inflation. Put your deflation worries away." The senior economist with Deutsche Bank
in New York estimates, "The chance of deflation is at most one
in 50" (apparently up from the 1 in 10,000 of a couple of years
ago). The President of the San Francisco Fed says, "The idea
that we are launching into a prolonged period of declining prices
I don't think has substance." A former government economist
jokes that deflation is "57th on my list of worries, right after the
56th — fear of being eaten by piranhas." These comments about
deflation represent entrenched professional opinion.

As you can see, anyone challenging virtually the entire army
of financial and economic thinkers, from academic to professional, from liberal to conservative, from Keynesian socialist to
Objectivist free-market, from Monetarist technocratic even to
many vocal proponents of the Austrian school, must respond
to their belief that inflation is virtually inevitable and deflation
impossible.

"Potent Directors"

The primary basis for today's belief in perpetual prosperity and inflation with *perhaps* an occasional recession is what I call the "potent directors" fallacy. It is nearly impossible to find a treatise on macroeconomics today that does not assert or assume that the Federal Reserve Board has learned to control both our money and our economy. Many believe that it also possesses immense power to manipulate the stock market.

The very idea that it *can* do these things is false. Last October, before the House and Senate Joint Economic committee, Chairman Alan Greenspan himself called the idea that the Fed could prevent recessions a "puzzling" notion, chalking up such events to exactly what causes them: "human psychology." In August 1999, he even more specifically described the stock market as being driven by "waves of optimism and pessimism." He's right on this point, but no one is listening.

The Chairman also expresses the view that the Fed has the power to temper economic swings for the better. Is that what it does? Politicians and most economists assert that a central bank is necessary for maximum growth. Is that the case?

This is not the place for a treatise on the subject, but a brief dose of reality should serve. Real economic growth in the U.S. was greater in the nineteenth century without a central bank than it has been in the twentieth century with one. Real economic growth in Hong Kong during the latter half of the twentieth century outstripped that of every other country in the entire world, and it had no central bank. Anyone who advocates a causal connection between central banking and economic performance must conclude that a central bank is harmful to economic growth. For recent examples of the failure of the idea of efficacious economic directors, just look around. Since Japan's boom ended in 1990, its regulators have been using every presumed macroeconomic "tool" to get the Land of the Sinking Sun rising again, as yet to no avail. The World Bank, the IMF, local central banks and government officials were "wisely managing" Southeast Asia's boom until it collapsed spectacularly in 1997. Prevent the bust? They expressed profound dismay that it even happened. As I write this paragraph, Argentina's economy has just crashed despite the machinations of its own presumed "potent directors." I say "despite," but the truth is that directors, whether they are Argentina's, Japan's or America's, *cannot* make things better and have *always* made things worse. It is a principle that meddling in the free market can only disable it. People think that the Fed has "managed" the economy brilliantly in the 1980s and 1990s. Most financial professionals believe that the only potential culprit of a deviation from the path to ever greater prosperity would be current-time central bank actions so flagrantly stupid as to be beyond the realm of possibility. But the deep flaws in the Fed's manipulation of the banking system to induce and facilitate the extension of credit will bear bitter fruit in the next depression. Economists who do not believe that a prolonged expansionary credit policy has consequences will soon be blasting the Fed for "mistakes" in the present, whereas the errors that matter most reside in the past. Regardless of whether this truth comes to light, the populace will disrespect the Fed and other central banks mightily by the time the depression is over. For many people, the single biggest financial shock and surprise over the next decade will be the revelation that the Fed has never really known what on earth it was doing. The spectacle of U.S. officials in recent weeks lecturing Japan on how to contain deflation will be revealed as the grossest hubris. Make sure that you avoid the disillusion and financial devastation that will afflict those who harbor a misguided faith in the world's central bankers and the idea that they can manage our money, our credit or our economy.

The Fed's Final Card

The Fed used to have two sources of power to expand the total amount of bank credit: It could lower reserve requirements or lower the discount rate, the rate at which it lends money to banks. In shepherding reserve requirements down to zero, it has expended all the power of the first source. In 2001, the Fed lowered its discount rate from 6 percent to 1.25 percent, an unprecedented amount in such a short time. By doing so, it has expended much of the power residing in the second source. What will it do if the economy resumes its contraction, lower interest rates to zero? *Then what?*

Why the Fed Cannot Stop Deflation

Countless people say that deflation is impossible because the Federal Reserve Bank can just *print money* to stave off deflation. If the Fed's main jobs were simply establishing new checking accounts and grinding out banknotes, that's what it might do. But in terms of *volume*, that has not been the Fed's primary function, which for 89 years has been in fact to foster the *expansion of credit*. Printed fiat currency depends almost entirely upon the whims of the issuer, but credit is another matter entirely.

What the Fed does is to set or influence certain very short-term interbank loan rates. It sets the discount rate, which is the Fed's nominal near-term lending rate to banks. This action is primarily a "signal" of the Fed's posture because banks almost never borrow from the Fed, as doing so implies desperation. (Whether they will do so more in coming years under duress is another question.) More actively, the Fed buys and sells overnight "repurchase agreements," which are collateralized loans among banks and dealers, to defend its chosen rate, called the "federal funds" rate. In stable times, the lower the rate at which banks can borrow short-term funds, the lower the rate at which they can offer long-term loans to the public. Thus, though the Fed

undertakes its operations to influence bank borrowing, its ultimate goal is to influence public borrowing from banks. Observe
that the Fed makes bank credit more available or less available
to two sets of *willing borrowers*.

During social-mood uptrends, this strategy appears to work,
because the borrowers — i.e., banks and their customers — are
confident, eager participants in the process. During monetary
crises, the Fed's attempts to target interest rates don't appear to
work because in such environments, the demands of creditors
overwhelm the Fed's desires. In the inflationary 1970s to early
1980s, rates of interest soared to 16 percent, and the Fed was
forced to follow, not because it wanted that interest rate but
because debt investors demanded it.

Regardless of the federal funds rate, banks set their own
lending rates to customers. During economic contractions, banks
can become fearful to make long-term loans even with cheap
short-term money. In that case, they raise their loan rates to
make up for the perceived risk of loss. In particularly scary times,
banks have been known virtually to cease new commercial and
consumer lending altogether. Thus, the ultimate success of the
Fed's attempts to influence the total amount of credit outstanding depends not only upon willing borrowers but also upon the
banks as *willing creditors*.

Economists hint at the Fed's occasional impotence in fostering credit expansion when they describe an ineffective monetary
strategy, i.e., a drop in the Fed's target rates that does not stimulate borrowing, as "pushing on a string." At such times, low
Fed-influenced rates cannot overcome creditors' disinclination
to lend and/or customers' unwillingness or inability to borrow.
That's what has been happening in Japan for over a decade, where
rates have fallen effectively to zero but the volume of credit is
still contracting. Unfortunately for would-be credit manipulators,
the leeway in interest-rate manipulation stops at zero percent.

When prices for goods fall rapidly during deflation, the value of money rises, so even a zero interest rate imposes a heavy real cost on borrowers, who are obligated to return more valuable dollars at a later date. No one with money wants to pay someone else to borrow it, so interest rates cannot go negative. (Some people have proposed various pay-to-borrow schemes for central banks to employ in combating deflation, but it is doubtful that the real world would accommodate any of them.)

When banks and investors are reluctant to lend, then only *higher* interest rates can induce them to do so. In deflationary times, the market accommodates this pressure with falling bond prices and higher lending rates for all but the most pristine debtors. But wait; it's not that simple, because higher interest rates do not serve only to *attract* capital; they can also make it flee. Once again, the determinant of the difference is market psychology: Creditors in a defensive frame of mind can perceive a borrower's willingness to pay high rates as desperation, in which case, the higher the offer, the more repelled is the creditor. In a deflationary crash, rising interest rates on bonds mean that creditors fear default.

A defensive credit market can scuttle the Fed's efforts to get lenders and borrowers to agree to transact at all, much less at some desired target rate. If people and corporations are unwilling to borrow or unable to finance debt, and if banks and investors are disinclined to lend, central banks cannot force them to do so. During deflation, they cannot even induce them to do so with a zero interest rate.

Thus, regardless of assertions to the contrary, the Fed's purported "control" of borrowing, lending and interest rates ultimately depends upon an accommodating market psychology and cannot be set by decree. So ultimately, the Fed does not control either interest rates or the total supply of credit; the market does.

There is an invisible group of lenders in the money game: *complacent depositors*, who — thanks to the FDIC (see Chapter 19) and general obliviousness — have been letting banks engage in whatever lending activities they like. Under pressure, bankers have occasionally testified that depositors might become highly skittish (if not horrified) if they knew how their money is being handled. During emotional times, the Fed will also have to try to maintain bank depositors' confidence by refraining from actions that appear to indicate panic. This balancing act will temper the Fed's potency and put it on the defensive yet further.

In contrast to the assumptions of conventional macroeconomic models, people are not machines. They get emotional. People become depressed, fearful, cautious and angry during depressions; that's essentially what causes them. A change in the population's mental state from a desire to expand to a desire to conserve is key to understanding why central bank machinations cannot avert deflation.

When ebullience makes people expansive, they often act on impulse, without full regard to reason. That's why, for example, consumers, corporations and governments can allow themselves to take on huge masses of debt, which they later regret. It is why creditors can be comfortable lending to weak borrowers, which they later regret. It is also why stocks can reach unprecedented valuations.

Conversely, when fear makes people defensive, they again often act on impulse, without full regard to reason. One example of action impelled by defensive psychology is governments' recurring drive toward protectionism during deflationary periods. Protectionism is correctly recognized among economists of all stripes as destructive, yet there is always a call for it when people's mental state changes to a defensive psychology. Voting blocs, whether corporate, union or regional, demand import tariffs and bans, and politicians provide them in order to get re-elected. If one country does not adopt protectionism, its trading partners will. Either way, the inevitable dampening effect on trade is inescapable. You will be reading about tariff wars in the newspapers before this cycle is over. Another example of defensive psychology is the increasing conservatism of bankers during a credit contraction. When lending officers become afraid, they call in loans and slow or stop their lending no matter how good their clients' credit may be in actuality. Instead of seeing opportunity, they see only danger. Ironically, much of the actual danger appears as a consequence of the reckless, impulsive decisions that they made in the preceding uptrend. In an environment of pessimism, corporations likewise reduce borrowing for expansion and acquisition, fearing the burden more than they believe in the opportunity. Consumers adopt a defensive strategy at such times by opting to save and conserve rather than to borrow, invest and spend. Anything the Fed does in such a climate will be seen through the lens of cynicism and fear. In such a mental state, people will interpret Fed actions differently from the way that they did when they were inclined toward confidence and hope.

With these thoughts in mind, let's return to the idea that the Fed could just print banknotes to stave off bank failures. One can imagine a scenario in which the Fed, beginning soon after the onset of deflation, trades banknotes for portfolios of bad loans, replacing a sea of bad debt with an equal ocean of banknotes, thus smoothly monetizing all defaults in the system without a ripple of protest, reaction or deflation. There are two problems with this scenario. One is that the Fed is a bank, and it would have no desire to go broke buying up worthless portfolios, debasing its own reserves to nothing. Only a government mandate triggered by crisis could compel such an action, which would come only after deflation had ravaged the system. Even in 1933, when the Fed agreed to monetize some banks' loans, it offered cash in exchange for only the very best loans in the banks'

portfolios, not the precarious ones. Second, the smooth refla-
tion scenario is an ivory-tower concoction that sounds plausible
only by omitting human beings from it. While the Fed could
embark on an aggressive plan to liquefy the banking system with
cash in response to a developing credit crisis, that action itself
ironically could serve to aggravate deflation, not relieve it. In a
defensive emotional environment, evidence that the Fed or the
government had decided to adopt a deliberate policy of inflating
the currency could give bondholders an excuse, justified or not,
to panic. It could be taken as evidence that the crisis is worse
than they thought, which would make them fear defaults among
weak borrowers, or that hyperinflation lay ahead, which could
make them fear the depreciation of all dollar-denominated debt.
Nervous holders of suspect debt that was near expiration could
simply decline to exercise their option to repurchase it once the
current holding term ran out. Fearful holders of suspect long-
term debt far from expiration could dump their notes and bonds
on the market, making prices collapse. If this were to happen,
the net result of an attempt at inflating would be a system-wide
reduction in the purchasing power of dollar-denominated debt,
in other words, a drop in the dollar value of total credit extended,
which is deflation.

The myth of Fed omnipotence has three main counter-
vailing forces: the bond market, the gold market and the currency
market. With today's full disclosure of central banks' activities,
governments and central banks cannot hide their monetary decisions. Indications that the Fed had adopted an unwelcome policy
would spread immediately around the world, and markets would
adjust accordingly. Downward adjustments in bond prices could
not only negate but also *outrun* the Fed's attempts at undesired
money or credit expansion.

The problems that the Fed faces are due to the fact that the
world is not so much awash in money as it is awash in credit.

Because today the amount of outstanding credit dwarfs the quantity of money, debt investors, who always have the option to sell
bonds in large quantities, are in the driver's seat with respect to
interest rates, currency values and the total quantity of credit,
which means that they, not the Fed, are now in charge of the
prospects for inflation and deflation. The Fed has become a slave
to trends that it has already fostered for seventy years, to events
that have already transpired. For the Fed, the mass of credit that
it has nursed into the world is like having raised King Kong from
babyhood as a pet. He might behave, but only if you can figure
out what he wants and keep him satisfied.

In the context of our discussion, the Fed has four relevant
tasks: to keep the banking system liquid, to maintain the public's
confidence in banks, to maintain the market's faith in the value
of Treasury securities, which constitute its own reserves, and to
maintain the integrity of the dollar relative to other currencies,
since dollars are the basis of the Fed's power. In a system-wide
financial crisis, these goals will conflict. If the Fed chooses to favor
any one of these goals, the others will be at least compromised,
possibly doomed.

The Fed may have taken its steps to eliminate reserve
requirements with these conflicts in mind, because whether
by unintended consequence or design, that regulatory change
transferred the full moral responsibility for depositors' money
onto the banks. The Fed has thus excused itself from responsibility in a system-wide banking crisis, giving itself the option of
defending the dollar or the Treasury's debt rather than your bank
deposits. Indeed, from 1928 to 1933, the Fed raised its holdings
of Treasury securities from 10.8 percent of its credit portfolio
to 91.5 percent, effectively fleeing to "quality" right along with
the rest of the market. What actual path the Fed will take under
pressure is unknown, but it is important to know that it is under
no *obligation* to save the banks, print money or pursue any other

rescue. Its primary legal obligation is to provide backing for the nation's currency, which it could quite merrily fulfill no matter what happens to the banking system.

Local Inflation by Repatriation?

Other countries hold Treasury securities in their central banks as reserves, and their citizens keep dollar bills as a store of value and medium of exchange. In fact, foreigners hold 45 percent of Treasury securities in the marketplace and 75 percent of all $100 bills. Repatriation of those instruments, it has been proposed, could cause a dramatic local inflation. If in fact investors around the world were to panic over the quality of the Treasury's debt, it would cause a price collapse in Treasury securities, which would be deflationary. As for currency repatriation, if overall money and credit were deflating in dollar terms, dollar bills would be rising in value. Foreigners would want to hold onto those remaining dollar bills with both hands. Even if foreigners did return their dollars, the Fed, as required by law, would offset returned dollar currency with sales of Treasury bonds, thus neutralizing the monetary effect.

Can Fiscal Policy Halt Deflation?

Can the government spend our way out of deflation and depression? Governments sometimes employ aspects of "fiscal policy," i.e., altering spending or taxing policies, to "pump up" demand for goods and services. Raising taxes for any reason would be harmful. Increasing government spending (with or without raising taxes) simply transfers wealth from savers to spenders, substituting a short-run stimulus for long-run financial deterioration. Japan has used this approach for twelve years, and it hasn't worked. Slashing taxes absent government spending cuts would be useless because the government would have to borrow the difference. Cutting government spending is a good thing, but politics will prevent its happening prior to a crisis.

Understand further that even the government's "tools" of macroeconomic manipulation are hardly mechanical levers on a machine; they are subject to psychology. Have you noticed the government's increasing fiscal conservatism over the past decade? Even Democrats have been voicing the virtues of a balanced budget! This is a sea change in *thinking*, and that is what ultimately causes trends such as inflation and deflation.

Endgame

The lack of solutions to the deflation problem is due to the fact that the problem results from prior excesses. Like the discomfort of drug addiction withdrawal, the discomfort of credit addiction withdrawal cannot be avoided. The time to have thought about avoiding a system-wide deflation was years ago. Now it's too late.

It does not matter how it happens; in the right psychological environment, *deflation will win*, at least initially. People today, raised in the benign, expansive environment of Supercycle wave (V), love to quote the conventional wisdom, "Don't fight the Fed." Now that the environment is about to change, I think that the cry of the truly wise should be, *"Don't fight the waves."*

Currency Hyperinflation

While I can discern no obvious forces that would counteract deflation, *after* deflation is another matter. At the bottom, when there is little credit left to destroy, currency inflation, perhaps even hyperinflation, could well come into play. In fact, I think this outcome has a fairly high probability in the next Kondratieff cycle.

When a government embarks on a policy of currency hyperinflation, such as the Confederate States did in the 1860s, Germany did in the early 1920s or France did after World War II, the monetary path is utterly different from that of deflation,

but ironically, the end result is about the same as that of a deflationary crash. At the end of hyperinflation, total bank accounts
denominated in the hyperinflated currency are worth far less than
they were, sometimes nothing at all. Total debts have shrunk or
disappeared because the notes were denominated in depreciated
money. In the severest cases, even the money disappears. In this
sense, even with hyperinflation, the end result is the destruction
of money and credit, which is deflation.

The Markets Will Signal Inflation

Despite my thoughts on the matter, I recognize that international money flows are massive, central bankers can be
ingenious, and politics can be volatile. Perhaps there is some
way that inflation, whether globally or locally, could accelerate
in the immediate future. How can you tell if my conclusion about
deflation is wrong and that inflation or hyperinflation is taking
place *instead* of deflation?

There are two sensitive barometers of major monetary trends.
One is the currency market. If the price of the dollar against other
currencies begins to plummet, it *might* mean that the market fears
dollar inflation, but it might simply mean that credit denominated
in other currencies is deflating faster than that denominated in
dollars. The other monetary barometer, which is more important,
is the gold market. If gold begins to soar in dollar terms, then
the market almost surely fears inflation. The bond market will
not make the best barometer of inflation because much of it will
fall under either scenario. I hope to recommend gold at lower
prices near the bottom of the deflationary trend, but if gold were
to move above $400 per ounce, I would probably be convinced
that a major low had passed. The ideas in Chapters 18 and 22
will show you how to protect yourself simultaneously against
deflation and a collapse in dollar value.

A High Degree of Complexity

Stocks are not registering a Supercycle top like that of 1929 but a Grand Supercycle top, per Figure 4-1. This means that the ultimate — if not the immediate — consequences will be more severe and more confounding than the consequences of the 1929-1932 crash. To balance the 64-year bear market of 1720-1784, the entirety of Grand Supercycle wave (IV) should last a century and comprise two or three major bear markets with one or two intervening bull markets. This book addresses primarily the first bear market, although the two preceding sections attempt to outline some of the longer-term risks. Because in some ways the financial world is in uncharted waters, this book may not have all the answers.

BOOK TWO

HOW TO PROTECT YOURSELF AND PROFIT FROM DEFLATION AND DEPRESSION

"...but Philamis...followed his ould course...thinking that the tide would have no ebb, the tune would have no ende."

— Thomas Lodge, *Euphues' Shadowe* (1592)

For Your Safety

Chapter 14:

Making Preparations and Taking Action

The ultimate effect of deflation is to reduce the supply of money and credit. Your goal is to make sure that it doesn't reduce the supply of *your* money and credit. The ultimate effect of depression is financial ruin. Your goal is to make sure that it doesn't ruin you.

Many investment advisors speak as if making money by investing is easy. It's not. What's easy is *losing* money, which is exactly what most investors do. They might make money for a while, but they lose eventually. Just keeping what you have over a lifetime of investing can be an achievement. That's what this book is designed to help you do, in perhaps the single most difficult financial environment that exists.

Protecting your liquid wealth against a deflationary crash and depression is pretty easy once you know what to do. Protecting your other assets and ensuring your livelihood can be serious challenges. Knowing how to proceed used to be the most difficult part of your task because almost no one writes about the issue. This book remedies that situation.

Preparing To Take the Right Actions

In a crash and depression, we will see stocks going down 90 percent and more, mutual funds collapsing, massive layoffs, high unemployment, corporate and municipal bankruptcies, bank and insurance company failures and ultimately financial and political crises. The average person, who has no inkling of the risks in the financial system, will be shocked that such things could happen, despite the fact that they have happened repeatedly throughout history.

Being unprepared will leave you vulnerable to a major disruption in your life. Being prepared will allow you to make exceptional profits both in the crash and in the ensuing recovery. For now, you should focus on making sure that you do not become a zombie-eyed victim of the depression.

The best news of all is that this depression should be relatively brief, though it will seem like an eternity while it is in force. The longest depression on record in the U.S. lasted three years and five months, from September 1929 to February 1933. The longest sustained stock market decline in U.S. history lasted seven years, from 1835 to 1842, and featured two depressions in close proximity. As the expected trend change is of one larger degree than those, it should be a commensurately large setback, but it should still be brief relative to the duration of the preceding advance.

Taking the Right Actions

Countless advisors have touted "stocks only," "gold only," "diversification," a "balanced portfolio" and other end-all solutions to the problem of attending to your investments. These approaches are usually delusions. As I try to make clear in the following pages, no investment strategy will provide stability *forever*. You will have to be nimble enough to see major trends coming and make changes accordingly. What follows is a good guide, I think, but it is only a guide.

The main goal of investing in a crash environment is *safety*. When deflation looms, almost every investment category becomes associated with immense risks. Most investors have no idea of these risks and will think you are a fool for taking precautions.

What's *that* for?

Many readers will object to taking certain prudent actions because of the presumed cost. For example: "I can't take a profit; I'll have to pay taxes!" My reply is, if you don't want to pay taxes, well, you'll get your wish; your profit will turn into a loss, and you won't have to pay any taxes. Or they say, "I can't sell my stocks for cash; interest rates are only 2 percent!" My reply is, if you can't abide a 2 percent annual gain, well, you'll get your wish there, too; you'll have a 30 percent annual loss instead. Others say, "I can't cash out my retirement plan; there's a penalty!" I reply, take your money out before there is none to get. Then there is the

venerable, "I can't sell now; I'd be taking a loss!" I say no, you
are recovering some capital that you can put to better use. My
advice always is, make the right move, and the costs will take
care of themselves.

If you are preoccupied with pedestrian concerns or blithely
going along with mainstream opinions, you need to wake up
now, while there is still time, and actively take charge of your
personal finances. First you must make your capital, your person
and your family safe. Then you can explore options for making
money during the crash and especially after it's over.

As the subtitle implies, this book is designed as a guide for
arranging your finances prior to any future deflationary depression, whether one occurs now, as I expect, or not. Although I
want this book to have value beyond the present situation, some
of the specifics of my suggestions are time-sensitive by nature. If
you need to know today where you can find the few exceptionally sound banks, insurers and other essential service providers,
if you want to locate the safest structures in the world for storing
your wealth, whether in paper monetary instruments or physical
assets such as precious metals, you will find the answers in these
chapters. Yet over time, the best institutions and services today
might be long gone, and others may have taken their place. For
a few years at least, we will post free updates to this information
at www.conquerthecrash.com/readerspage. But if you read this
book 50 years from now, you may have to do your own research
to fit the investment options and service providers available at
the time. Nevertheless, the general nature of your goals should
be much as outlined herein.

Most people do not have the foggiest idea how to prepare
their investments for a deflationary crash and depression, so the
techniques are almost like secrets today. The following chapters
show you a few steps that will make your finances secure despite
almost anything that such an environment can throw at them.

Chapter 15:

Should You Invest in Bonds?

If there is one bit of conventional wisdom that we hear repeatedly with respect to investing for a deflationary depression, it is that long-term bonds are the best possible investment. This assertion is wrong. Any bond issued by a borrower who cannot pay goes to *zero* in a depression. In the Great Depression, bonds of many companies, municipalities and foreign governments were crushed. They became wallpaper as their issuers went bankrupt and defaulted. Bonds of *suspect* issuers also went way down, at least for a time. Understand that in a crash, no one knows its depth, and almost everyone becomes afraid. That makes investors sell bonds of any issuers that they fear could default. Even when people trust the bonds they own, they are sometimes forced to sell them to raise cash to live on. For this reason, even the safest bonds can go down, at least temporarily, as AAA bonds did in 1931 and 1932.

Figure 15-1 shows what happened to bonds of various grades in the last deflationary crash. Figure 15-2 shows what happened to the Dow Jones 40-bond average, which lost 30 percent of its value in four years. Observe that the collapse of the early 1930s brought these bonds' prices *below* — and their interest rates above — where they were in 1920 near the peak in the intense inflation of the 'Teens. Figure 15-3 shows a comparable data series (the Bond Buyer 20-Bond average) in recent decades. Notice

Figure 15-1

how similar the pattern is to that of 1915-1928. If bonds follow the path that they did in the 1930s, their prices will fall *below the 1981 low, and their interest rates will exceed that year's peak of 13+ percent.*

Conventional analysts who have not studied the Great Depression or who expect bonds to move "contra-cyclically" to stocks are going to be shocked to see their bonds plummeting in value right along with the stock market. Ironically, economists will see the first wave down in bonds as a sign of inflation and recovery, when in fact, it will be the opposite.

The Specter of Downgrading

The main problem with even these cautionary graphs is that they do not show the full impact of *downgrades*. They show what bonds *of a certain quality* sold for at each data point. Bonds rated AAA or BBB at the start of a depression generally do not keep those ratings throughout it. Many go straight to D and then become de-listed because of default. Figure 15-1 does not take the price devastation of these issues into account. Like keepers of stock market averages who replace the companies that fail along the way, keepers of the bond averages of Figures 15-2 and 15-3 stand ready to replace component bonds whose ratings fall too far. As scary as they look, these graphs fail to depict the real misery that a depression inflicts upon bond investors.

High-Yield Bonds

When rating services rate bonds between BBB and AAA, they imply that they are considered safe investments. Anything rated BB or lower is considered speculative, implying that there is a risk that the borrower someday could default. The lower the rating, the greater that risk. Because of this risk, Wall Street, in a rare display of honesty, calls bonds rated BB or lower "junk." They appear to have "high yields," so people still buy them.

1915 TO 1933 IN THE
DOW JONES 40-BOND AVERAGE
arithmetic scale

investment mania top
(1928)

inflation
low
(1920)

© 2002 Elliott Wave International

depression
low
(1932)

Figure 15-2

That very yield, though, compounds the risk to principal. In a bad economy, companies and municipalities that have issued bonds at high yields find it increasingly difficult to meet their interest payments. The prices of those bonds fall as investors perceive increased risk and sell them. The real result in such cases is a *low* yield or a *negative* yield, particularly if the issuer defaults and your principal is gone.

Figure 15-3

The converse is not necessarily true. We are *told* that in a good economy, high-yield bonds are safe because the economic expansion means good business conditions, which should support the company that issued the bond. Can you rely on this reasoning? Figure 15-4 shows what has been happening to junk bonds over the past 14 years. As you can see, they have been crashing in value *even though the economy was mostly expanding during that*

Figure 15-4

time. At least with respect to this debt class, the late Franz Pick, who used to call bonds "certificates of guaranteed confiscation," seems not to have been overly strident.

In recent weeks, advisors have been assuring readers that the recession is ending, so it is the "perfect time" to buy "depressed" junk bonds. The main entities that will be further greatly depressed in coming years besides these junk bonds are the suckers who buy them. Way back in 1988, I published a special analysis urging readers to avoid junk bonds entirely. I added, "If you can figure out a way to short junk bonds, do it." That's when they started down. Their "high yields" have been a chimera, as the bonds' prices have fallen 70 percent on average since then. Most of these issues are headed straight for default.

Today's "High-Grade" Bonds

Don't think that you will be safe buying bonds rated BBB or above. The unprecedented mass of vulnerable bonds extant today is on the verge of a waterfall of downgrading. Many bonds that are currently rated investment grade will be downgraded to junk status and then go into default. The downgrades will go hand-in-hand with falling prices, so you will not be afforded advance warning of loss. When the big slide begins, I doubt that the rating services will even be able to keep up with the downgrades at the rate that they will be required.

An added problem with owning government bonds is the political risk. Governments have a long record of stiffing their creditors in a crisis, and no government is immune from adopting that solution to its financial problems. A new regime especially may have little regard for previously squandered credit.

Today, millions of individuals and institutions own tax-exempt municipal bonds. While there are assuredly many exceptions, this class of bonds is the riskiest among popular government issues. In the United States, default could happen to municipal bonds at any time after times get difficult. Politicians in many jurisdictions have borrowed and spent way more money than is likely ever to be paid back. Merely paying the interest on that debt in tough economic times will become an acute problem for many issuers. In such cases, default for many cities and counties will be inevitable. Even the debt of some higher-level government agencies is at serious risk of default in a worst-case scenario.

The Answer To Bond Selection

So if conventional wisdom is wrong, what is the correct way to frame the problem of investment opportunity and risk with respect to bonds in a deflationary depression? It is this: Any bond that is AAA at the start of the depression *and remains AAA throughout it* will be a satisfactory investment. The problem is, who can figure out which bonds those are? As we will see in Chapter 25, you cannot rely on bond rating services to guide you in a crunch.

If a crash and depression take place, some corporations whose products or services are important in that environment will become special situations, and their bonds will shine as viable investments. Unfortunately, I don't have the expertise to pick out the handful of long-term corporate bonds that will hold their value in a deflationary crash; I can only speculate on what will obviously be some of the worst. Since you can't short individual bonds, there's no point in making a list.

As debt prices fall, yields rise. If you're in long-term bonds, you're stuck with only the "falling prices" part of the equation. It's better to own short-term debt instruments, which can keep rolling over at ever-higher yields to compensate substantially for price losses. So, generally speaking, for safety, it is better to own high-quality *short-term* debt than long-term debt. We will explore that option in Chapter 18.

Chapter 16:

Should You Invest in Real Estate?

So bonds are risky. But we all know that property values never go down. Right?

After the stock experience of 2000-2001, people are saying, "Maybe stocks *can* come down for a few months from time to time, but real estate won't; real estate never has." They are saying it because real estate is the last thing still soaring at the top of the Great Asset Mania, but it, too, will fall in conjunction with a deflationary depression. Property values collapsed along with the depression of the 1930s. Few know that many values associated with property — such as rents — continued to fall through most of the 1940s, even after stocks had recovered substantially.

The worst thing about real estate is its *lack of liquidity* during a bear market. At least in the stock market, when your stock is down 60 percent and you realize you've made a horrendous mistake, you can call your broker and *get out* (unless you're a mutual fund, insurance company or other institution with millions of shares, in which case, you're stuck). With real estate, you can't pick up the phone and sell. You need to find a *buyer* for your house in order to sell it. In a depression, buyers just go away. Mom and Pop move in with the kids, or the kids move in with Mom and Pop. People start living in their offices or moving their offices into their living quarters. Businesses close down. In time, there is a massive glut of real estate.

In the initial stages of a depression, sellers remain under an illusion about what their property is really worth. They keep a high list price on their house, reflecting what it was worth last year. I know people who are doing that now. This stubbornness leads to a drop in sales volume. At some point, a few owners cave in and sell at much lower prices. Then others are forced to drop their prices, too. What is the potential *buyer's* psychology at that point? "Well, gee, property prices have been coming down. Why should I rush? I'll wait till they come down further." The further they come down, the more the buyer wants to wait. It's a downward spiral.

When Real Estate Falls

Real estate prices have always fallen hard when stock prices have fallen hard. Figure 16-1 displays this reliable relationship.

The overwhelming evidence for a major stock market decline presented in Chapters 4 through 7 is enough by itself to portend a tumble in real estate prices. Usually the culprit behind these joint declines is a credit deflation. If there were ever a time we were poised for such a decline, it is now.

The Extension of Credit

What screams "bubble" — giant, historic bubble — in real estate today is the system-wide extension of *massive* amounts of credit to finance property purchases. As a result, a record percentage of Americans today are nominal "homeowners" via $7.6 trillion in mortgage debt. Two-thirds of them owe an average of two-thirds of the value of their homes, plus interest, and both ratios have been increasing at a blistering pace.

People can buy a house with little or no down payment in many cases. They can refinance a house for its entire value. "How can this be?" you ask. "Isn't at least 20 percent homeowner equity required?" Well, sort of. Credit institutions are supposed to be

Figure 16-1

penalized for lending more than 80 percent on an uninsured mortgage. But if they get it insured, which is generally not difficult,
the limit can go up to 90 percent. With VA or FHA approval, it
can go up to 95 percent. "Prime borrowers" can refinance for up
to 125 percent of a home's appraised value.

What if none of these exceptions apply? Real estate insiders
on a quiet Saturday afternoon will tell you that many banks skirt
the intent of laws aimed to ensure some homeowner equity in
refinancing deals. For example, suppose the owner of a $500,000

home wants to refinance it at the full amount, but the bank is restricted to lending him only 80 percent of the value of the property, which is $400,000. If the homeowner wants the whole half-million anyway, the bank will send in an appraiser who magically discerns that the property is actually worth $625,000. Get it? 80 percent of $625,000 is $500,000. The homeowner has his 100 percent loan, the bank earns more interest, and the rules are satisfied. If you are creative, you can wangle even more than 100 percent out of a deal. The principle (and maybe later the principal) is out the window, and no one's the wiser, at least until a bear market imparts wisdom.

The problem with these schemes is that their success and continuation depend upon continuously rising property prices. Once the bank extends a loan of that size, it owns the house at full value. *Then, any drop in that value directly causes a drop in the value of the bank's capital.* By contrast, when the bank lends only half of the value of a home, its value can drop as much as half, and the bank can still get all of its depositors' money out of the deal by selling the house. With these latest methods of "creative financing," depositors' money is utterly unprotected from market risk.

Bank loans to home buyers are bad enough, but government-sponsored mortgage lenders — the Federal National Mortgage Corp. (Fannie Mae), the Federal Home Loan Mortgage Corp. (Freddie Mac) and the Federal Home Loan Bank — have extended $3 *trillion* worth of mortgage credit. Major financial institutions actually *invest* in huge packages of these mortgages, an investment that they and their clients (which may include you) will surely regret. *Money* magazine (December 2001) reports that the CEO of Fannie Mae "may be the most confident CEO in America." Certainly his stockholders, clients and mortgage-package investors had better share that feeling, because confidence is the only thing holding up this giant house of cards. When real estate prices begin to fall in a deflationary crash, lenders will experience a rising number of defaults on the mortgages they hold. My guess is that the Treasury will lose the $7 billion line of credit that it is required by law to extend to these quasi-government companies and even more if it attempts a bailout.

Another remarkable trend of recent years adds to the precarious nature of mortgage debt. Many people have been rushing to borrow the last pennies possible on their homes. They have been taking out home equity loans so they can buy stocks and TVs and cars and whatever else their hearts desire at the moment. This widespread practice is brewing a *terrible* disaster. Taking out a home equity loan is nothing but turning ownership of your home over to your bank in exchange for whatever other items you would like to own or consume. It's a reckless course, and it stems from the extreme confidence that accompanies a major top in social mood.

At the bottom of the depression, banks are going to own many, many homes, and their previous owners will be out in the street. That's not so bad; at least they got their money's worth from the TVs and cars. It will be a disaster for the banks' depositors, though, because there will be no one to buy the homes at mortgage-value prices. Depositors' money will be stuck in lifeless property deals, marked down 50 percent, 90 percent or (as happened in the Great Depression) even more.

Credit expansion has supported real estate prices, but it is late in the game. The dramatic tumble in interest rates in 2001 has spurred a record number of home sales because financing rates appear low. Marginal buyers, who had waited on the sidelines, are finally taking the plunge. People around the country are nearly unanimous in thinking that this is their last great opportunity to buy a house. Naturally, it is the opposite: It's your last chance to sell. The market is becoming as bought up as it can get, and there is little interest-rate ammunition left to win the battle for even more borrowers.

Some Things To Do

The prospect for property value is negative. To avoid the bust, you can take the following steps:

- Make sure you avoid real estate investment trusts, which are perhaps the worst property-related investments during a bear market. Some REITs valued at $100 a share in the early 1970s fell to ¼ by late 1974, and most of them never recovered. REITs are sold to the public because the people who do the deals don't want to stick with them. The public falls for REITs cycle after cycle. These "investments" hold up in the best part of bull markets, but they are disasters in bear markets.

- If you are in the real estate business, wrap up any sales deals you are working and get out of all investment real estate holdings that are not special situations about which you know much more than the market. In general, wait for lower prices to re-invest.

- If you hold a big mortgage on expensive property that depends upon massive public patronage, such as an arena, playhouse, amusement park, arts center or other such facility, consider selling it or subleasing it insured.

- If you are a banker, sell off your largest-percentage mortgages and get into safer investments.

- If you rent your living or office space, make sure that your lease either allows you to leave on short notice or has a clause lowering your rent if like units are reduced in price to new renters.

- If you have a huge mortgage on a McMansion or condo that you cannot afford unless your current income maintains, sell it and move into something more reasonable. If at all possible, join the 1/3 of title-holding Americans who own their homes outright. Be willing to trade down to make it happen. See Chapter 29 for more on this topic.

- If you consider your home a consumption item, and you wish to keep it on that basis, fine. If you are just as happy renting your residence as owning, do so.

- At the bottom, buy the home, office building or business facility of your dreams for ten cents or less per dollar of its peak value.

Chapter 17:

Should You Invest in Collectibles?

Collecting for Investment

Collecting for investment purposes is almost always foolish. Never buy anything *marketed* as a collectible. The chances of losing money when collectibility is priced into an item are huge. Usually, collecting trends are fads. They might be short-run or long-run fads, but they eventually dissolve. The inflation of the 1970s pushed gold and silver higher, so rare coins got a free ride of new interest. What did coin rarity have to do with inflation? Nothing.

Except perhaps for certain enduring masters' works, the focus of art appreciation goes through cycles. So do prices, even for the best art. The Japanese investors who bought paintings at record prices a decade ago have lost much of the value of their "investments."

There are times when collecting makes sense, but you have to be in on the ground floor. When I was a kid, I collected coins. You could find rare coins in everyday pocket change. In the 1950s, my grandmother persuaded the local parking meter collector to let her sort through the town's weekly take of coins and exchange them one for one. There was *no downside* to the hobby because the coins were always worth at least face value.

If you have speculated in rare coins or other collectibles that you do not want for their aesthetic or nostalgic value, sell them at today's prices, before they fall further in the crash. In depressions, people care about gold or silver content in coins, not rarity. One company that specializes in liquidating U.S. coin collections is American Federal, which can broker your coins or buy them outright. Be sure to compare prices with other dealers, some of which are listed in Chapter 22. Here is the contact information:

American Federal Rare Coin & Bullion

Website: americanfederal.com

Email: info@americanfederal.com

Address: 14602 North Cave Creek Rd., Ste. C,
Phoenix, AZ 85022

Phone: 1-800-221-7694 or 602-992-6857

Fax: 602-493-8158

CEO: Nick Grovich

Also taking a hard-nosed, consumer-advocacy stance is the *Rosen Numismatic Advisory*, which has won many awards over its 27 years of publication. If you prefer handling your own financial dealings, this is a good source of buy-and-sell coin strategies, information and advice. Here's how to get in touch:

Rosen Numismatic Advisory

Numismatic Counseling, Inc.

Email: mauricerosen@aol.com

Address: PO Box 38, Plainview, NY 11803

Phone: 516-433-5800

Fax: 516-433-5801

CEO: Maurice Rosen

Rock 'n' roll memorabilia and other baby-boomer collectibles are probably at an all-time top. Baby boomers who covet reminders of their youth will die off in the next 30 years, and most of their collectibles will be considered little more than curios.

For many supposed collectibles, such as Beanie Babies and such, it's already too late. Others, such as baseball cards, comic books and Barbie dolls, still have some value. If you want to sell your pedestrian collectibles, few venues are better than Ebay on the web, at www.ebay.com. For fine art sales, contact:

Christie's
Website: christies.com
Address: 20 Rockefeller Place, New York, NY 10020
Phone: 212-646-2000
Fax: 212-636-2399

Sotheby's
Website: sothebys.com
Address: 1334 York Ave, New York, NY 10021
Phone: 212-606-7000/541-312-5682
Fax: 212-606-7107/541-312-5684

Collecting for Pleasure

If you collect certain items for the love of them, you are about to be made very happy. Prices for art and collectibles, so outrageous today, will fall to joyously affordable levels in a depression. If you want to enhance your collection, keep your capital safe, wait until the bottom, and buy up all the items you want at pennies on today's dollar value.

Chapter 18:

Should You Invest in "Cash"?

The Wonder of Cash

For those among the public who have recently become concerned that being fully invested in one stock or stock fund is not risk-free, the analysts' battle cry is "diversification." They recommend having your assets spread out in numerous different *stocks*, numerous different stock *funds* and/or numerous different (foreign) stock *markets*. Advocates of junk bonds likewise counsel prospective investors that having lots of different issues will reduce risk.

This "strategy" is bogus. Why invest in anything unless you have a strong opinion about where it's going and a game plan for when to get out? Diversification is gospel today because investment assets of so many kinds have gone up for so long, but the future is another matter. Owning an array of investments is financial *suicide* during deflation. They all go down, and the logistics of getting out of them can be a nightmare. There can be weird exceptions to this rule, such as gold in the early 1930s when the government fixed the price, or perhaps some commodity that is crucial in a war, but otherwise, *all assets go down in price during deflation except one: cash.*

Today, few people give cash a thought. They sneer at the mere suggestion. "Cash is trash," goes the popular saying. Because interest rates are "too low," investors claim that they have "no choice" but to invest in something with more "upside potential." Ironically but obviously necessarily, the last major interest-rate cycle was perfectly aligned to convince people to do the wrong thing. Two decades ago, when rates were high, people insisted that stocks were not worth buying. Now that rates are low, they insist that cash is not worth holding. It's a psychological trap keeping investors from doing the right thing: buying stocks at the bottom (when rates were high) and selling them at the top (when rates are low).

Figure 18-1

Now let's dispose of the idea that the return on cash is "low." How would you like to own an asset that goes up *four times in value* in eleven years? Figure 18-1 is a picture of the soaring value of cash in Japan from 1990 through 2001. Cash has appreciated 300 percent in eleven years in terms of how many shares of Japanese stocks it can buy. Figure 18-2 is one picture of the rising value of cash in the United States, which appreciated nearly 250 percent from March 2000 to the present in terms of how many shares of the NASDAQ index it can buy. Wouldn't you like to enjoy this

Figure 18-2

kind of performance, too? You can, if you move into cash before a major deflation. Then when the stock markets reach bottom, you can buy incredibly cheap shares that almost no one else can afford because they lost it all when their stocks collapsed.

"If I hadn't lost everything I'd definitely be buying right now."

reproduced by permission of Leo Cullum

Cash is the only asset that assuredly rises in value during deflation. One safe "parking place" for capital during a deflationary crash is cash notes — for example, $100 bills, £50 notes or the equivalent in your home currency — in a safe depository to which you will always have access. That way, you will have money if the bank fails, you will have money if credit collapses, and you will have money if the government defaults on its debt. I suggest that you have at least *some* currency on hand if you expect a deflationary crash.

Unfortunately, currency has no yield, it is destructible, and it cannot be transferred with a phone call. Carefully selected "cash equivalents" can solve those problems.

The Risk in Many "Cash Equivalents"

Cash equivalents are high-quality short-term debt. They are extremely attractive investments in a deflationary crash. Choosing them, however, can be tricky. You must own *safe* instruments stored in a *safe* facility.

Most cautious investors think that their funds are utterly safe, even guaranteed, in any money market fund. Do not fall for this illusion. Money market funds are *relatively* safe, but they are still nothing but portfolios of debt, short-term debt to be sure, but debt nonetheless. When a company or government goes bankrupt, it stops paying interest on its debts, short-term or long, *right then.* If you own any of it at the time, your investment is compromised, if not gone.

In a strong economy, few give this risk any thought. They do not imagine that companies, governments and their agencies will ever cease paying interest due. Many people also erroneously believe that the debt issued by government-sponsored enterprises, such as U.S. mortgage insurers Fannie Mae and Freddie Mac, are government-guaranteed, but they're not. *You* take the risk when you buy their debt or their investment products.

Some money market funds realized early on that they could buy slightly riskier debt issues in order to squeeze out an extra 0.1 percent annual yield above that of their competitors, which they could then advertise to attract deposits. Others began to try to top *them* using the same tactics. Some funds have ended up owning a lot of weak debt. To the extent that a money-market fund's holdings are downgraded, the fund is that much riskier. Funds do not report downgrades to you or warn you if they think any of their holdings may be at risk. You hear about it only when it has to explain to you the loss statement that you receive in the mail.

In a depression, many money market funds will shock their depositors when they report losses. Once the process of debt defaults begins, to whom — and at what price — will the funds sell their portfolios if they wish to replace their risky assets with safer ones? They are all on the same ship, and there are few lifeboats.

The Safest Cash Equivalents Inside the U.S.

The safest cash equivalents in a depression are the very best near-term debt instruments, issued by a strong enterprise or government. The strongest such issues today lie *outside* the United States. In the U.S., the primary option is short-term Treasury securities, which includes not only Treasury bills but also longer-term notes and bonds that are within months of maturity, which can be purchased on the secondary market. For the time being, and for the investor who must or prefers to keep all assets inside the United States, Treasury bills or money market funds that hold only short-term U.S. Treasury debt appear to be the best financial haven available next to bullion-type gold and silver coins. These investments might also be attractive for some investors outside the U.S., although there is always currency risk to take into account, because if the dollar falls against your home currency, you will lose money.

The beauty of safe near-term debt is that instead of getting killed by rising interest rates, you can benefit from them. In 1931, the Fed was forced to raise its discount rate in the face of deflation in order to prop up the value of a falling dollar. Other investments fell harder as a result, but holders of very short-term T-bills who kept purchasing new ones at expiration watched their returns increase. This is a good way to defend your portfolio against rising interest rates.

Treasury bills and "Treasury only" money market funds have the added advantage of incurring no state income tax obligation on the interest they pay, which saves you some money if you live in a state with an income tax. Most of these funds also allow you to write checks on the account, so you will be getting a fairly safe yield on what amounts to your checking account. Usually they limit check amounts to $100 or more each, so you will still need a bank checking account for smaller checks, but that shouldn't put much of your total wealth at risk.

You could choose to buy Treasury bills directly from a broker or the U.S. Treasury Department from instructions available at its websites www.publicdebt.treas.gov. and www.treasurydirect.gov. For the record, you no longer get actual Treasury bills for your money. You get a bookkeeping entry that *says* you own Treasury bills. The Treasury department makes it easy to roll over your position automatically upon expiration, but on the other hand, you get none of the amenities of a money-market fund. You do get a modicum of additional safety from more direct ownership. Like many money-market funds, Treasury-only funds are bonded by insurance companies against fraud or theft. However, in a depression environment, such a bond is only as good as its insurer (see Chapter 24). Also, if the fund's custodial bank fails, your T-bills could be under wraps until things are sorted out. So buying T-bills directly from the government has the same advantage as holding actual gold in your hand as opposed to stock shares or warehouse receipts: There is no middleman. If top domestic safety and uninterrupted liquidity are crucial to your investment plan, go ahead and buy T-bills directly. Otherwise, the funds should serve. Personally, I prefer to err on the side of being as safe as possible.

Despite the assumptions of virtually everyone, there are some risks in owning T-bills, directly or indirectly. For example, you could lose some of the value of your certificates or fund shares if there were a rush to sell debt assets in general or merely a panic over possible U.S. government insolvency, either of which could drive the prices of short-term Treasury debt down (and their interest rates up) until the market recovered its equilibrium or confidence. Aside from the above-mentioned risks associated with funds, the only way for holders of Treasury bills to lose all their money would be for the U.S. government to default on its debt.

A federal government default is not impossible. The U.S. Treasury's $3.4 trillion debt and extensive unfunded government liabilities will present significant financial burdens in a depression. The deepest depression in three centuries could force Treasury issues down to junk status, like so many South American IOUs. Despite this risk, the U.S. government still has immense taxing power, and its world-class reputation should attract a share of capital if there is a "flight to quality" during a worldwide monetary crisis. As many stocks and bonds collapse during the crash, those who thought they were pretty smart investing in historically overpriced stocks, Russian and Argentinean bonds, retail consumer debt, junk bonds and worse will come to realize, "We need to sell these losers for what we can get and buy something else with the money we have left." In such a situation, money is likely to flow into what investors perceive as stronger issues. These could well include Treasury bills, making their issuer, the U.S. Treasury, even more liquid. Of course, politics could scuttle this potential. Foreign governments could outlaw money exports, or the U.S. could become politically unstable, reducing its status as an investment haven. The truth is that no one can know exactly how Treasury securities will fare in a major depression. What I *can* say is that, apart from special situations in the corporate realm that I dare not attempt to anticipate, T-bills are probably the safest U.S.-based interest-bearing investment. The next section will present attractive alternatives to holding short-term U.S. Treasury securities.

5 LARGEST TREASURY-ONLY MONEY MARKET FUNDS WITH NO CHARGES OR TRANSACTION LIMITS Source: Weiss Ratings, Inc.		
Fund Name	**Toll-Free No.**	**Web Address**
Alliance Treasury Reserves	(800) 247-4154	www.alliancecapital.com
American Century Capital Presv Fund I	(800) 345-2021	www.americancentury.com
Dreyfus 100% US Treasury MMF	(800) 242-8671	www.dreyfus.com
Evergreen Treasury MMF/CI A	(800) 343-2898	www.evergreen-funds.com
One Group US Treas Secs MMF/CI A	(800) 480-4111	www.onegroup.com

Table 18-1   *(see updated list at end of book)*

Of the many hundreds of money market funds in the United States, surprisingly few hold exclusively short-term U.S. Treasury obligations. Among the largest fifteen of these funds, only five have all these features: no other required accounts, no transaction limits, and no separate charges for printing checks, bounced checks or wire transfers into or out of your account. Table 18-1 provides a list. All of these funds' costs are covered by their "expense ratios," i.e., the percentage of your account that they charge as a management fee. They do vary, so do some comparative shopping. If you would like to examine the full list of Treasury-only money-market funds, contact the following:

Weiss Ratings, Inc.

Website: www.weissratings.com

Email: wr@weissinc.com

Address: P.O. Box 109665, Palm Beach Gardens, FL 33410

Phone: 800-289-9222 and 561-627-3300

Fax: 561-625-6685

See end of book for updated contact information

While I am comfortable saying that T-bills are the safest asset to hold inside the United States this side of gold and silver, some day even Treasury bills would probably become risky. If the dollar ever re-enters its long-term bear market, and particularly if it goes into free-fall, then even soaring short-term Treasury yields might not be able to overcome investors' imperative to get out. Each uptick in yield would be a yet greater burden to the government in the form of debt service, a fact that might frighten T-bill investors as much as entice them. If the federal government defaults, it might resort to a desperate action such as declaring that Treasury bills are now long-term bonds, to be paid off in ten years instead of ten weeks. You don't want to be stuck with any such deal.

If you come to believe that T-bills will get into trouble, you should buy safe foreign short-term debt or gold and silver to protect your capital. For details, see the next section and Chapter 22. Always be vigilant; always be practical; always try to get out of a potentially risky investment *before* others perceive that risk. If you need help, Elliott Wave International continuously monitors risks and opportunities in these markets from the standpoint of price trends and investor psychology.

Finding the Safest Cash Equivalents Outside the U.S.

For the globally sophisticated investor, there are excellent alternatives to U.S.-based debt. Most people hesitate to look outside their own areas, but if you have substantial capital to protect, you should expand your geographical horizons. The first reason is for the sake of diversity (*targeted* diversity, not the willy-nilly type), but there is a better reason: The safest investment debt resides within the safest financial systems.

Even if a debt-issuing *entity* is financially secure, events that are barely its fault might compromise it. For example, a manufacturer or municipality might be fully sound, except that it unwarily entrusts all its reserves to a single bank, and the bank fails. Suddenly, the issuing entity is in financial trouble, and its debt is much riskier.

So ideally, you should begin by identifying a country whose financial system is among the soundest available. According to SafeWealth Group, a firm of wealth preservation experts, *Switzerland* is the standout in this respect in Europe, and *Singapore* is the standout in Asia, currently and for the immediately foreseeable future.

Swiss voters are financially conservative. Under the Swiss Constitution, citizen-led referendums and initiatives can, and often do, challenge or revoke government policies or legislation, keeping excesses in check. Swiss citizens also have the highest savings rate in Europe, which helps liquefy the local banking system. Singapore issues little short-term debt because the government, with its conservative spending policy, doesn't need much short-term money. The country's bank reserves are strong because its citizens have a 25 percent savings rate mandated by law, which they routinely exceed. For comparison, the savings rate in the U.S. has fallen in the past 18 years from an average rate of 10 percent all the way down to zero. (Figures actually dropped to a 4 percent *negative* savings rate — i.e., spending exceeding income — but U.S. statisticians adjusted the definition of savings, so the lowest rate officially recognized to date is 0.2 percent of disposable income.) Moreover, each of these countries has a small total government debt relative to its financial base. Switzerland's national debt load is only about 170 billion Swiss francs, a fraction of the 3 trillion Sfr deposited in that country's banks, much of which would surely be freely available to refinance Swiss government debt given difficult times, when capital seeks conservative investments. Thus, while keeping in mind that politics can change, it appears at this time far less likely that a Swiss or Singaporean government entity will renege on its jurisdiction's obligations than perhaps any other government entities in the world.

The next step is to find the safest debt issues within one or both of the safest countries. In Switzerland, Swiss Money Market Claims (the equivalent of T-bills), near-term Swiss Confederation bonds and carefully selected cantonal (a canton is a state) bonds are probably as close to safe debt as you can get. Singapore's safest offerings are long-term government bonds with nearby maturities.

To be even safer, you will want to get more specific. While most Swiss cantons' paper has a top safety rating, the standard rating services, as we will see in Chapter 25, do not take the possibility of severe system-wide financial pressures into account. It is advisable, then, to invest in cantons that have little debt and whose bonds have a modicum of liquidity.

As you can probably tell by now, this is a field for specialists. I am not one of them. If you are a major institution or Arab oil magnate, you may already get good advice. But as far as I know, the SafeWealth Group is the best option. It has researched banks, insurance companies and debt issuers and isolated those that it believes have the highest level of safety on the planet. It has also identified wealth managers who focus primarily on protecting and preserving capital as opposed to aggressive growth with risk. Wherever you reside, if you would like to own a portfolio of the safest short-term foreign debt or even a fund of U.S. Treasury bills through a safe Swiss institution, this is a good place to start. Be aware that the available custodial institutions typically require minimum investments beginning at 100,000 Sfr or more. You may contact the firm as follows:

SafeWealth Group Service Center
Cari Lima, Senior Vice President
Email: clientservices@safewealthgroup.ch
Address: CP 476, 1000 Lausanne, 30 Grey, Switzerland
Phone: (from U.S. 011) 41-21-641-1640
Fax: (from U.S. 011) 41-21-641-1640-1390

See end of book for updated contact information

Equally comforting, SafeWealth traditionally counsels people as if a global financial disaster lay immediately around the corner, so you don't have to explain concerns that most investment counselors view as little different from paranoia. As the old saying goes, I may be paranoid, but that doesn't mean there isn't someone following me. In the final analysis, it is better to be safe and wrong than exposed and wrong.

Protecting Against Hyperinflation

When a state follows the course of printing banknotes rapidly to fund its spending, the result is hyperinflation. I expect deflation in the U.S., not inflation. Nevertheless, I conceded in Chapter 13 that monetary foresight cannot be 20/20. Also, you may live in a country that is in a position to hyperinflate.

If you face a currency-based hyperinflation, some aspects of your financial defense are substantially different from those that you will use to protect against deflation. For example, you do not want to hold *anything* denominated in the hyperinflating currency, and you do not want to sell local stocks short. You can protect yourself best with a portfolio of notes and bills denominated in stable foreign currencies, along with gold and silver (see Chapter 22).

Small investors in qualified countries outside Europe who are afraid of home currency hyperinflation have an option, too. The Prudent Safe Harbor Fund issues from the same fund family that offers the Prudent Bear Fund (see contact information in Chapter 20). This fund invests primarily in sovereign foreign notes and bonds of major European nations, but part of the fund (typically around 15 percent) is invested in gold stocks and gold bullion. The fund is also appropriate for Europeans who anticipate deflation. The minimum is an affordable $2000. Keep in mind that European currencies can fall in value, too, and interest rates for European bonds can fluctuate as much as those in other areas.

This fund is fine for some of your holdings, but you must be sure of your market analysis to use it for the bulk of your assets.

A Combination Strategy

Observe that one defense works for both a deflationary crash *and* a local hyperinflation: *holding notes and bills of strong issuers, denominated in a stable currency.* If you are worried about either deflation or hyperinflation in your country and want to protect against it, you should explore a mechanism through which you can hold a portfolio of the highest-grade near-term debt with the option of switching its denomination easily from one currency to another so that you can keep your money continuously lodged with the most conservative and stable governments. If you want to have a handle on the most likely future trends among the world's currencies, Elliott Wave International's services can help you. Of course, if a worldwide hyperinflation were to spare no currency at all, then precious metals would be your primary recourse. To prepare even for that remote possibility, you should also have a mechanism already in place to convert your holdings quickly to precious metals. If you can meet the minimums associated with their recommended institutions, SafeWealth Group can help you make all these arrangements under one roof. If you are a small investor, you can still achieve close to the desired result by choosing the most liquid banks, money market funds and precious metals available to you, using the lists and leads in this chapter and Chapters 19 and 22 as a guide.

Chapter 19:

How To Find a Safe Bank

Risks in Banking

Between 1929 and 1933, 9000 banks in the United States closed their doors. President Roosevelt shut down *all* banks for a short time after his inauguration. In December 2001, the government of Argentina froze virtually all bank deposits, barring customers from withdrawing the money they thought they had. Sometimes such restrictions happen naturally, when banks fail; sometimes they are imposed. Sometimes the restrictions are temporary; sometimes they remain for a long time.

Why do banks fail? For nearly 200 years, the courts have sanctioned an interpretation of the term "deposits" to mean *not* funds that you deliver for safekeeping but a *loan* to your bank. Your bank balance, then, is an IOU from the bank to you, even though there is no loan contract and no required interest payment. Thus, legally speaking, you have a claim on your money deposited in a bank, but practically speaking, you have a claim only on the loans that the bank makes with your money. If a large portion of those loans is tied up or becomes worthless, your money claim is compromised. A bank failure simply means that the bank has reneged on its promise to pay you back. The bottom line is that your money is only as safe as the bank's loans. In boom times, banks become imprudent and lend to almost anyone. In busts, they can't get much of that money back due to widespread defaults. If the bank's portfolio collapses in value, say, like those of the Savings & Loan institutions in the U.S. in the late 1980s and early 1990s, the bank is broke, and its depositors' savings are gone.

Because U.S. banks are no longer required to hold any of their deposits in reserve (see Chapter 10), many banks keep on hand just the bare minimum amount of cash needed for everyday transactions. Others keep a bit more. According to the latest Fed figures, the net loan-to-deposit ratio at U.S. commercial banks is 90 percent. This figure omits loans considered "securities" such as corporate, municipal and mortgage-backed bonds, which from my point of view are just as dangerous as everyday bank loans. The true loan-to-deposit ratio, then, is 125 percent and rising. Banks are not just lent to the hilt; they're past it. Some bank loans, at least in the current benign environment, could be liquidated quickly, but in a fearful market, liquidity even on these so-called "securities" will dry up. If just a few more depositors than normal were to withdraw money, banks would have to sell some of these assets, depressing prices and depleting the value of the securities remaining in their portfolios. If enough depositors were to attempt simultaneous withdrawals, banks would have to refuse. Banks with the lowest liquidity ratios will be particularly susceptible to runs in a depression. They may not be technically broke, but you still couldn't get your money, at least until the banks' loans were paid off.

You would think that banks would learn to behave differently with centuries of history to guide them, but for the most part, they don't. The pressure to show good earnings to stockholders and to offer competitive interest rates to depositors induces them to make risky loans. The Federal Reserve's monopoly powers have allowed U.S. banks to lend aggressively, so far without repercussion. For bankers to educate depositors about safety would be to disturb their main source of profits. The U.S. government's

Federal Deposit Insurance Corporation guarantees to refund depositors' losses up to $100,000, which *seems* to make safety a moot point. Actually, this guarantee just makes things far worse, for two reasons. First, it removes a major motivation for banks to be conservative with your money. Depositors feel safe, so who cares what's going on behind closed doors? Second, did you know that most of the FDIC's money comes from other banks? This funding scheme makes prudent banks pay to save the imprudent ones, imparting weak banks' frailty to the strong ones. When the FDIC rescues weak banks by charging healthier ones higher "premiums," overall bank deposits are depleted, causing the net loan-to-deposit ratio to rise. This result, in turn, means that in times of bank stress, *it will take a progressively smaller percentage of depositors to cause unmanageable bank runs.* If banks collapse in great enough quantity, the FDIC will be unable to rescue them all, and the more it charges surviving banks in "premiums," the more banks it will endanger. Thus, this form of insurance compromises the entire system. Ultimately, the federal government guarantees the FDIC's deposit insurance, which sounds like a sure thing. But if tax receipts fall, the government will be hard pressed to save a large number of banks with its own diminishing supply of capital. The FDIC calls its sticker "a symbol of confidence," and that's exactly what it is.

Some states in the U.S., in a fit of deadly "compassion," have made it illegal for a bank to seize the home of someone who has declared bankruptcy. In such situations, the bank and its depositors are on the hook indefinitely for a borrower's unthrift. Other states have made it illegal for a bank attempting to recover the value of a loan to seize any of a defaulting mortgage holder's assets other than the mortgaged property. In such situations, the bank assumes the price risk in the real estate market. These states' banks are vulnerable to severe losses in their mortgage portfolios and are at far greater risk of failure.

Many major national and international banks around the world have huge portfolios of "emerging market" debt, mortgage debt, consumer debt and weak corporate debt. I cannot understand how a bank trusted with the custody of your money could ever even *think* of buying bonds issued by Russia or Argentina or any other unstable or spendthrift government. As I have put it, "Today's emerging markets will soon be *sub*merging markets." That metamorphosis began two years later. The fact that banks and other investment companies can repeatedly ride such "investments" all the way down to *write-offs* is outrageous.

Many banks today also have a shockingly large exposure to leveraged derivatives such as futures, options and even more exotic instruments. The underlying value of assets represented by such financial derivatives at quite a few big banks is greater than the total value of all their deposits. The estimated representative value of all derivatives in the world today is $90 trillion, over half of which is held by U.S. banks. Many banks use derivatives to hedge against investment exposure, but that strategy works only if the speculator on the other side of the trade can pay off if he's wrong.

Relying upon, or worse, speculating in, leveraged derivatives poses one of the greatest risks to banks that have succumbed to the lure. Leverage almost *always* causes massive losses eventually because of the psychological stress that owning them induces. You have already read of the tremendous debacles at Barings Bank, Long-Term [sic] Capital Management, Enron and other institutions due to speculating in leveraged derivatives. It is traditional to discount the representative value of derivatives because traders will presumably get out of losing positions well before they cost as much as what they represent. Well, maybe. It is at least as common a human reaction for speculators to double their bets when the market goes against a big position. At least, that's what bankers might do with your money.

Today's bank analysts assure us, as a headline from *The Atlanta Journal-Constitution* put it on December 29, 2001, that "Banks [Are] Well-Capitalized." Banks today are indeed generally considered well capitalized compared to their situation in the 1980s. Unfortunately, that condition is mostly thanks to the great asset mania of the 1990s, which, as explained in Book One, is probably over. Much of the record amount of credit that banks have extended, such as that lent for productive enterprise or directly to strong governments, is relatively safe. Much of what has been lent to weak governments, real estate developers, government-sponsored enterprises, stock market speculators, venture capitalists, consumers (via credit cards and consumer-debt "investment" packages), and so on, is not. One expert advises, "The larger, more diversified banks at this point are the safer place to be." That assertion will surely be severely tested in the coming depression.

There are five major conditions in place at many banks that pose a danger: (1) low liquidity levels, (2) dangerous exposure to leveraged derivatives, (3) the optimistic safety ratings of banks' debt investments, (4) the inflated values of the property that borrowers have put up as collateral on loans and (5) the substantial size of the mortgages that their clients hold compared both to those property values and to the clients' potential inability to pay under adverse circumstances. All of these conditions compound the risk to the banking system of deflation and depression.

Financial companies are enjoying big advances in the current stock market rally. Depositors today trust their banks more than they trust government or business in general. For example, a recent poll asked web surfers which among a list of seven types of institutions they would most trust to operate a secure identity service. Banks got nearly 50 percent of the vote. General bank trustworthiness is yet another faith that will be shattered in a depression.

Well before a worldwide depression dominates our daily lives, you will need to deposit your capital into safe institutions. I suggest using two or more to spread the risk even further. They must be far better than the ones that today are too optimistically deemed "liquid" and "safe" by rating services and banking officials.

Safe Banking in the United States

If you must bank in the U.S., or if you prefer it, choose the best bank(s) available. I believe that even in a deflationary crash, many of the safest U.S. banks have a good shot at survival and even prosperity. The reason is that relatively safe banks, if they have the sense to inform the public of their safety advantage, are likely to become *even safer* during difficult times. Why? Because depositors in a developing financial crisis will move funds out of the weakest banks into the strongest ones, making the weak ones weaker and the strong ones stronger. One of the great ironies of banking is that the more liquid a bank, the less likely it is that depositors will conduct a run on it in the first place.

Weiss Ratings, Inc. provides one of the most reliable bank-rating services in America. (See Chapter 18 or the last section of this book for contact information.) CEO Martin Weiss has graciously consented to provide a practical guide for this book. Table 19-1 lists what his researchers consider the two strongest banks in each state in the union. Table 19-2 lists what they consider the 24 strongest *large* banks in the U.S. For our purposes, I see little point in listing the weakest banks, but if you want to know which ones they are, you can find them listed in the brand-new *Ultimate Safe Money Guide*, by Martin Weiss (John Wiley & Sons, 2002). Weiss' book is a good complement to this one for many reasons. Aside from banks and insurance companies (see Chapter 24), his firm also rates mutual funds, brokerage firms, HMOs and corporations with common stock.

THE TWO HIGHEST-RATED BANKS IN EACH STATE
Source: TheStreet.com Ratings, Inc. (based on 9/30/01 data)

Name	City	State	Total Assets in millions	TheStreet Safety Rating
Alabama				
FIRST NB OF SCOTTSBORO	SCOTTSBORO	AL	284.74	A-
FIRST UNITED SECURITY BANK	THOMASVILLE	AL	513.4	B+
Alaska				
FIRST NB ALASKA	ANCHORAGE	AK	1779.6	A+
MOUNT MCKINLEY MSB	FAIRBANKS	AK	174.1	A
Arizona				
SEARS NB	TEMPE	AZ	178.4	A-
MOHAVE ST BK	LAKE HAVASU CITY	AZ	160.7	A-
Arkansas				
FIRST NB OF FT SMITH	FORT SMITH	AR	633.8	A-
FIRST FEDERAL BANK OF AR	HARRISON	AR	697.7	B+
California				
FARMERS & MERCHANTS BK	LONG BEACH	CA	2094.0	A+
SAVINGS BK OF MENDOCINO CTY	UKIAH	CA	519.8	A+
Colorado				
AMERICAN BUSINESS BK NA	DENVER	CO	878.0	A-
ALPINE BANK	GLENWOOD SPRINGS	CO	883.5	B+
Connecticut				
NEW HAVEN SVGS BK	NEW HAVEN	CT	2223.9	A+
AMERICAN SVGS BK	NEW BRITAIN	CT	1907.9	A+
Delaware				
PNC BANK	WILMINGTON	DE	2417.4	A-
CITIBANK-DELAWARE	NEW CASTLE	DE	6290.9	B+
District of Columbia				
NATIONAL CAPITAL BK OF WA	WASHINGTON	DC	153.2	A+
ADAMS NB	WASHINGTON	DC	168.2	A-
Florida				
HARBOR FEDERAL SVGS BK	FORT PIERCE	FL	1747.6	A+
MELLON UNITED NB	MIAMI	FL	1555.4	A-
Georgia				
COLUMBUS B&TC	COLUMBUS	GA	3747.5	A-
MAIN STREET BK	COVINGTON	GA	1075.9	A-
Hawaii				
BANK OF HAWAII	HONOLULU	HI	10,085.2	B+
CENTRAL PACIFIC BANK	HONOLULU	HI	1860.7	B+
Idaho				
BANK OF COMMERCE	IDAHO FALLS	ID	431.5	A+
IDAHO INDEPENDENT BK	COEUR D'ALENE	ID	270.4	B+
Illinois				
CORUS BK NA	CHICAGO	IL	2568.6	A
COMMERCE BK NA	PEORIA	IL	917.9	B+
Indiana				
FIRST SOURCE BK	SOUTH BEND	IN	3362.1	A-
TERRE HAUTE FIRST NB	TERRE HAUTE	IN	1299.3	B+
Iowa				
WEST DES MOINES ST BK	W DES MOINES	IA	807.5	A-
HILLS B&TC	HILLS	IA	885.8	B+

Table 19-1   *(see updated list at end of book)*

Kansas				
VALLEY VIEW ST BK	CLEVELAND PARK	KS	557.2	A+
CAPITOL FEDERAL SAVINGS BK	TOPEKA	KS	8666.0	A-
Kentucky				
AREA BK	OWENSBORO	KY	2625.7	A-
BANK OF LOUISVILLE	LOUISVILLE	KY	1679.1	B+
Louisana				
WHITNEW NB OF NEW ORLEANS	NEW ORLEANS	LA	6874.3	B+
HANCOCK BK OF LOUISIANA	BATON ROUGE	LA	1348.8	B+
Maine				
KENNEBECK SVGS BK	AUGUSTA	ME	404.0	B+
OCEAN NB	KENNEBUNK	ME	276.2	B+
Maryland				
PENINSULA BK	PRINCESS ANNE	MD	702.7	A+
WESTMINSTER UNION BK	WESTMINSTER	MD	544.1	A+
Massachusetts				
BRISTOL COUNTY SVGS BK	TAUNTON	MA	679.1	A+
COUNTRY BK FOR SVGS	WARE	MA	772.6	A
Michigan				
CHEMICAL B&TC	MIDLAND	MI	1479.7	A
CHEMICAL BK WET	CADILLAC	MI	762.3	A
Minnesota				
FIRST NB OF BEMIDJI	BEMIDJI	MN	305.0	A+
MIDWAY NB OF ST PAUL	ST PAUL	MN	437.3	B+
Mississippi				
TRUSTMARK NB	JACKSON	MS	6834.8	A-
NATIONAL BK OF COMMERCE	STARKVILLE	MS	1027.8	A-
Missouri				
BANK MIDWEST NA	KANSAS CITY	MO	2696.9	A-
COMMERCE BK NA	KANSAS CITY	MO	10363.6	B+
Montana				
YELLOWSTONE BK	LAUREL	MT	242.5	A+
FIRST SECURITY BK	BOZEMAN	MT	295.6	A-
Nebraska				
PINNACLE BK	PAPILLION	NE	1386.9	B+
FIVE POINTS BK	GRAND ISLAND	NE	323.8	B+
Nevada				
HOUSEHOLD BK NEVADA NA	LAS VEGAS	NV	1591.3	A-
FIRST NB OF ELY	ELY	NV	38.5	B+
New Hampshire				
MEREDITH VILLAGE SVGS BK	MEREDITH	NH	314.2	B+
CLAREMONT SVGS BK	CLAREMONT	NH	241.6	B+
New Jersey				
HUDSON CITY SVGS BK	PARAMUS	NJ	10815.4	A+
KEARNY FSB	KEARNY	NJ	1176.8	A
New Mexico				
WESTERN COMMERCE BK	CARLSBAD	NM	256.6	A-
FIRST NATIONAL BANK - SANTA FE	SANTA FE	NM	339.6	B+
New York				
MASPETH FS&LA	MASPETH	NY	1093.8	A+
SUMITOMO TR & BNKG CO USA	NEW YORK	NY	973.8	A+
North Carolina				
PIEDMONT FS&LA	WINSTON-SALEM	NC	811.0	A
HIGH POINT B&TC	HIGH POINT	NC	567.6	A

Table 19-1 (cont'd)

North Dakota				
GATE CITY BANK	FARGO	ND	676.6	B+
FARMERS & MRCH BK VALLEY CIT	VALLEY CITY	ND	87.5	B+
Ohio				
PEOPLES BK NA	MARIETTA	OH	1165.4	A-
FARMERS NB OF CANFIELD	CANFIELD	OH	642.6	A-
Oklahoma				
FIRST NB&TC MCALESTER	MCALESTER	OK	440.0	A
RCB BK	CLAREMORE	OK	574.6	A-
Oregon				
KLAMATH FIRST FS&LA	KLAMATH FALLS	OR	1419.2	B+
WEST COAST BK	LAKE OSWEGO	OR	1384.2	B+
Pennsylvania				
OMEGA BK NA	STATE COLLEGE	PA	628.5	A+
FIRST NB&TC	NEWTOWN	PA	501.1	A
Rhode Island				
CENTREVILLE SVGS BK	W WARWICK	RI	645.5	A
FIRST B&TC	PROVIDENCE	RI	173.5	A-
South Carolina				
ENTERPRISE BK S CAROLINA	EHRHARDT	SC	252.6	A+
CONWAY NB	CONWAY	SC	512.0	A-
South Dakota				
PIONEER B&TC	BELLE FOURCHE	SD	269.6	A
FIRST WESTERN BANK	STURGIS	SD	260.8	A-
Tennessee				
HOME FEDERAL BANK OF TN	KNOXVILLE	TN	1427.2	A
FIRST FARMERS & MERCHANTS NB	COLUMBIA	TN	824.8	A-
Texas				
CITIZENS 1ST BK	TYLER	TX	505.8	A+
AMARILLO NB	AMARILLO	TX	1372.9	A-
Utah				
MORGAN STANLEY DEAN WITTER B	W VALLEY CITY	UT	2709.6	A-
ADVANTA BK CORP	DRAPER	UT	1003.2	A-
Vermont				
MERCHANTS BK	BURLINGTON	VT	784.7	B+
UNION BK	MORRISVILLE	VT	224.9	B+
Virginia				
BURKE & HERBERT B&TC	ALEXANDRIA	VA	854.8	A+
AMERICAN NB&TC	DANVILLE	VA	564.3	A+
Washington				
WASHINGTON FS&LA	SEATTLE	WA	6991.1	A+
HORIZON BK	BELLINGHAM	WA	743.4	A+
West Virginia				
BANK OF CHARLES TOWN	CHARLES TOWN	WV	167.7	A
WESBANCO BK	WHEELING	WV	2451.1	A-
Wisconsin				
NATIONAL EXCHANGE B&TC	FOND DU LAC	WI	721.4	A
TRI CITY NB	OAK CREEK	WI	583.4	A
Wyoming				
WELLS FARGO BK WY NA	CASPER	WY	2542.1	B+
PINNACLE BK WY	TORRINGTON	WY	316.6	B+

Table 19-1 (cont'd)

STRONGEST LARGE BANKS IN AMERICA			
Source: Weiss Ratings, Inc. (based on 9/30/01 data)			
Bank Name	State	Weiss Safety Rating	Total Assets (in millions of $)
Apple Bk for Svgs	NY	A-	6,117
Bancorpsouth Bk	MS	B+	9,390
Bank of Tokyo Mitsubishi TC	NY	A-	4,128
Capital Federal Savings Bank	KS	A	8,423
Central Carolina B&TC	NC	B+	9,489
Citibank-Delaware	DE	B+	6,160
Columbus B&TC	GA	A-	3,353
Comerica Bk-Texas	TX	B+	3,803
Commerce Bk NA	MO	B+	9,867
Emigrant Svg Bk	NY	A	8,535
First Charter NB	NC	B+	3,061
First Commonwealth Bk	PA	B+	3,430
First Source Bk	IN	A-	3,148
Hudson City Svgs Bk	NJ	A+	9,618
Israel Discount Bk of NY	NY	B+	5,695
Mercantile Safe Deposit & TC	MD	A	3,489
North Fork Bk	NY	B+	14,685
Sanwa Bk Calfornia	CA	B+	9,013
Trustmark NB	MS	A-	6,822
Union Bk of CA NA	CA	B+	35,467
United States TC of NY	NY	B+	3,988
Valley NB	NJ	B+	7,957
Washington FS&LA	WA	A+	6,990
Whitney NB of New Orleans	LA	B+	6,630

Table 19-2

There are other independent and reliable bank rating sources. Among them, Veribanc, Inc. has been in the ratings business the longest. The service covers banks, S&Ls and credit unions. The company's classifications rank financial institutions not just on their present standing but also on their future outlook, which is what you should care about. Using a clear, simple rating system, it assesses capital strength, asset quality, management ability, earnings sufficiency, liquidity and sensitivity to market risk.

IDC Financial Publishing, Inc. also publishes highly specific and easy-to-interpret quarterly financial ratings that track the financial safety of U.S.-based banks, savings and loan institutions and credit unions. You will find their contact information below:

Veribanc, Inc.

Website: www.veribanc.com

Email: service@veribanc.com

Address: P.O. Box 1610, Woonsocket, RI 02895

Phone: 800-837-4226/800-442-2657

Fax: 781-246-5291

See end of book for updated contact information

IDC Financial Publishing, Inc.

Website: www.idcfp.com

Email: info@idcfp.com

Address: P.O. Box 140, Hartland, WI 53029

Phone: 800-525-5457 and 262-367-7231

Fax: 262-367-6497

See end of book for updated contact information

If, despite all your precautions, you come to suspect that any of your chosen banks face the risk of closure, move your money to a safer bank immediately. If you cannot identify a safer bank, then do not hesitate to withdraw all of your money in cash. If you are not first in line, you may forfeit the opportunity.

Safe Banking Worldwide

A free market in banking would provide every imaginable service, from 100% safekeeping for a fee to 100% lending with a large return. To preserve their reputations, bankers would have an incentive to be extremely careful with your money. Monopoly money and regulated banking have produced quite another result. Nevertheless, there still exist a few banks in the world that mainly provide a wealth preservation service as opposed to interest income and daily transactional conveniences. If you want the utmost safety for capital storage, if a bit less convenience, you must use these banks. The safest banking institutions in the world reside in countries that (1) do not have, and are unlikely to impose, exchange controls or wealth transfer restrictions and (2) have a low ratio of illiquid debts to deposits. Not surprisingly, the top candidates are the same as those with the safest debt: Switzerland and Singapore.

Nevertheless, do not fall into the trap of choosing any Swiss bank just because it's Swiss. Today's largest Swiss banks, with their fat portfolios of derivatives, are at immense risk of failure if a depression occurs. Furthermore, they have branches worldwide and are thus vulnerable to the whims of numerous governments. The best course of action is to locate smaller, safer local Swiss banks. Austria's low debt per capita makes it a good backup alternative. If you want to find a safe bank, these jurisdictions are the place to begin.

Using stringent bank-rating requirements, SafeWealth Group has identified banks in these countries that earn its highest rating for survivability in a global depression. This "Class 1" rating requires an aggressively discounted liquidity ratio of at least 75 percent, an otherwise nearly unheard-of 35 percent net liquid equity ratio (i.e., the percentage of a bank's capital that is free and accessible at all times), a low derivatives/capital ratio, no derivatives held for the bank's account on a speculative basis, a low amount of deposits held at other banks and that the bank operate in a single nation so that the rules it must follow are clearly defined.

A 75 percent aggressively discounted liquidity ratio means that deposits are held in such liquid investments that even if the bank were suddenly faced with demands from depositors to withdraw 75 percent of the total money in the bank, given a few days or weeks, it could do so. There are even a very few banks in the world with liquidity ratios at or above 100 percent. In other words, they could pay off *all* their depositors, *in full*, on very short notice. Many banks couldn't pay off 10 percent of their depositors quickly, and the world's weakest banks would be hard-pressed to service *any* above-normal level of simultaneous withdrawals. And that is in *today's* benign financial environment, never mind a depression environment.

If you are serious about safety and can meet a recommended bank's account minimum, you should set up a relationship with a Class 1 bank. SafeWealth Group can help you cut through red tape to establish relationships with such banks and other institutions. The reason you need to go through a representative is that these private Swiss banks do not readily accept accounts from any individual, corporation or trust representative that walks through the door, a policy that reflects their general conservatism. They will accept a new account only if its ownership and purpose are completely above board and will not endanger the bank's reputation. If you meet these standards, SafeWealth Group can secure the proper introductions for you in most cases and guide you through the process. (See Chapter 18 or the final section of this book for contact information and typical minimums.) If you are a Swiss or Singaporean resident and have ready access to such institutions, by all means stay put as long as local politics remain stable.

Act While You Can

When it comes to safety, it is always best to act early. Due largely to aggressive governmental policing of illegal activities such as the drug trade, money laundering, tax evasion and terrorist financing, average honest people do not enjoy the free, ready access to financial institutions that they did a few years ago. Some banks are now obliged to meet with prospective clients in person to satisfy suitability rules. There can be little doubt that if a crisis climate comes to pass, you could face many more obstacles if not outright denial of service. If you are truly intent on preserving your wealth, you should resist the temptation to procrastinate under the presumption that you can rely on the status quo. Opportunities close down all the time. For example, the two safest banks in London no longer accept non-British clients. In the U.S., the bank deemed the safest in the nation two years ago no longer takes out-of-state accounts. A few of my prudent subscribers got in after I recommended it, but now the procrastinators have to look elsewhere. This is a lesson. Don't delay, or the institutions now available to protect your savings may close their doors to you. Another word of warning: Bank ratings can change. The smart approach is to keep in touch with the services that rate banks seriously to make sure your bank(s) continue to qualify for a high safety rating.

Once you move the bulk of your investment funds into the safest cash equivalents, and after you have chosen a safe bank or two for savings and transactions, then and only then should you consider speculating in the stock market with a small portion of your capital. That is the subject of the next chapter.

Chapter 20:

Should You Speculate in Stocks?

Perhaps the number one precaution to take at the start of a deflationary crash is to make sure that your investment capital is *not* invested "long" in stocks, stock mutual funds, stock index futures, stock options or any other equity-based investment or speculation. That advice alone should be worth the time you spent to read this book.

In 2000 and 2001, countless Internet stocks fell from $50 or $100 a share to near zero in a matter of months. In 2001, Enron went from $85 to pennies a share in less than a year. These are the early casualties of debt, leverage and incautious speculation. Countless investors, including the managers of insurance companies, pension funds and mutual funds, express great confidence that their "diverse holdings" will keep major portfolio risk at bay. Aside from piles of questionable debt, what are those diverse holdings? Stocks, stocks and more stocks. Despite current optimism that the bull market is back, there will be many more casualties to come when stock prices turn back down again.

Don't presume that the Fed will rescue the stock market, either. In theory, the Fed could declare a support price for certain stocks, but which ones? And how much money would it commit to buying them? If the Fed were actually to buy equities or stock-index futures, the temporary result might be a brief rally, but the ultimate result would be a collapse in the value of the Fed's own assets when the market turned back down, making the

Fed look foolish and compromising its primary goals, as cited in Chapter 13. It wouldn't want to keep repeating that experience. The bankers' pools of 1929 gave up on this strategy, and so will the Fed if it tries it.

Short Selling Stocks and Trading in Futures and Options

Short selling is a great idea at the onset of a deflationary depression, at least from a *timing* standpoint. Shares of vulnerable banks and other financial companies in particular are a great downside bet. The current stock-market rally, so far a pitifully weak response to record Fed-induced liquidity in 2001, is providing a great general short-selling opportunity, per all the evidence in Chapters 6 and 7. You should avoid shorting special situations such as defense and natural resource stocks, which can move counter-trend, or at least fall less precipitously, when international tensions rise. Buying "leaps," which are long-term puts, on stocks and stock indexes would be a fine speculation. If you do not already know by experience what the terms "short selling" and "leaps" mean, I recommend that you avoid engaging in these activities.

Unfortunately, there could well be *structural* risks in dealing with stocks and associated derivatives during a major retrenchment. Trading stocks, options and futures could be extremely problematic during a stock market panic. One reason is that trading systems tend to break down when volume surges and the system's operators become emotional. When the exchange floor became a hurricane of paper in 1929, it would sometimes take days to sort out who had bought and sold what and then determine whether investors and traders could afford to pay for their positions. You can experience the turmoil vicariously in any good history of the 1929 crash. To give you a flavor of what goes on, read this description, from one of my subscribers, of the tumult during a comparatively mild panic forty years ago:

I worked for Merrill Lynch in New York in 1962 during the collapse. I well recall the failure of the teletype in our office and inexperienced clerks calling in the orders to the main office. I recall many of the screw-ups: buys called in as sells and vice versa. Some stocks had nicknames like Bessie (Bethlehem Steel), Peggy (Public Service Electric and Gas), and I recall the clerks calling in the orders by the stocks' nicknames and the person on the other end not knowing what the hell they were talking about. All the while, the market was collapsing.

Do you think investors and brokers will behave differently now that so much stock trading is done on-line? I don't. Do you think the experience will be "smoother" because modern computers are involved? I don't. In fact, today's system — much improved, to be sure — is nevertheless a recipe for an even bigger mess during a panic. Investors will be so nervous that they will screw up their orders. Huge volume will clog website servers, disrupting orders entered on-line. Orders may go in, but confirmations may not come out. A trader *might not know* if his sale or purchase went through. Is he in or out? Quote systems will falter at just the wrong time. Phone lines from you to the broker and from the broker to the floor will be jammed, and some will go down. Computer technicians will be working overtime while being distracted worrying about their own investments. Brokers will be operating on little sleep and at peak agitation, since most brokers are themselves bullish speculators. They will be entering orders wrong. Firms will begin to enact and enforce tighter restrictions on trading and margin. Price gaps will trigger stops at prices beyond the ability of some account holders to pay. You, the wise short seller, could survive all these problems only to discover that your broker has gone bankrupt or has been shut down by the SEC or that its associated bank has had a computer breakdown or that its assets are depleted or frozen.

Unless you are prepared for such an environment, don't get suckered into this maelstrom thinking that the bear market will be business as usual, just in the other direction. If you want to try making a killing being short in the collapse, make sure that you are not overexposed. Make sure that if the system locks up for days or weeks, you will not be in a panic yourself. Make sure that in a worst-case scenario, the funds you place at risk are funds you could lose.

Inverse Index ("Short") Mutual Funds

A somewhat more conservative speculation would be to invest in inverse index funds, also called short funds or bear funds, which are bets on falling stock indexes. These funds go up in value as stock index futures fall in value, and vice versa. I recommended inverse index funds in *The Dick Davis Digest* for both 2000 and 2001, and they beat everything else both years. The stock market should have several more down years ahead, and bigger ones at that.

In the U.S., you will find inverse S&P index funds at Rydex and ProFunds. Rydex has Ursa, which is the largest inverse index fund available, and ProFunds has the Bear ProFund. Rydex also has Arktos, which moves inversely to the NASDAQ 100 Index.

For seasoned speculators who can time the market well, Rydex offers Tempest, which is *doubly* short the S&P index, and Venture Fund, which is doubly short the NASDAQ 100. Also, they may be traded twice a day, not just at the close. ProFunds has the UltraBear fund and the UltraShort OTC fund, which are doubly short the S&P and NASDAQ 100, respectively. I am serious about using such funds *only if you are already a seasoned speculator.* You must be extra careful any time you use leverage, because leverage heightens your emotions, making them an even worse enemy to success.

The companies that offer short funds also offer money market funds and "long" index funds too, so with a brief phone call, you can easily move your money to take advantage of swings in either direction or "park" it for safety. Speaking of parking, Rydex's money market fund owns only instruments issued, guaranteed or backed by the U.S. government or its agencies or instrumentalities, making it safer than the average money market fund.

For information on these two mutual fund companies, contact the following:

Ursa Fund, Arktos Fund, Tempest Fund, Venture Fund
Website: www.rydexfunds.com
Address: Rydex Series Funds, 9601 Blackwell Rd,
    Suite 500, Rockville, MD 20850
Phone: 800-820-0888 and 301-296-5406
Minimum: $10,000

Bear ProFund, UltraBear, UltraShort 100
Website: www.profunds.com
Address: ProFunds, 7501 Wisconsin Ave, Suite 1000,
    Bethesda, MD 20814
Phone: 888-776-1970 or 240-497-6400
Minimum: $15,000

Before you invest in bear index funds, you need to understand something important about how they work, which can be a good or bad thing, depending upon the market environment. Holders of shares make money depending upon the short-term *percentage change* that the market undergoes each day or half day. In a persistently trending market, this situation is better than a short sale. Theoretically, the market can go down five percent per week indefinitely. If the market does fall a long way in a straight line, these funds could compound your return well beyond that of a normal short sale, which at most can gain 100 percent. Also, while the shares of these funds lose value in an up market, they do not lose all of their value, as a short sale can when a stock doubles.

On the other hand, this attribute in some circumstances can present a big problem. To understand it, follow this example: You invest $100,000 in a doubly leveraged short S&P 500 fund with the index at 1000, which is a $200,000 short S&P 500 exposure. The next day, the index rises 10%, so you have lost $20,000. The short fund automatically resets your exposure to twice your equity at the end of the day, so your new exposure is short $160,000. The next day, the index returns to 1000, but your equity rises only to $94,545 because the percentage decline from the higher level is only 9.09 percent, and you didn't have enough exposure on the way back to make up your initial loss. The index is unchanged, but you lost money. The same negative result occurs when the index initially goes your way and then returns to its starting point. Critics call this attribute "beta slippage." This problem is compounded when markets are in a trading range and further when leveraged funds reset twice a day. Since markets do tend to fluctuate a lot, this is usually a negative attribute for long-term investors. To make these funds work in all environments, you have to be a short-term market timer. Being a successful one when you are restricted to trading in and out only once or twice a day *at a particular time* is nearly impossible. If you can do it, then use these vehicles. If not, there is an alternative to the rescue.

Customized Dynamic Index Allocation

The brainchild of Stanford M.B.A. Robert R. Champion, Bermuda-based Invesdex, Ltd has developed an Internet-based instrument called MarketPlus, which is a liquid, fully asset-backed over-the-counter investment contract that has the look and feel of an online trading account. It offers a selection of major world equity and debt indexes, currencies, commodities, and a money-market index. You create your own return parameters by customizing your contract to the performance of one or more of these assets, long or short. You also get to choose the leverage you want, from zero (conservative) up to 3-to-1. To avoid beta slippage, your exposure is normally not reset unless and until you choose to do so. You can adjust allocations as often as every half-hour, far more often than index funds allow. This frequency is somewhat restricted compared to a futures account, but with MarketPlus, you cannot lose more than your investment because the system resets your exposure to your initial ratio if your loss exceeds certain limits. What's more, all gains — even when indexed to the money-market rate — are capital gains and are not taxed until funds are withdrawn from the instrument. To invest in MarketPlus, you must be a professional financial adviser, money manager or experienced "Qualified Investor," which means that you must have a net worth in excess of US$1 million and be able to invest at least US$100,000 in the contract. Currently available only to non-U.S. investors, MarketPlus is due to become available to U.S. investors later in 2002. For information, contact the following:

Invesdex, Ltd
Website: www.invesdex.com
Email: info@invesdex.com
Address: P.O. Box HM 1788, Hamilton HM HX,
    Bermuda
Phone: 441-296-4400
Fax: 441-295-2377
President & CEO: Valere B. Costello
Minimum: $100,000

Managed Bear Funds

You may also wish to consider a portfolio of short or hedged stocks, managed by an expert. Actively managed bearish stock funds are designed to benefit from a declining stock market. There are very few around today because the stock mania of the 1990s drove most of them out of business. The public hasn't been interested; in fact, it has moved money out of bear funds since the 2000 top! A few courageous money managers have maintained this alternative.

One example in the U.S. is the Prudent Bear Fund, which maintains short positions in individual stocks and indexes and also buys put options. The fund is about 70 percent short. This short percentage typically does not vary greatly, says president David Tice. The fund maintains some long positions, which account for up to 15 percent of its assets. Longs include special situations such as shares of certain small-cap companies and natural resource stocks such as gold and silver mining companies. The fund is no-load. It is about $200 million in size. Tice is fully apprised of the long-term risk in the stock market and the financial world.

Another example is the Comstock Capital Value Fund, which is positioned to profit from a declining market with a combination of index puts and shorts of both individual stocks and stock futures. With the leverage of puts taken into account, the fund is the equivalent of over 100 percent short. The fund also has positions in long-term U.S. Treasury bonds and the Euro currency. The firm's other fund is the Comstock Strategy Fund, which is conservatively positioned to benefit from a bear market, using puts to approximate a 70% net short position. The funds' managers, Charles Minter and Martin Weiner, have been writing free web commentary which (amazingly) calls for a long-term bear market in a deflationary environment. You can read it free on their website.

Another bear fund is the Gabelli Mathers Fund. Manager Henry van der Eb takes a conservative approach, making it attractive if you are unconvinced of the bear's imminence or ultimate severity. The fund also offers tax-sheltered gains due to tax-loss carry-forwards, "earned" during the bull market.

For information on these funds, contact the following:

See end of book for updated contact information

Prudent Bear Fund
Website: www.prudentbear.com
Email: info@prudentbear.com
Address: 8140 Walnut Hill Lane, Suite 300,
    Dallas, TX 75231
Phone: 800-711-1848 and 214-696-5474
Manager: David Tice
Minimum: $2000

See end of book for updated contact information

Comstock Capital Value Fund and Strategy Fund
Website: www.comstockfunds.com
Email: info@comstockfunds.com
Address: 24 S. Main St, Yardley PA 19067
Phone: 215-493-7076
Fax: 215-493-8083
Managers: Charles Minter and Martin Weiner
Minimum $1000

See end of book for updated contact information

Gabelli Mathers Fund
Website: www.gabelli.com/mathers.html
Email: info@gabelli.com
Address: One Corporate Center, Rye NY 10580
Phone: 800-422-3554
Manager: Henry van der Eb
Minimum: $1000

Insurance-Based Manager Combinations

Well-heeled investors in the United States have an interesting option. Access Fund Management LLC ("AFM") offers qualified purchasers multi-manager portfolios within private-placement insurance products. AFM utilizes the Performex® Proprietary Analytical System, which maintains the track records of thousands of managers and among them profiles a number of theoretically idealized allocations.

AFM has set up what it calls *market-neutral* strategies. Its methodology allocates assets among several equity and hedge fund managers, including those with a successful record of selecting securities to buy long and others with a successful record of selecting securities to sell short. The expectation is that those managers investing in the direction of the market do extremely well, while the other managers' selection expertise mitigates losses on their counter-trend positions. Ideally, the market is thereby "neutralized," so you get good stock selection on both sides without one-sided exposure to market-trend risk.

According to its reports, Performex®-based investment structures have had strong gains in both rising and falling markets in recent years. Of course, such performance can change.

The insurance product embodying multi-manager allocations provides tax-deferred growth for qualified purchasers. Under current law, some states also provide asset protection from creditors within this type of insurance product. Although I am convinced that the safest insurance companies are in Switzerland, AFM says it chooses only North American insurance companies with high financial ratings. It further points out that each policy's assets are held in separate custodial accounts at stock exchange member firms utilized by the individual investment managers. These separate accounts are not subject to claims by general creditors of the insurance companies, increasing the qualified buyer's overall safety. When choosing such products, make sure that its specific arrangements meet your safety requirements.

The minimum investment for this insurance alternative is high, at $1,000,000. These portfolio structures are also available for taxable and retirement accounts (IRAs, 401Ks, etc.), which have a minimum investment level of half that amount. Access Fund Management LLC can be reached as follows:

Access Fund Management, LLC
Address: 28050 Highway 19 North, Suite 301,
    Clearwater, FL 33761
Phone: (800) 638-5760
Fax: (877) 577-6744
Contact name: Michael V. Williams
Email: info@AccessFundManagement.com

Portfolio Managers Who Are Not Afraid To Be Bearish

You can also find portfolio managers who are not afraid to be bearish. There are surely many in the world. I personally know of only a few, and they may or may not be the best. In the U.S., examples are Lang Asset Management (www.langasset.com), which selects medium-to-large-cap stocks that look overpriced and shorts them, staying reasonably fully invested, sometimes "hedging" with options or by other means. In Asia, Marc Faber Ltd. (www.gloomboomdoom.com), and in Europe, Zulauf Asset Management AG (Grafenauweg 4, CH-6300 Zug, Switzerland; phone: (US: 011) 41-41-724-57-01), provide bearishly oriented management. Minimum funding requirements range between $100,000 and $3 million.

To find more leads, check out the Hedge Fund Association at http://www.thehfa.org and Planet Hedge Fund at http://planethedgefund.com/catlinks/indi.html. Hedge funds are only as good as their managers. Some fund managers use huge leverage and can "blow up," losing everything on a bad bet. The more spectacular of those make the newspapers; there are others that just go quietly. If you want to go this route, choose wisely and make sure that you satisfy yourself that the money manager you choose deals with safe banks. I have not investigated that aspect of any of these funds.

Temporary Opportunity?

The opportunity to make money on the downside in a deflationary crash can hardly be overstated, because *you will be making more dollars as the value of dollars* is soaring. It's a double benefit. Will it always be there?

I recall only one time when authorities banned buying in a bull market. The Comex futures exchange banned orders "to open" in silver futures in January 1980 to save their own skins, since many exchange members were short. Most investors were long, so their only allowed course was to sell. By changing the rules, the exchange profited and investors got killed. (For more on that story, read *Silver Bonanza*, by James Blanchard and Franklin Sanders, published by Jefferson Financial, 2400 Jefferson Highway, Suite 600, Jefferson, LA 70121, phone 504-837-3033.)

In a bear market, bullish investors always come to believe that short sellers are "driving the market down," when in fact, the decline is almost entirely due to selling from within their own over-invested ranks. Sometimes authorities outlaw short selling. In doing so, they remove the one class of investors that *must* buy. Every short sale (except when stocks go to zero) must be *covered*, i.e., the stock or derivative contract must be purchased to close the trade. A ban on short selling creates a market with no latent buying power at all, making it even less liquid than it was. Then it can dribble down day after day, unhindered by the buying of nervous shorts. Like all other bans on free exchange, a ban on short selling hurts those whom it is designed to help.

The Japanese government is currently discussing a ban on short selling. If authorities in your country decide to disallow short selling, the bad news is that this option will be closed to you. The good news is that they usually take such actions near major bottoms, so it will probably be about the proper time to cover shorts and start composing your "buy" list anyway.

Chapter 21:

Should You Invest in Commodities?

Figures 21-1 through 21-9 show what happened to commodities in dollar terms from 1929 through 1938. Pay particular attention to what happened in 1929-1932, the three years of intense deflation in which the stock market crashed. As you can see, commodities crashed, too.

You can get rich being short commodity futures in a deflationary crash. This is a player's game, though, and I am not about to urge a typical investor to follow that course. If you are a seasoned commodity trader, avoid the long side and use rallies to sell short. Make sure that your broker keeps your liquid funds in T-bills or an equally safe medium.

There can be exceptions to the broad trend. A commodity can rise against the trend on a war, a war scare, a shortage or a disruption of transport. Oil is an example of a commodity with that type of risk. This commodity *should* have nowhere to go but down during a depression. From 1929 to 1933, for example, after oil had already fallen substantially over preceding years, it plummeted another 80 percent in price. The odds of a repeat performance, however, are lessened by the fact that 4/5 of the world's known oil reserves are in Asia. Aside from France, political entities in general have squandered their nations' forty-year opportunity to have responsible companies replace the cumbersome, costly and dangerous old models of energy production with nuclear power

Figure 21-1 through 21-4

Figure 21-5 through 21-8

Figure 21-9

plants, which (absent politics) can produce multiples more energy at far less cost, risk and pollution. Because of these policies, many nations are deeply vulnerable to a cessation of oil shipments from unstable nations. So oil may be a good short, but it's a risky one. Be careful with any commodities that could experience shortages.

Some people today who are concerned about economic upset are touting commodities, mostly because they look for a replay of the inflationary 1970s. Commodities have been jumping higher since October, and advocates are vehement. I do not buy this argument, at least not as of today. As shown in Figure 21-10, the Commodity Research Bureau (CRB) commodity index has tracked the S&P, with a slight lag, since mid-1998. Gold and silver have also joined in the latest stock rally. As I see it, this correlation means that most assets lately are moving up and down more or less together, probably as liquidity expands and contracts. If so, then any deflation will crush hard-asset prices right along with share prices, just as it always has.

Even if I came to expect the prices of hard assets to rise, I still would not put commodities on the top of my list. I would buy gold and silver, for three reasons: First, unless you own an oil company or the like, you can't own physical commodities; you

Figure 21-10

have to own them through a promise to deliver, called a futures
contract. With respect to gold and silver, you can own the physical asset. Second, gold and silver are cheap, and third, they have
monetary value. If there truly is a panic into real goods, I cannot
imagine a scenario in which those two would be excluded.

Chapter 22:

Should You Invest in Precious Metals?

Precious metals are likely one day to become the most important asset class to own. From the mid-1970s to the mid-1980s, investors were dedicated to owning gold and silver for safety. Today, people are utterly disinterested in gold or silver, which is what sets the stage for an opportunity.

First, some brief background. Currencies today are utter fictions, but few realize it. Sometime during this century, people will question the validity of the fiat money system. The 1970s may prove to have been just a warm-up in a world battle for real money. Governments may exercise their powers to keep the fiat paper money system afloat, defending their currencies with various schemes and legal restrictions, but in the end, gold will win.

Why is gold such a desirable commodity? At the top of the list is its impeccable utility as a store of value. Relentless inflating has caused chronic value losses in currencies. The U.S. dollar has dropped in value by an estimated 94 percent (exact values depend upon the benchmark) since the Fed came into being. These collapses have destroyed the financial security of the working class, the middle class and retirees. Had modern money a tangible basis, then workers could have saved for their retirement in a true store of value, and retirees would have far more buying power in their golden years. It is already a pity to observe hard-working people unable to save a penny. It will be heart wrenching to see innocent people suffer during the ultimate resolution of central banks' credit-expansion policies. Gold also contributes to long-run productive stability. By setting up central banks with monopoly powers dedicated to paper money, governments traded that stability for an international casino in which money manipulators thrive at the expense of both producers and savers.

It is dangerous to entrust any service crucial to survival to a statutory monopoly or government regulation. When the Russian government handled food production and distribution, central planners reported over seven straight decades of "bad weather," food shortages and starvation. Similarly, with the Bank of England, the Fed and their worldwide counterparts in charge, central planners report decades of "rising prices," monetary debasement and the impoverishment of savers. Periodic credit inflation would occur in a free market as well, but its effects would be limited because real money cannot be inflated, and prudent people and institutions could choose to opt out of a credit binge in favor of real money. A free people would choose the best money, and I have no doubt that it would be gold.

Is the Precious Metals' Bear Market Over?

Despite the verity of gold as the best form of money, there is a right time for everything. Advisors who have insisted upon inflation's inevitability have kept their followers in gold and silver for 21 years as they plummeted 70 percent and 93 percent respectively in dollar terms, while the dollar was losing purchasing power at the local store. This is no mean feat insomuch as no other commodity has accomplished it. These losses, even forgetting the massive opportunity costs, have been staggering.

Right now, I think it likely that gold and silver will fall into their final dollar price lows at the bottom of the deflation because that is what happened to silver in the last great deflation. Figure

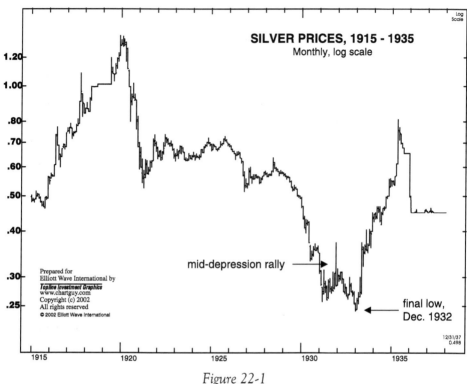

Figure 22-1

22-1 shows that although silver had undergone most of its bear market by the time of the 1929 high in the stock market, it still followed commodities and paper assets down during the deflation to a final low in December 1932. There is rarely sufficient reason to bet heavily on cycles doing something different from what they have typically done, and this cycle's history implies that the precious metals' bear market is not quite over yet. If this deflation acts like the last one, then at the coming bottom, we will have a great buying opportunity for gold and silver — maybe the greatest ever.

Most gold bugs today assert that gold and silver are a "deflation hedge," a "war hedge," and a "depression hedge," claims that the record does not convincingly support. The price history of 1931 is instructive in showing that there was a year-long mid-depression rally in the price of silver, which ended on a spike, indicating brief panic buying. Investors of that time were likewise convinced that silver would provide counter-trend solace during monetary difficulty. They were remembering silver's positive performance during the preceding difficult times of 1914-1919, which were inflationary. Similarly, today's precious metals enthusiasts have the inflationary 1970s in mind. However, the actual troubles in the 1930s were, and in this case are expected to be, deflationary.

The fact that people "rushed into gold" in the early 1930s has been a mainstay of the gold advocates' argument. They rarely tell the whole story. I suspect that people bought gold then because the U.S. government had fixed the price, at $20.67 per ounce. While everything else collapsed, gold was soaring in relative value, and its value gains were guaranteed. Who wouldn't buy it? If the government had fixed the price of any other substance, people would have invested in that instead. Like silver in the 1930s, gold today is free to trade at market price, which means that it can go down during a dollar deflation. I cannot guarantee that it will; I can only state that there is no good case to be made that history indicates otherwise.

Buy Gold and Silver Anyway

You might be surprised to find that I advocate holding a healthy amount of gold and silver anyway. There are several reasons for this stance:

First, it could be different this time, for some reason I cannot foresee. In a world of fiat currencies, prudence demands hedging against a rush to tangible money.

Second, these metals should perform well on a relative basis compared to most other investments. Unlike so many commodities, they will not fall 90 percent from today's prices, much less to zero, like so many stocks and bonds. These metals are downright inexpensive compared to their top values in 1980. Silver today costs only about 8 percent of its peak dollar value. Relative to home prices and stock prices, the metals have never been cheaper. So even if the precious metals continue to decline, they will fall much less in percentage terms than most other assets because they have already fallen so far.

Third, the question of whether there will be further bear market in the metals is really one for speculators and quibblers. Gold and silver have declined in dollar value for over two decades, which is between 90 percent and 100 percent of the total time I had expected them to fall. It may not be prudent to try to finesse the final months.

Fourth, the metals should soar once the period of deflation is over. Notice in Figure 22-1 that silver rebounded ferociously after it bottomed in 1932, tripling in just two years, rewarding those who continued to hold it. If deflation again keeps precious metals prices down, the rebound after the bottom should be no less robust. Given the likely political inflationary forces, it could well be much stronger. So by all means, you want to own precious metals prior to the onset of the post-depression recovery.

Fifth and foremost, if you buy gold and silver now, *you'll have it*. If investors worldwide begin to panic into hard assets, locking up supplies, if governments ban gold sales, if gold and silver prices go through the roof, you won't be stuck entirely in paper currency. You will already own something that everyone else wants.

Be aware that the present legalities of gold and silver ownership could change. This political risk isn't fantasy, even in the Land of the Free. In 1933, President Roosevelt outlawed gold ownership for U.S. citizens and imposed a ten-year prison sentence on anyone who refused to surrender his gold to a Federal Reserve Bank within 25 days. (The following year, the government began a long campaign of fixing the price of newly mined silver, though each level was temporary and closely reflected market forces.) The ban on gold stayed in place for over four decades, until President Ford lifted it on the first day of 1975.

Should you buy gold and silver now? The answer depends on how much you are willing to pay for the added breadth in your portfolio and for their current availability. If you are willing to see the dollar value of the precious metals drop another 30 percent or more before they rise substantially, then I would say, that's the price you're willing to pay for its current availability and for the "insurance" of greater portfolio stability under an unexpected inflation scenario. If you want to arrange for capital safety in every way that you can manage, then diversification into real money is a necessary part of that effort.

How To Buy Gold and Silver

I do not advocate buying gold and silver in paper form by way of futures contracts, gold-backed bonds from the Russian government or ownership certificates connected to commingled accounts at storage facilities. After all, which is better — owning actual gold or some entity's promise to pay it? For maximum safety, you should own gold and silver in physical form, outright.

One-kilo bars are widely traded globally, but "standard bars" of 400 fine ounces are the primary form of gold and silver used by central banks and recognized by the U.S. Comex, the London Bullion Market Association and the Tokyo Commodity Exchange (TOCOM). So that is the most liquid medium for storing substantial wealth in gold.

Coins are a good medium for smaller portfolios. Even larger ones should include their share of coins, because some day tangible money could once again become a medium of exchange, at least temporarily. To that end, be sure to avoid rare coins that have a "collectibility" premium. Many dealers recommend paying up for rare coins because in 1933 some collectible gold coins were exempt from U.S. government confiscation. The "cutoff" point for rarity was never codified, though, and there is no guarantee that any such law, much less exactly the same law, will go into effect in your jurisdiction. Any future confiscation in your country may include gold coins with a small collectibility premium because investment strategies built around them are well known. By all means, though, if the argument makes sense to you, pay the premium and sleep better for it.

The best-known and most liquid "bullion" style gold coins are American Eagles, South African Krugerrands, Canadian Maple Leafs and Australian Nuggets. As for silver, Americans should own a bag or two of circulated U.S. silver coins. Most coin dealers can get you these items. After you have a core position, accumulate the metals at a pace with which you are comfortable, preferably on price declines. Every time myopic central banks and panicked debtors push the price of gold and silver down, buy some more.

It is probably not as good an idea to invest in gold stocks, either. In common stock bear markets, stocks of gold mining companies have more often gone down than up except in relatively rare five to ten-year periods of accelerating inflation. Few people know that from the top day in the Dow in 1929 to the bottom day in 1932, gold mining shares rose only slightly *even though the U.S. government propped up the companies' product by fixing its price.* Mining shares did not soar in value until the stock market as a whole turned up. Today the government does not fix the price of gold, so in the deflation we currently face, gold mines will enjoy no false advantage over any other companies. Their stocks will probably rally when the overall stock market rallies (as they are doing now), but they have no built-in support as they did in the 1930s, so they are likely to disappoint those who invest in them. (Of course, if the government's policy on gold changes, then so might the outlook for mining share prices.)

Also be aware that there are risks attending the independence of mining companies. Owning gold shares means betting that no government will nationalize the mines whose shares you own. Owning gold shares is fine at the top of a Kondratieff economic cycle when inflation is raging, such as occurred in the 1970s, but not in its final years when deflation is raging and political tensions are their most severe.

In 1933, Roosevelt's Executive Order stated, "Your possession of these proscribed metals and/or your maintenance of a safe-deposit box to store them is known to the Government from bank and insurance records. Therefore, be advised that your vault box must remain sealed, and may only be opened in the presence of an agent of The Internal Revenue Service." Most banks were only too happy to comply because gold prohibition promised their salvation, or so they believed. If your government decides to confiscate gold, your country's banks will be recruited in the operation. If it happens sometime in the coming crash, the reason will probably be "fighting terrorism." By the way, this potential is a good reason to refrain from keeping any important personal papers in bank safe deposit boxes in any jurisdiction where such an action is possible. Otherwise, you may have to wait a while for permission to access the contents.

If you would like to buy gold and silver, your options are much more limited than they were twenty years ago, when everyone seemed to be in the business. Here are some suggestions. If you want to buy at least $100,000 worth of gold and/or silver bars and store them in one or more of the safest depositories in the world, contact SafeStore, Ltd., via the SafeWealth Group. If you want to buy bullion-style gold coins or circulated silver coins inside the U.S. and store them domestically, check out the dealers listed below. (Fidelitrade also offers an exchange-approved depository.) Be sure to cross-check prices before buying.

Fidelitrade
Website: www.fidelitrade.com
Email: info@fidelitrade.com
Address: 3601 North Market Street,
        Wilmington, DE 19802
Phone: 800-223-1080 and 302-762-6200
Fax: 302-762-2902
CEO: Mike Clark

See end of book for updated contact information

Hancock & Harwell
Website: www.raregold.com
Email: info@raregold.com
Address: Suite 310, 3155 Roswell Rd.,
        Atlanta, GA 30305
Phone: 888-877-1782 and 404-261-6566
CEO: Robert L. Harwell

See end of book for updated contact information

Investment Rarities, Inc.
Website: www.gloomdoom.com
Email: jcook@investmentrarities.com
Address: 7850 Metro Parkway, Suite 213,
        Minneapolis, MN 55425-1521
Phone: 800-328-1860 and 612-853-0700
CEO: James R. Cook

See end of book for updated contact information

Miles Franklin Ltd.
Website: www.milesfranklin.com
Email: milesf@ix.netcom.com
Address: 3601 Park Center Building, Suite 120,
        St. Louis Park, MN 55416
Phone: 800-822-8080 and 952-929-7006
Fax: 952-925-0143
CEO: David M. Schectman

See end of book for updated contact information

See end of book for updated contact information

Straight Talk Assets, Inc.
Website: www.coinmoney.com
Email: straighttalk@mindspring.com
Address: P.O. Box 1301, Gainesville, GA 30503
Phone: 800-944-9249 and 770-536-8045
CEO: Glenn R. Fried

Well-heeled investors should round out their holdings with platinum. Platinum is a precious metal, and in recent decades, its coinage has established it as an emerging monetary metal as well. Platinum has several advantages over gold and silver, not the least of which is that it packs more value per ounce. If you can afford to diversify to this extent, ask your metals dealer about platinum bars and coins.

Chapter 23:

What To Do With Your Pension Plan

As most of us know, banks and mortgage companies lend money to consumers via credit cards, auto loans and mortgages. You may not know that they then package and re-sell those loans as investments to pension funds (perhaps yours) as well as portfolio managers, insurance companies and even trust departments at other banks. The issuing banks keep most of the interest paid by the consumers in exchange for guaranteeing a small interest payment (today less than 2.5 percent) on the package. These investments are called "securitized loans," and banks and mortgage companies have issued $6 trillion worth of them. This high sum implies that if you have a managed trust, invest in a debt fund or have insurance or a pension, you are almost surely dependent upon some of these deals.

When banks sell the packages, they get back as much money as they lent out in the first place, so guess what. They can go right out and roll the same percentage of their deposits out again and again as new consumer loans. Investors in the packages are, in a sense, new depositors.

If the issuing banks get in trouble some day and can't pay, the owners of the debt packages will then have dibs on the interest payments from the consumers. If those payments dry up, they have that great collateral to fall back on: vacant homes, used cars and household junk. If a depression is on, what will that collateral be worth?

If such deals don't sound that solid to you, then why are so many institutions making these investments? Because they're buying them with OPM: Other People's Money…your money.

And besides, it's "guaranteed" and backed by "collateral"!

This scheme, like so many others in existence today, works only as long as the debtors and the economy can keep up the pace of interest payments, some of which are as high as 17 percent. In a major economic downturn, this credit structure will implode.

Make sure you fully understand all aspects of your government's *individual* retirement plans as well. In the U.S., this includes such structures as IRAs, 401Ks and Keoghs. If you anticipate severe system-wide financial and political stresses, you may decide to liquidate any such plans and pay whatever penalty is required. Why? Because there are strings attached to the perk of having your money sheltered from taxes. You may do only what the government allows you to do with the money. It restricts certain investments and can change the list at any time. It charges a penalty for early withdrawal and can change the amount of the penalty at any time.

What is the worst that could happen? In Argentina, the government continued to spend more than it took in until it went broke trying to pay the interest on its debt. In December 2001, it seized $2.3 billion dollars worth of deposits in *private pension funds* to pay its bills.

In the 1930s, the world heard a lot of populist rhetoric about why "rich" people should be plundered for the public good. It is easy to imagine such talk in the next crisis, directed at requiring wealthy people to forfeit their retirement savings for the good of the nation.

With the retirement setup in the U.S., the government need not be as direct as Argentina's. It need merely assert, after a stock market fall decimates many people's savings, that stocks are too risky to hold for retirement purposes. Under the guise of protecting you, it could ban stocks and perhaps other investments in tax-exempt pension plans and restrict assets to one category: "safe" long-term U.S. Treasury bonds. Then it could raise the penalty of early withdrawal to 100 percent. Bingo. The government will have seized the entire $2 trillion — or what's left of it given a crash — that today is held in government-sponsored, tax-deferred 401K private pension plans. I'm not saying it will happen, but it could, and wouldn't you rather have your money safely under your own discretion?

By the way, if you are normally in a high tax bracket and find yourself in a year with zero income or significant business losses, you can cash out part or all of your plan with either less tax (since you will be in a lower tax bracket) or no tax, if your earned-income losses cancel out the income from the plan. If you are under the age of 59½, you will normally have to pay a penalty, which is currently 10 percent of the value of the distribution. If you use the funds to pay for college tuition, though, you can even avoid the penalty. When you cash out your plan, you can still keep the money in the same investments if you wish, but then they will be in your own name, not in the name of a plan. Be sure to consult a tax advisor before proceeding.

Perhaps you have no such opportunity for tax saving and do not want to pay the penalty attached to premature withdrawal. If your balance is high enough, you may wish to consider converting your retirement plan investments into an annuity at a safe insurance company (see Chapter 24). It is highly likely (though not assured) that such investments would be left alone even in a national financial emergency.

If you have money in a personally directed corporate or government employee retirement plan with limited options, move it out of stock and bond funds. Park it in the safest money market fund available within the plan. Investigate the rules that pertain to cashing out and decide your next course of action.

If you or your family owns its own small company and is the sole beneficiary of its pension or profit sharing plan, you should lodge its assets in a safe bank or money market fund. As an alternative, depending upon your age and requirements, you may consider converting it into an annuity, issued by a safe insurance company. Such insurance companies are few and far between, but the next chapter shows you where to find them.

Chapter 24:

What To Do With Your Insurance and Annuities

If you believe that your fortunes are not dependent upon junk bonds, you might be in for a surprise. If you have life insurance, especially if you have a "guaranteed rate of return" insurance policy, your policy may be dependent upon the performance of junk bonds. Many large insurance companies failed in the comparatively mild recession of the early 1990s because they backed their policies with junk bonds. The economic contraction that insurance companies now face is *three degrees larger* than that one (Grand Supercycle as opposed to Primary). Your insurance nest egg, to put it bluntly, may be at risk.

Some insurance companies guarantee a minimum return on "equity-indexed annuities" while letting you participate in the market's gains but not its losses. An article in a major financial magazine calls these plans "a bear-proof way to ride the market" that "removes downside risk," but the way it's done involves zero-coupon bonds, index options and other exotic vehicles. This scheme will surely blow up, and if it does, the guarantee will stress the insurance companies that sell these policies.

Even traditionally safe insurance companies are massively exposed to losses during a major deflation because they invest in standard vehicles such as stocks, bonds and real estate. Some venerable insurance companies in Europe have become compromised not from their own investments but because banks that today are awash in leveraged derivatives purchased them some time in the past ten years.

A deflationary vise will put double pressure on the solvency of insurance companies. As the values of most investments fall, the value of insurance companies' portfolios will fall. Conversely, as the economy weakens, more and more people will decide to cash out their policies. Insurance companies become hard-pressed to honor the value of whole-life policies when there is a net outflow of cash at the same time that their property and stock investments are declining in value.

When insurance companies implode, they file for bankruptcy, and you can be left out in the cold. I know, because my insurance broker placed our insurance with, of all the companies in the world, Confederation Life. In 1994, it collapsed, along with Baldwin United and First Executive Corporation, which were huge institutions. See what happened when I didn't do the necessary research? If you think that you can rely on your broker to recommend a safe insurance company, think again. Brokers shop mainly for price, and when they do look into safety, they rely on rating services that don't do a good job (see Chapter 25). As it turned out, I was lucky. Government and industry leaders in both the U.S. and Canada worked for three years to distribute the policies to other companies. When my policy moved, it carried another full year's cash-out restriction, and all the while, I was still required to pay the premiums. The only reason that the deal finally made it through was that the North American financial boom continued throughout the 1990s, and other insurance companies felt safe taking on the additional obligations.

When a bust is in force, few insurance companies are willing or able to take over a stressed company's policy obligations, which have little collateral behind them. If your insurance company fails, your investment of a lifetime will be gone. It's happened to many people and will happen to many more.

Whole-life policies are almost always a terrible idea under a fiat money system. During inflationary times, their real value grows far more slowly than it appears, if at all, because the purchasing power of the monetary unit declines. During deflationary times, the policy your family is counting on to protect against death or old age can disappear if the company fails.

One option is to cash out such policies and buy term insurance instead. With term insurance, you can keep an eye on the fortunes of various companies and switch from one to another. Talk to your insurance broker about the courses of action open to you.

On the other hand, an interesting "deflation bonus" can also come available if you're careful. If you have whole-life insurance or an annuity with a *sound company*, you can actually come out way ahead because *the values and payouts are denominated in currency*. During deflation, the value of cash rises, so in terms of purchasing power, each dollar of value in your policy will be able to purchase more goods and services than it previously did. All you need to do is find a sound company.

Where To Buy Your Insurance Policies

At minimum, you should move your whole-life insurance policy or annuity to a sound insurer as soon as possible. If you delay one day too long in moving your policy, and the company's assets are frozen, you will have no recourse.

As far as I can tell, Weiss Ratings, Inc. produces the most reliable ratings of U.S. insurance companies. Their system is also simple and straightforward. Unlike the maze of gradations such as "Bbb+" and so on that other services use, the Weiss system simply reads like a report card, from A+ down to F, adding only a set of "E" grades prior to F. Weiss considers any company rated B- or above to have "good" financial safety but recommends that you do business with companies rated B+ or better. In normal times, that assessment is probably all you need. However, if you believe that there is a reasonable risk of that rare and devastating event, a deflationary crash and depression, why not demand the absolute best? Table 24-1 lists all U.S. insurance companies that Weiss rates A+. The three companies on this list that are also on Weiss' list of the 25 largest insurance companies rated B+ or higher are marked with an asterisk. To investigate a larger list of companies, see Weiss' book, *The Ultimate Safe Money Guide*.

Of course, as prudent as these judgments may be, these ratings do not fully take into account other considerations that will be crucial in a depression. For example, what bank(s) does your

THE SAFEST U.S. INSURERS			
Source: Weiss Ratings, Inc. (based on 12/31/01 data)			
Company Name	Domicile State	Weiss Safety Rating	Total Assets (in millions of $)
LIFE & HEALTH INSURERS			
American Family Life Ins Co	WI	A+	2,541.2
Country Life Ins Co	IL	A+	4,118.9
Northwestern Mutual Life Ins Co*	WI	A+	99,660.8
State Farm Life & Accident Asr Co	IL	A+	991.2
State Farm Life Ins Co*	IL	A+	29,344.9
Teachers Ins & Annuity Asn Of Am *	NY	A+	124,606.7
PROPERTY & CASUALTY INSURERS			
Alfa Mutual Ins	AL	A+	1,136.6
Amica Mutual Ins	RI	A+	2,912.4
Associates Ins	IN	A+	529.6
Auto-Owners Ins	MI	A+	5,514.3
Canal Ins	SC	A+	661.2
Government Employees Ins	MD	A+	8,157.9
Home-Owners Ins	MI	A+	323.6
Interins Exch of the Automobile Club	CA	A+	3,366.1
Kentucky Farm Bureau Mutual Ins	KY	A+	1,108.2
Protective Ins	IN	A+	412.6
State Farm Mutual Automobile Ins	IL	A+	73,397.5
Tennessee Farmers Asr	TN	A+	470.0
Tennessee Farmers Mutual Ins	TN	A+	1,212.3
United Services Automobile Asn	TX	A+	10,278.6
USAA Casualty Ins	TX	A+	3,145.5

*These are among the largest 25 insurers rated B+ or higher.

Table 24-1

insurer use to hold its assets and make transactions? If an insurer's main bank implodes, its situation could become chaotic. This one factor could override even an insurer's A+ credit rating. Ratings can change for all sorts of reasons. For maximum confidence, keep abreast of Weiss' ratings as they pertain to the companies you choose. (See contact information in the last section of this book.)

As if there were not already enough to worry about, the currency denomination of your policy may also prove crucial. If the currency in which you expect to be paid collapses in value, so will your plans for retirement.

Again, SafeWealth Group specializes in minimizing all these risks by identifying the safest insurance companies in the world as well as those among them that use safe banks as custodians of their funds. Better yet, it can identify the ones that also allow you to designate the currency denomination(s) of your choice within their policies. Such provisions for ultimate safety are particularly important for annuity arrangements, estate planning and capital-preservation programs that utilize insurance contracts.

The main point is to make sure that you assess the vulnerability of your insurance policies and annuities now. If you are satisfied, fine. If not, then you can take appropriate action before your insurance company, its bank, or you, become too stressed to adapt.

Chapter 25:

Reliable Sources for Financial Warnings

Safety Ratings for Financial Institutions

The most widely utilized rating services are almost always woefully late in warning you of problems within financial institutions. They often seem to get news about a company around the time that everyone else does, which means that the price of the associated stock or bond has already changed to reflect that news. In severe cases, a company can collapse before the standard rating services know what hit it. When all you can see is dust, they just skip the downgrading process and shift the company's rating from "investment grade" to "default" status.

Examples abound. The debt of the largest real estate developer in the world, Olympia & York of Canada, had an AA rating in 1991. A year later, it was bankrupt. Rating services missed the historic debacles at Barings Bank, Sumitomo Bank and Enron. Enron's bonds enjoyed an "investment grade" rating four days before the company went bankrupt. In my view, Enron's bonds in particular were transparently junk well before their collapse. Why? Because the firm employed an army of traders in derivatives, which is an absolute guarantee of ultimate failure even when it's *not* a company's main business.

Sometimes there are structural reasons for the overvaluation of debt issues. For example, investors buy the debt offerings of

Fannie Mae, Freddie Mac and the FHLB because they think that the U.S. government guarantees them. It doesn't. All that these companies have is the right to borrow money from the U.S. Treasury, $2.5 billion in the case of Fannie and Freddie and $4 billion in the case of the FHLB. That credit line represents less than ¼ of 1 percent of each company's outstanding mortgage loans, so it is a drop in the bucket. Worse, because of that advantage, the bonds that these companies issue are exempt from SEC registration and disclosure requirements because they are simply *presumed* to be safe. Managers of these companies are going to be utterly shocked when a depression devastates their portfolios and their earnings. Investors in these companies' stocks and bonds will be just as surprised when the stock prices and bond ratings collapse. Most rating services will not see it coming.

A few companies take a stringent approach to rating institutional safety. I listed three good U.S. bank-rating firms in Chapter 19. Weiss Ratings, Inc. has quite reliable, detailed ratings on a broader range of U.S. institutions. For example, while most analysts never saw the Enron disaster coming, Weiss placed Enron on its "Corporate Earnings Blacklist" in April 2001 and cited the company as being "highly suspect of manipulating its earnings reports." Two quarters later, the scandal broke, and countless employees and investors — people who hadn't the foggiest notion about taking the precautions I'm suggesting to you in this book — lost everything.

SafeWealth Group uses an even more stringent "survivability indicator" for financial institutions globally, taking not just the present balance sheet and corporate structure into account but also the institution's projected viability in a financial crisis or depression. SafeWealth is not in the ratings publishing business, but in response to inquiries, it will introduce qualified individuals, companies and trusts to its highest-rated institutions.

Investment Advice from Brokers

Throughout my career, I have advised people not to trust a brokerage firm's "fundamental" (as opposed to technical) analysts to warn you about anything. Brokerage firm analysts are notoriously poor at market timing. Besides being beholden to their corporate clients, which gives them an extreme bullish bias, most of these analysts use the wrong tools. Even when they are independent thinkers, they are usually not students of market psychology and thus have no idea how to figure out when a stock is probably topping. In fact, brokerage firm analysts are typically cheerleaders for a stock just as it is topping out and during most of its fall. Over 20 years ago, when I worked as a Technical Market Specialist at Merrill Lynch, I watched as an analyst kept a "buy" rating on a maker of CB radios while its stock dropped from 19 to 1. Nothing has changed. According to reports, 11 out of 16 analysts covering Enron had a "buy" (some even emphasized "strong buy") on the stock four weeks before the company declared bankruptcy and well after the decline in the stock price had wiped out its investors. As most people have subsequently learned, brokerage firm analysts almost never use the word "sell." If they really think a company's stock is dangerous, they label it a "hold." The problem with trying to follow this guideline, though, is that they usually label a stock that way after its bear market has run most or all of its course. To avoid being hurt by these strategists, you need independent market analysis.

Useful Newsletters in a Bear Market

Most newsletters these days are wet behind the ears. Their focus is touting stocks to buy. That was fine for the bull market, but it probably isn't now. At all times ideally, but particularly in a global bear market, you need input from seasoned analysts who cover the financial world with healthy skepticism and are as good at warning you about what investments to avoid as they are at suggesting what actions to take. Besides my own company's publications (see final section of this book), here are a few that I like:

The Gloom, Boom & Doom Report

Website: www.gloomboomdoom.com

Email: info@gloomboomdoom.com

Address: 3308 The Center, 99 Queens Rd. Central,
  Hong Kong

Phone: (U.S. dial 011) 852-2-801-5410

Fax: 852-2-845-9192

Editor: Marc Faber

See end of book for updated contact information

Grant's Interest Rate Observer

Website: www.grantspub.com

Email: webmaster@grantspub.com

Address: 30 Wall Street, New York, NY 10005

Phone: 212-809-7994

Fax: 212-809-8426

Editor: James Grant

See end of book for updated contact information

The International Speculator

Website: www.internationalspeculator.com

Email: info@internationalspeculator.com

Address: P.O. Box 84911, Phoenix AZ 85071

Phone: 800-528-0559 and 602-252-4477

Fax: 602-943-2363

Editor: Doug Casey

See end of book for updated contact information

Safe Money Report

Website: www.safemoneyreport.com

Email: wr@weissinc.com

Address: Weiss Research, P.O. Box 31689,
  Palm Beach Gardens, FL 33420

See end of book for updated contact information

Phone: 800-236-0407 and 561-627-3300
Fax: 561-625-6685
Editor: Martin D. Weiss

SafeWealth Report
Email: clientservices@safewealthadvisory.com
Address: SafeWealth Advisory Ltd. – Service Center,
      P.O. Box 1995, Windsor, Berkshire SL4 5LL, U.K.
Phone: (in U.S., dial 011) 44-1753-554-461
Fax: (in U.S., dial 011) 44-1753-554-642
Production Manager: Jane V. Scott

All that most of these services can do is offer you ideas. In the end, you will have to make up your own mind with the evidence that they present.

Chapter 26:

How To Ensure Your Physical Safety

In essence, bull and bear markets are social mood trends. Social mood trends have consequences.

A positive social mood has positive social consequences. The great bull market of the past quarter-century created a wonderful world. Major antagonists in the areas of politics, religion and race kissed and made up. The Cold War ended. Communism collapsed. Markets became global and sophisticated. The world embraced, to one degree or another, capitalism and freedom. The Information Age was born. Even country music got raucous and happy. In the 1990s, people felt secure, and today wealth abounds.

Generally speaking, that environment has been safe, profitable and fun. However, social mood trends are a two-way street. When the positive trend ends, a negative one takes over for a while. Those trends have social consequences, too: destructive ones, which affect finance, the economy, politics and all kinds of social relationships.

This book focuses mostly on finance. If you get out of investments that will lose most of their value in a crash and keep your money safe, you will be quite wealthy in terms of your purchasing power. Unfortunately, that's not all there is to a major bear market. Depressions are a mess. You may have money, but certain goods might be scarce or rationed. You might be financially smart yet get caught in a war zone.

It may not be much fun to contemplate the social effects of downtrends, but it is important. It's true that if you become financially devastated, you can't take advantage of great investment opportunities. But if you encounter physical risk, you may not even be around to try.

In order to profit from and enjoy an uptrend, you and your family must be fully protected during the preceding downtrend. Then, at the bottom, you can rise above the general despair and take full advantage both financially and emotionally of the next expansive increase in positive social mood.

Elliott waves portend many social changes, and you can anticipate them to some degree by understanding what I call socionomics. There is not room to explain the idea in this book. For a taste of how useful socionomics can be, review these comments on one result of social mood change that the forecasted bear market was expected to exhibit:

"Foreigners will commit terrorist acts on U.S. soil...."
— *At the Crest of the Tidal Wave* (1995)
Chapter 21, p.435

"The impulse to build shows up in the construction of record-breaking skyscraper buildings at social-mood peaks. At troughs, few buildings are built, and many of those already in place may be burned or bombed out of existence."
— *The Wave Principle of Human Social Behavior and the New Science of Socionomics* (1999)
Chapter 14, pp.229-230

"The Middle East should be a complete disaster. You've got at least three major religions in that area that all dislike each other, and the truce of the bull market has already been tenuous, so that area is going to blow up."
— *The Elliott Wave Theorist*, August 2001 issue

The 9/11/01 attack on the World Trade Center and the ensuing war in Afghanistan have borne out these observations, and we are as of yet only two mild years into the bear market.

By the way, some commentators write as if the terrorist attack caused the recession, but the stock market topped out a year and a half earlier, and the economy began contracting half a year earlier. Attacks such as this *result* from negative social-mood trends, which is why a socionomist can generally anticipate the tenor of behavior that manifests in such acts. Such manifestations are always a matter of frequency and degree. There is always some social unrest, even in the late stages of a bull market, but conflict always escalates in a bear market. For more on this theme, please see Chapters 14-16 of *The Wave Principle of Human Social Behavior and the New Science of Socionomics.*

Polarization and Conflict

The main social influence of a bear market is to cause society to polarize in countless ways. That polarity shows up in every imaginable context — social, religious, political, racial, corporate and by class. In a bear market, people in whatever way are impelled to identify themselves as belonging to a smaller social unit than they did before and to belong more passionately. It is probably a product of the anger that accompanies bear markets, because each social unit seems invariably to find reasons to be angry with and to attack its opposing unit. In the 1930s bear market, communists and fascists challenged political institutions. In the 1970s bear market, students challenged police, and blacks challenged whites. In both cases, labor challenged management and third parties challenged the status quo. In bear markets, rallies, marches and protests become common events. Separatism becomes a force as territories polarize. Populism becomes a force as classes polarize. Third parties, fourth parties, and more, find constituents. Bear markets engender labor strikes, racial conflict, religious persecution, political unrest, trade protectionism, coups and wars. In the area of personal behavior, part of the population gets more conservative, and part gets more hedonistic, and each side describes the other as something that needs reform. One reason that conflicts gain such scope in depressions is that much of the middle class gets wiped out by the financial debacle, increasing the number of people with little or nothing to lose and anger to spare.

The Erroneous Timing of Previous Concerns

In the late 1970s and early 1980s, survival was a big topic. There were million-seller books about where to buy electric generators, how to choose bulletproof vests, storing dried foods and so on. This occupation of course coincided with an approaching major bottom in a 16-year bear market (in inflation-adjusted terms). By then, you shouldn't have been wasting your time with it; you should have been buying stocks and bonds. The ideal time to address safety concerns is at the beginning of a downtrend, not at the end.

In 1999, near the all-time high in stocks, many people were again concerned for their physical safety, but this time, it was for the wrong reason. They feared that the "Y2K" computer glitch would shut down the civilized world. In the heat of the international obsession over this issue and in answer to many emails to the Message Board on our website, I answered that the free market would take care of that problem. Until the social mood trend turned down, as evidenced by a major downturn in the stock averages, there was little to fear on that scale.

Anticipated events such as those rarely cause global disruption. Major trends of increasing pessimism, anger and fear do cause global disruption, and that's what a bear market is. After

January 1, 2000, all the worriers over Y2K evaporated. Complacency reigned again, just when financial risk was at its greatest. That's also when physical safety should have become a real concern. The eruption of terrorist activity in recent months is a product of a bear market, so you see my point.

Some Thoughts on Preparedness

Exactly what to do about your physical safety is a difficult problem. Living in a populous area or near a military installation or an important infrastructure site is somewhat dangerous in times of social unrest. If you are physically tied to a job in such a spot, decisions about relocating are even more difficult than otherwise.

I know people who have farmland in the country, a retreat in the mountains or a self-sufficient home. Others buy guns or learn self-defense. These are fine ideas if you can fit them into the requirements and desires of your life. But for such preparations to be useful, you have to find yourself in a position where you need them. Usually in a major bear market, you are less likely to encounter a mob, a criminal or a terrorist than to face state-sponsored controls within your own country or military attack from without, and there may be little that a retreat or karate can do for you in those situations.

Nevertheless, if you determine that you need this type of preparation, now is a good time to dig out that old list of "Y2K" items and buy from it whatever you would like to have — such as an electric generator, a few months' worth of emergency dried foods, a video surveillance system, defensive weapons, etc. — some at half the prices that they were selling for in late 1999. Being prepared for terrorism is hardly an unreasonable idea.

Here are some web locations to help you with aspects of physical preparedness. Some of them link to other sites, so once you get in the loop, you will find many more resources.

Disaster Preparedness
   http://www.oism.org/nwss/s73p908.htm
   http://www.fema.gov

Basic Survival
   http://www.survivalcenter.com
   http://www.ki4u.com/nuclearsurvival/list.htm

Home Security, Disaster Information
   www.joelskousen.com

Dried Foods
   www.alpineaire.com
   www.freezedryguy.com
   www.fcs.uga.edu/pubs/current/FDNS-E-34-CS.html
   http://foodsafety.nal.usda.gov/

Self Defense
   www.kravmagainc.com

Some disaster-related literature can be more upsetting than helpful. Always stop and think: Is this course of action necessary? Is there a more sensible alternative? There is little point in taking much time and effort and cost to prepare for disastrous events that are highly unlikely or which can be judiciously avoided.

Chapter 27:

Preparing for a Change in Politics

The Elected Leader's Fortunes

Figure 27-1 uses U.S. electoral history to show that when the stock market is rising, reflecting a positive social-mood trend, voters tend to maintain the incumbent leader. When stocks collapse, the leader is thrown out in a landslide or by other means; though the instances are rare, there are no exceptions to this rule. Voters do not appear to care which party is in power at such times; they just throw whomever they perceive to be in charge, and his party, out of power.

National leaders always make things worse for themselves by (1) claiming credit when the economy does well, thereby implying that it's their fault when it doesn't, and (2) vowing to enact economy-boosting measures when the economy weakens, thereby supporting the fiction that they can control it, which puts their opponents in a position to claim that those policies failed.

A leader doesn't control his country's economy, but the economy mightily controls his image. When the economy contracts, that image suffers, and the voters throw him out. This is true of elected rulers all over the earth. For an instructive case in point, study the fortunes of U.S. president Richard Nixon, who won a second term in a landslide in late 1972 at a major top and was hounded from office less than two years later as the Dow

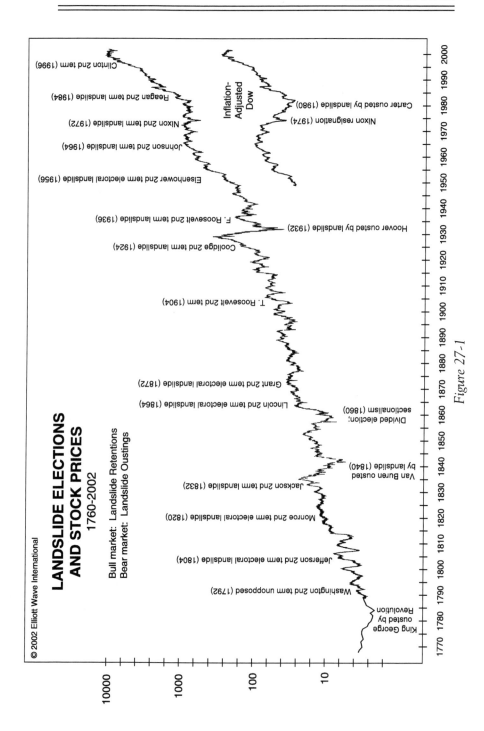

© 2002 Elliott Wave International

**LANDSLIDE ELECTIONS
AND STOCK PRICES**
1760-2002

Bull market: Landslide Retentions
Bear market: Landslide Oustings

King George ousted by Revolution

Washington 2nd term unopposed (1792)

Jefferson 2nd term electoral landslide (1804)

Monroe 2nd term electoral landslide (1820)

Jackson 2nd term landslide (1832)

Van Buren ousted by landslide (1840)

Lincoln 2nd term electoral landslide (1864)

Divided election; sectionalism (1860)

Grant 2nd term electoral landslide (1872)

T. Roosevelt 2nd term (1904)

Coolidge 2nd term landslide (1924)

Hoover ousted by landslide (1932)

F. Roosevelt 2nd term landslide (1936)

Eisenhower 2nd term electoral landslide (1956)

Johnson 2nd term landslide (1964)

Nixon 2nd term landslide (1972)

Reagan 2nd term landslide (1984)

Clinton 2nd term (1996)

Inflation-Adjusted Dow

Carter ousted by landslide (1980)

Nixon resignation (1974)

Figure 27-1

suffered its largest decline since 1937-1938. Or consider George Bush, who enjoyed record presidential approval ratings in 1991 yet lost the election just a year later amidst the deepest slide in S&P companies' earnings since the 1940s. In Argentina, which recently has suffered financial ruin after a deflationary crash, the president saw his public approval drop from 70 percent to 4.5 percent in just two years. The country then ran through four successive presidents in a matter of weeks. Those voters wanted all the bums thrown out.

If there is a deflationary crash, the incumbent leader of your nation, no matter how popular he is early in his term, will not win re-election if stock prices are much lower on election day. The financial and economic decline during his term and the defeat that follows will not be primarily his fault, though the majority will insist that they are. If the decline is a drawn-out affair, more than one successive leader could suffer defeat at its hands.

The Public, Not the President, Controls the Trend

People who hear me say in speeches that the markets and the economy affect the election of the leader more so than vice versa invariably gasp in incredulity. In the U.S., Republicans say, "How can you say that Ronald Reagan's conservative policies cannot be credited for the economic improvement of the 1980s, which led to 8 out of 10 years of expansion?" To which I reply, "Then do you also credit Franklin Roosevelt's liberal policies for the economic improvement of the 1930s, which led to 11 out of 12 years of economic expansion?" (You can switch these lines when a Democrat asks you the question.) Or more poignantly, "Do you credit Adolf Hitler for the dramatic economic upturn in Germany after he assumed power in 1933?"

What is really happening is that these leaders got into power because the people, despairing over their depression, demanded the ouster of the incumbents. The trend turned, and the new leader got the credit. Sometimes, voters at market bottoms do elect leaders with better economic policies. Usually, they don't.

Conversely, leaders in power during financial collapses are rarely directly at fault. Usually years of mismanagement by others set the stage. The leaders in power at the time, though, always appear inept, because they take actions designed to "help the economy," which fail, or they decline to take actions and are blamed for fiddling while Rome burns. Regardless of what they do or don't do, the public blames them and their party and kicks them out.

Political Stresses in Major Bear Markets

As we discussed in Chapter 26, bear markets create social polarization; in the political realm, that means radical politics. That much I can guarantee in the upcoming depression. Who wins the battles or the war is not scripted beforehand, except that the incumbents perceived to be in power lose.

In recent years, voter turnout has been low, races have been lackluster and close, and politics have been middle-of-the-road, with little difference between the major parties. Get ready for dramatic political changes.

In the U.S. stock collapse of 1835-1842, a brand-new political party (the Whigs) won the presidential election in 1840 and another (the Democrat Republicans), which had held power for forty years, soon afterward dissolved. In the election of 1860, following the stock bottom and deep recession of 1859, politics were so polarized that many states did not list all the presidential candidates on their ballots. A new party (Republican) won its first election. The following year, the Civil War broke out. The election of 1932, near the bottom of the Great Depression, was less tense but still a watershed, which led to the transformation of the United States into a semi-socialist state.

Given the projected size of this bear market, look for nations and states to split and shrink. Look for regional governments to challenge national ones. There is no way to know exactly where such splits will erupt, but they will erupt somewhere.

International politics will become increasingly dangerous. The number of annual nuclear explosions, whether for testing or attack, waxes and wanes inversely with the stock market. (For a graph, see Chapter 16 in *The Wave Principle of Human Social Behavior*.) Look for an increased number of nuclear explosions during the bear market.

Debt and fiat money create political risks. Overseas investors and central banks own 45 percent of the U.S. Treasury's bonds in the marketplace. The largest investors are Japan and China. Ultimately, the turmoil of a record-breaking debt liquidation could force the Treasury or the Fed to renege on some of its obligations, which could have extreme political consequences and turn global sentiment viciously against the U.S. On the other hand, an irony arises in the area of currency. The Fed's September 2001 bulletin reports that an estimated 90 percent of the new $100 bills ordered by the Federal Reserve Bank of New York are used to "satisfy foreign demand." According to a 1994 *New York Times* article, "In Russia, Romania, Tajikstan, China, Vietnam and other countries [the U.S. dollar] has become 'the official unofficial tender.'" Since 70 percent of dollar currency is overseas, a major dollar-based credit deflation would transfer 70 percent of the surviving dollars' expanding purchasing power to non-U.S. holders of dollar bills. Americans hold a larger percentage of IOUs, while others hold a larger percentage of the real thing, that is, to the extent that it is real. What political decisions such a situation may cause are anyone's guess, and so are the consequences.

What To Do If You Have Political Aspirations

If there is a major stock market crash, you want to run for office near the bottom. You will be revered by the public and historians if you win. George Washington, Abraham Lincoln, Franklin Roosevelt and Ronald Reagan were all elected at or near the bottom of severe downtrends, and all have an exalted place in American history.

Third parties do well in tough times; so do outsiders and radicals; incumbents do poorly. So if you are a non-incumbent political animal, you can plan now to take advantage of the situation. If you want to be a politician, plan to run for office on any party ticket but that of the leader(s) in your country who rode the trend down.

Why Politics Matter in the Context of This Book

At some point during a financial crisis, money flows typically become a political issue. You should keep a sharp eye on political trends in your home country. In severe economic times, governments have been known to ban foreign investment, demand capital repatriation, outlaw money transfers abroad, close banks, freeze bank accounts, restrict or seize private pensions, raise taxes, fix prices and impose currency exchange values. They have been known to use force to change the course of who gets hurt and who is spared, which means that the prudent are punished and the thriftless are rewarded, reversing the result from what it would be according to who *deserves* to be spared or get hurt. In extreme cases, such as when authoritarians assume power, they simply appropriate or take *de facto* control of your property.

You cannot anticipate every possible law, regulation or political event that will be implemented to thwart your attempt at safety, liquidity and solvency. This is why you must plan ahead and pay attention. As you do, think about these issues so that when political forces troll for victims, you are legally outside the scope of the dragnet.

Chapter 28:

How To Identify a Safe Haven

As I said in Chapter 26, the real risk of social unrest will probably involve not so much roving itinerant bands looting your home — a classic fear that is rarely realized — as much as *international conflict* and *domestic repression*. In a bear market, both international and domestic tensions increase, and the resulting social actions can be devastating.

Far more people in the past century had their lives wrecked or terminated by domestic implosions than by war. Whether you lived in Russia in the 1920s, Germany in the 1930s, Europe in the 1940s, China in the late 1940s, Cuba in 1959 or Cambodia in the 1970s, the smart thing to do early was to get out of Dodge. However, if you ever make such a decision, you will have to be lucky as well as smart. The people in Europe who decided in 1937 to move away before things got worse were the prudent ones. But one or two of them might have said, "Let's go somewhere far away and safe. Let's go out to the Pacific and live on one of those sleepy islands in the Philippines." In other words, you might guess wrong.

One good guide to the world's developing crisis spots is Richard Maybury's *Early Warning Report*. If you are an Asian, African or Middle Eastern resident, his analysis is especially pertinent. Maybury has also published some excellent primers on inflation and justice. You may contact him through the following means:

See end of book for updated contact information

Early Warning Report
Website: www.richardmaybury.com
Email: pmc701@aol.com
Address: P.O. Box 84908, Phoenix, AZ 85701
Phone: 800-509-5400 and 602-252-4477
Fax: 602-943-2363
Editor: Richard Maybury

If you live in a country with unstable politics, you should think about where you might go if things get oppressive. Like everything in a developing crisis, it is imperative to be prepared well before you have to make a final decision.

Some readers, admittedly only a few, may find merit in the idea of spending some time outside of their home countries while a depression unfolds. After researching the international scene for free and stable Western-style English-speaking countries, I find five top candidates: the United States, Canada, Australia, New Zealand and Ireland.

The world's #1 choice for refuge is the United States. Indeed, the philosophical foundation of the United States and its (some-times dormant) embodiment by many of its citizens may bode well for a low likelihood of severe domestic repression. Nothing is impossible, of course, and some people argue that the history of civilizations suggests that, on a multi-century basis at least, the peak of U.S. world power is at hand and repression will fol-low. Potentially more dangerous is the international threat. The U.S.'s penchant for involving itself in other countries' disputes has made it a prime target for terrorists and certain governments. Any sustained or coordinated effort by America's enemies could make domestic life highly unstable. Alternatively, if authori-tarians assume power at the federal level near the bottom of a depression (which happened throughout Europe and Asia in the 1930s and 1940s), difficulties could arise from domestic sources.

Simply *preparing* to move might not prove to be enough. Before you actually take that crucial action, your country of choice might shut its borders. Your country of *origin* might shut its borders. If terrorists infect a city in your nation with a biological warfare agent, you may be banned from entering any other nation. If you ever reach the point that you are sure you want a foreign refuge, you should move right then. If you choose a safe haven, and if the threats pass, you can always return to your home country.

At minimum, make sure that your passport is current, since demand for passports may increase later and delay processing. Another great idea is to obtain a "green card" or permanent resident visa in the country to which you would probably move if you came to such a decision. Usually they are issued for a period of five years or so, at which time you must renew them from inside that country. Permanent-resident visas generally cost about $US 4000 in legal fees to obtain, although most attractive countries have do-it-yourself forms available on the Internet. Like everything else, though, getting an extended visa takes time. You have to fill out forms and meet fairly stringent requirements. Even if you are quick and efficient, your legal representative or your host government might not be. Silly roadblocks can crop up that require another piece of paper, and so on. The point is, to get what you want, act early. Before actually packing up to move, you should consult an attorney in your chosen country so that you understand its laws.

A great way to get to know other countries from your armchair is by way of the *Eyewitness Travel Guides*, by Dorling Kindersley Publishing. They are not only packed with information, like most travel guides, but they are also loaded with breathtaking and informative photos. Their current cost is $24.95 each. For specific information about these countries' visitation and extended visitation policies, investigate the following websites:

United States: www.bcis.gov
Canada: www.cic.gc.ca/english
Australia: www.immi.gov.au
New Zealand: www.immigration.govt.nz
Ireland: www.justice.ie

Some of these sites are easier to use than others; you may have to poke around to find what you want. Sometimes web addresses change. If any of these sites move, or if you wish to investigate countries other than those listed above, just perform an Internet search on key words. Most immigration offices have their own websites.

I thought about filling up a couple of chapters with the pros and cons of these and other nations, but in the end, what really matters is what matters to *you*. Some of these countries have a better set of laws, others better weather, others a better culture, others better infrastructure, others more convenience. I am unfamiliar with non-English speaking countries that other people have been recommending, such as Argentina, Chile and Costa Rica, partly for the reason that I am unconvinced that they would be stellar havens of peace in a global depression. There are also many beautiful small island countries around the world, which rarely seem to be the focus of international conflict. You will have to sift through the data, the books and the brochures and decide for yourself. Of course, the best way to approach such a question is to visit selected locations personally. They make great vacation spots, so you will hardly regret it. Who says contemplating a depression can't have its pleasures?

Chapter 29:

Calling in Loans and Paying off Debt

People and institutions that best weather the system-wide debt liquidation of a deflationary crash and depression are those that take on *no debt* and extend *no risky credit*. This is the ideal situation for most people most of the time, anyway.

Handling Credit

In this book, we have already covered many topics that pertain to the problem of risky credit. Make sure that you do not lend your money to a weak debt issuer, whether corporate, governmental or any other entity. If you have already done so, trade it for something better.

There is also the question of personal credit extension. Have you lent money to friends, relatives or co-workers? The odds of collecting any of these debts are usually slim to none, but if you can prod your personal debtors into paying you back before they get further strapped for cash, it will not only help you but it will also give you some additional wherewithal to help those very same people if they become destitute later.

Handling Debt

If at all possible, remain or become debt-free. Being debt-free means that you are freer, period. You don't have to sweat credit card payments. You don't have to sweat home or auto repossession or loss of your business. You don't have to work 6 percent more, or 10 percent more, or 18 percent more just to stay even.

If you can afford it, the best mortgage is none at all. If you own your home outright and lose your job, you will still have a residence. When banks are throwing others out of their homes, you will still have a place to live. If you can't pay the rent on your business space, you can move your business into your house. And so on. I would rather own a crackerbox outright than have a mansion with mortgage payments I can barely make.

Consider the bank's situation in times of financial stress. Suppose you have paid off enough of your mortgage so that you own 50 percent of your home, which reflects the average equity held by homeowners nationwide. Suddenly, you find that you can't make further payments because of money problems in a depression. At that point, even if house prices had fallen by a whopping 50 percent, your bank would see it as no drop at all. It can place your property (actually *its* property) on the market. If the house sells for only 50 percent of its peak value, the bank gets 100 percent of its outstanding loan back. You can see why banks are pressured to sell properties in such situations. Of course, you end up homeless after slaving to pay off half the mortgage on the house over many years. That's what happens to many homeowners in a depression.

I suppose it might be possible to be creative in an otherwise impossible situation. Some people might decide to borrow as much of the home's value as possible, put the proceeds in a safe money-market fund and use those funds to meet the mortgage, thus assuring no missed payments for the duration. The problem with this idea is that many people are their own worst enemies, and they lack the discipline to protect the needed cash. They can find themselves both broke and homeless either way.

One way out of a debt load is personal bankruptcy. I don't recommend it because it isn't honest. People lent you their hard-earned money; you should pay it back. If you truly are a victim of unforeseen circumstances and must declare bankruptcy, apologize to your creditors and tell them that you hope the experience taught them a lesson about under-collateralized lending.

Chapter 30:

What You Should Do If You Run a Business

Avoid long-term employment contracts with employees. Try to locate in a state with "at-will" employment laws. Red tape and legal impediments to firing could bankrupt your company in a financial crunch, thus putting everyone in your company out of work.

If you run a business that normally carries a large business inventory (such as an auto or boat dealership), try to reduce it. If your business requires certain manufactured specialty items that may be hard to obtain in a depression, stock up.

If you are an employer, start making plans for what you will do if the company's cash flow declines and you have to cut expenditures. Would it be best to fire certain people? Would it be better to adjust all salaries downward an equal percentage so that you can keep everyone employed?

A cynic might recommend that if you are an employer, you should try to pay in stock or options, but if you share the expectations presented in this book, that course of action would be dishonest. Besides, an employee who gets gypped is hardly going to serve your company well. Don't forget, depressions don't last forever; when the next upturn comes, you will want a loyal staff to help you prosper in it, and they will want a healthy company to help them prosper, too. To encourage that result, pay what and how you need to for the talent you require.

If you manage a bank, insurance company, money management firm or other financial institution, try to work out of your speculative derivative positions, particularly bullish ones. Reduce stock market risk as much as possible. If you must be heavily invested in stocks — for example if you manage a stock mutual fund — hedge your positions with options. Tidy up your mortgage portfolio. Get rid of all second-tier debt paper. If you have invested in municipal bonds, consumer debt, real estate debt, junk bonds or anything other than top-grade paper, sell it at today's lofty prices. Get on a solid footing with investments that are high quality, liquid and commonly understood.

Perhaps most important, plan how you will take advantage of the next major bottom in the economy. Positioning your company properly at that time could ensure success for decades to come.

Chapter 31:

What You Should Do with Respect to Your Employment

Over the past decade, more and more companies have been compensating employees with stock options instead of money. In 2001, over half of America's large public companies were paying over half of their employees in stock options. As a market analyst, I am fascinated with the value of these figures as a reflection of society-wide stock-market optimism. As someone trying to help you, I see them as a trap that you should avoid.

If you have no special reason to believe that the company you work for will prosper so much in a contracting economy that its stock will rise in a bear market, then cash out any stock or stock options that your company has issued to you (or that you bought on your own).

If your remuneration is tied to the same company's fortunes in the form of stock or stock options, try to convert it to a liquid income stream. Make sure you get paid actual money for your labor.

If you have a choice of employment, try to think about which job will best weather the coming financial and economic storm. Then go get it.

If you are entrepreneurial, start thinking of ways to serve people in a depression so that you will prosper in it. For example,

I am writing this book. Think about what people will need when times get hard. Some people automatically think that providing services for strapped people is the right choice when they think "depression." Certainly, opportunities are there. At the same time, that's not where much of the money is. Many people will *not* have their assets tied up in the stock market or other risky investments, and if deflation occurs, their real purchasing power will soar. At the bottom of the Great Depression, 70 percent of the population had jobs, and they were quite well off. You can prosper by providing services to the solvent and the wealthy. Offering services to creditors may also yield steady employment. For example, because so much of today's debt is consumer debt, the repo business will probably thrive. There will also be a boom in bankruptcy services in a depression; maybe you can keep out of debt by helping others manage theirs.

If you have charitable impulses, this is the time to exercise them. Government services will shrink in a depression, and many people will be suffering. If you are *really* creative, find a way to help destitute people and make money doing so.

Unfortunately, I don't have all the answers for your situation. You know your skills and tastes better than I do. Now is the time to take account of them.

Chapter 32:

Should You Rely on Government To Protect You?

In one sense, the answer is yes. You always have to live somewhere. If you are fortunate enough to live in a safe, free country, you can probably tell that those benefits are greatly a product of its philosophy of government. To that extent, you should rely on the best government you can find. Other than that, government can be a disappointing guardian.

Compounding the Problems

Government is rarely prepared for national financial calamities or economic depressions, and when it is, they are unlikely to occur. This is not a result of personal failures so much as an aspect of collective human nature. People are often prepared for the past but rarely for the future.

Generally speaking, the intelligent way for an individual to approach the vagaries of his or her financial future is to have *savings* or buy *insurance*. Governments almost invariably do the opposite. They spend and borrow throughout the good times and find themselves strapped in bad times, when tax receipts fall. Like their counterparts around the world, the Social Security, Medicare, Medicaid and "welfare" systems in the U.S. have been dispersing billions of dollars throughout decades of mostly good times. Even today, political forces are trying to raise the government's payouts, for example to include coverage of mental as well as physical illness, which seems to be another express ticket to insolvency.

When the bust occurs, governments won't have the money required to service truly needy people in unfortunate circumstances. They are likely then to make things worse by extending "unemployment benefits," which sucks money away from employers and makes them lay off more workers, by raising the cap on retirement benefit taxes, which takes money away from employees and makes them unable to save and spend, and by increasing taxes generally, which impoverishes productive people so that they cannot spend and invest. It's sad, but the pattern is almost always the same.

Dependencies To Avoid

Don't rely on government programs for your old age. Retirement programs such as Social Security in the U.S. are wealth-transfer schemes, not funded insurance, so they rely upon the government's tax receipts. Likewise, Medicaid is a federally subsidized state-funded health insurance program, and as such, it relies upon transfers of states' tax receipts. When people's earnings collapse in a depression, so does the amount of taxes paid, which forces the value of wealth transfers downward. Every conceivable method of shoring up these programs can lead only to worse problems. A "crisis" in government wealth-transfer programs is inevitable.

Don't rely on projected government budget surpluses. A couple of years ago, the U.S. government declared a budget surplus, projected it years into the future and predicted healthy trends for its wealth-transfer programs. Was that a proper conclusion? Well, in 1835, after over two decades of economic boom, U.S. government debt became essentially fully paid off for the first (and only) time. Conventional economists would cite such an achievement as a bullish "fundamental" condition. (Any time an analyst claims to be using "fundamentals" for macroeconomic or financial forecasting, run, don't walk, to the nearest exit.) In actuality, that degree of government solvency occurred the very year of the onset of a 7-year bear market that produced two back-to-back depressions. Government surpluses generated by something other than a permanent policy of thrift are the product of exceptionally high tax receipts during boom times and therefore signal major tops. They're not bullish; they're bearish and ironically portend huge deficits directly around the corner.

Don't rely on any government's bank-deposit "insurance." The money available through the FDIC, for example, is enough to cover only a small fraction of U.S. bank deposits. As Japan's troubles increase, its government has proposed lowering the value of insured deposits; that could happen in any country. The whole idea of having other banks and taxpayers guarantee bank deposits is theft in the first place and thus morally wrong and thus ultimately practically wrong. Government sponsored deposit insurance has lulled depositors into a false sense of security. After the 1930s, when thousands of banks failed, depositors became properly wary of profligate banks. Today they don't know or care what their bank officers are doing with their money because they think that the government insures their deposits. Deposit insurance will probably save accounts in the first few distressed banks, but if there is a system-wide money and credit implosion, this insurance won't protect you.

Don't rely incautiously on government's obligations to you if you are a retired government worker. In Argentina in recent weeks, the government suspended state pension payments to 1.4 million retired state employees. It had no money to pay because times got tough, and it had never saved when times were good. The same thing could happen to many governments around the world, whether national, state or local, which pay billions of dollars annually in pensions. All of them are dependent either upon wealth transfer or upon managed funds that may or may not be properly invested.

Don't rely on all governments to pay their debts. In the 1930s, Fulton County, Georgia, where I grew up, was formed from two bankrupt counties that defaulted on their bonds. By 1938, state and local municipalities had defaulted on approximately 30 percent of the total value of their outstanding debt. Much of it was eventually resolved; some wasn't. U.S. investors today own billions of dollars worth of municipal bonds, thinking they are getting a great deal because that bond income is tax-exempt. This tax break may be a bonus in good times, but like so many seemingly great deals, this one will ultimately trap investors into a risky position. Governments that have borrowed to the hilt were running deficits even in the booming 1990s, so the risk of default in a depression is huge. If the issuers of your tax-exempt bonds default, you will have the ultimate tax haven: being broke. Quite a few munis are "insured," which salesmen will tell you means the same as "guaranteed." Such guarantees work fine until defaults drag down the insurers. That is to say, when you really need the supposed guarantees, they can fail. Given the huge extent of today's municipal indebtedness, such failures are inevitable.

Don't rely on your central bank, either. Ultimately, it is not in control of your country's stock market, bond market or interest rates. It mostly reacts to market forces. People think that the Fed "lowered interest rates" in 2001. For the most part, the *market* lowered interest rates. Declining interest rates are not a "first cause" designed to induce borrowing; rather, a dearth of borrowing is a "first cause" that makes interest rates decline. Interest rates on perceived safe debt always fall when an economy begins to deflate. So the record-breaking decline in short-term U.S. interest rates last year was not any kind of "medicine." It was not primarily administered but an effect. Japan's prime interest rate fell to nearly zero over the past decade because of its ongoing deflation. That drop in the cost of borrowing didn't change the economy. Why? Because the economy was in charge of the drop. The most that a central bank can do is distort normal market trends and make credit a bit tighter or looser than it would otherwise be. Unfortunately, every such distortion has a counterbalancing market-induced correction later. The Fed's record-breaking monetary looseness during 2001 has revived the economy and propped up asset markets for a few months, but it probably won't last much longer than that. Ultimately, it will simply serve to make the contraction worse.

Don't rely on government to bail out the banking system. When Barings Bank failed, the Bank of England declined to save Barings' depositors. The World Bank and the IMF did not bail out the banks that collapsed in Southeast Asia in 1997. The Japanese Ministry of Finance has not been bailing out troubled Japanese banks. No one is bailing out Argentina's banks today. The French government bailed out Credit Lyonnais in a series of bailouts from 1994 through 1998 that drained more than $20 billion from France's tax intake. This was not much of an exception, though, because the bank was state-owned. Financial institutions and the U.S. government, through the FSLIC and then the Resolution Trust Corporation, bailed out the Savings & Loan industry a dozen years ago to the tune of $481 billion. These were unfortunate actions. Yes, unfortunate, because they lulled French and American bank depositors, who might otherwise have become wary, into thinking that they are protected against anything. How many more bailouts can France afford? Or the U.S.? If many big banks get in trouble, prudence will dictate that even the richest governments stand aside. If instead they leap unwisely into bailout schemes, they will risk damaging the integrity of their own debt, triggering a fall in its price. Either way, again, deflation will put the brakes on their actions.

Don't expect government services to remain at their current levels. The ocean of money required to run the union- bloated, administration-stultified public school systems will be unavailable in a depression. School districts will have to adopt cost-cutting measures, and most of them will result in even worse service. Encourage low-cost free-market solutions, which will benefit both children and teachers. The tax receipts that pay for roads, police and jails, fire departments, trash pickup, emergency (911) monitoring, water systems and so on will fall to such low levels that services will be restricted. Look for ways to get better services elsewhere wherever it is legal and possible.

Don't rely on government "watchdogs." They rarely foresee disasters. U.S. regulators did not anticipate the Savings & Loan industry collapse. Subsequent investigation revealed several years of immense corruption. Enron created some 850 suspicious partnerships and employed an army of "inventive" accountants. Still, the SEC and the FASB were clueless about anything being amiss. A $68 billion company collapsed, impoverishing countless employees and creditors. Now the watchdogs in Congress are holding "hearings." Do you think this will help the employees and investors who bet the farm on Enron? Well, when the Insull utility trust similarly collapsed in 1931-1932, no investor was reimbursed a nickel; no manager ever went to jail. With 20/20 hindsight, Congress passed a few new laws.

Be smart. Don't let your financial future end up depending upon proceedings covered by C-Span.

Chapter 33:

A Short List of Imperative "Do's" and Crucial "Don'ts"

Recall the old Chinese character that entwines crisis and opportunity in the same glyph. Position yourself to take advantage of what's coming.

Don't:

- Generally speaking, don't own stocks.

- Don't own any but the most pristine bonds.

- Generally speaking, don't invest in real estate.

- Generally speaking, don't buy commodities.

- Don't invest in collectibles.

- Don't trust standard rating services.

- Don't presume that government agencies will protect your finances.

- Don't buy goods you don't need just because they are a bargain. They will probably get cheaper.

Do:

• Fight the inertia that will keep you from taking action to prepare for the downturn. Start taking steps now.

• Involve your significant others in your decisions. Put your home or business partners in tune with your thinking before it's too late.

• Talk to heavily invested parents or in-laws who may be planning to pass on their investments to you. See if you can get them to become safe and liquid.

• Think globally, not just domestically.

• Open accounts at two or three of the safest banks in the world.

• Invest in short-term money market instruments issued by the soundest governments.

• Own some physical gold, silver and platinum.

• Have some cash on hand.

• Make sure that you have insurance policies only with the safest firms and make sure that they deal only with safe banks.

• If you are so inclined, speculate conservatively in anticipation of a declining stock market.

• Sell any collectibles that you own for investment purposes.

• If it is right for your circumstances, sell your business.

• Make a list of things you want to buy at much lower prices when they go on "liquidation sale."

• If you want to have kids, hurry up. Statistics show that fewer people feel like doing so during a bear market.

• Give friends a copy of this book.

• Keep up with our *Bear Market Strategies* page, a continually updated report on-line at http://www.conquerthecrash. com/readerspage.

• *Contact the services mentioned in this book!* I am a market analyst and forecaster, not a banker, insurer, money manager, institution rater or depression strategist. These services can help guide you through the maze. Some of them can help you design your whole strategy in a matter of days.

• Plan how to take advantage of the next major uptrend. For example, go back to school during the decline and come out with extra skills just as the economy begins to recover. Apprentice in a job for low pay and learn enough to start your own business at the bottom so you can ride the next big upwave of prosperity. Investigate troubled businesses to buy at the bottom at deep discounts.

• Smile! because you will not be jumping out of the window; you'll be preparing for the incredible opportunities listed in the next chapter.

Chapter 34:

What To Do at the Bottom of a Deflationary Crash and Depression

At the bottom of a crash and depression, reverse most of Chapter 33's investment "do's" and "don'ts." When the Elliott wave pattern in the major stock market averages indicates that the collapse is over, take a good portion of your safely stored cash and do the following:

- Cover shorts and buy stocks of surviving companies at fire sale prices.

- Buy depressed bonds from issuers that have survived.

- Buy more gold, silver and platinum.

- Buy prime pieces of investment property from distressed banks.

- Buy your favorite uninhabited home or mansion at pennies on the dollar.

- Buy the under rented office building or the abandoned business facility you need for the cost of back taxes.

- Buy your favorite art and collectibles at bargain prices.

- Buy your own business back, start a business, or buy a distressed business cheap.

- Keep an eye on commodities. Generally, one would wait about two decades, when inflation begins to accelerate as the Kondratieff liquidity cycle approaches its peak, to buy them aggressively. Because a financial crisis could ignite hyperinflationary political forces at the bottom of the deflation, you might decide to buy some commodities then as a safety hedge. If the futures market survives the crash, the Rogers Raw Materials Fund should provide an excellent vehicle. It invests in an international basket of 35 commodities, continually adjusting it to maintain constant percentage weightings for each commodity. These maneuvers are a mechanical method of buying relative weakness and selling relative strength, which helps the fund's profitability. You can learn more about the fund at its website, www. rogersrawmaterials.com or by calling 800-775-9352 or 866-304-0450.

- Choose your location well and remain watchful of world affairs, because wars often break out during or shortly after depressions. (For more specifics, see Chapter 16 of *The Wave Principle of Human Social Behavior.*)

- Sit back and watch the investment markets in which you have invested turn up strongly and surprise the world.

You've survived! Now prosper!

Media and Misc. References

Chapter 1

Seigler, Mark V. (1998, June). "Real output and business cycle volatility, 1869-1993: U.S. experience in international perspective." *Journal of Economic History*.

Chapter 3

Elliott, Ralph Nelson. (series of books and articles published from 1938-1946). Republished: (1994) R.N. *Elliott's Masterworks—The Definitive Collection*, Prechter, Jr., Robert Rougelot. (Ed.) Gainesville, GA: New Classics Library.

Mandelbrot, Benoit. (1988). *The Fractal Geometry of Nature*. New York: W.H. Freeman.

Frost, Alfred John and Prechter, Robert Rougelot. (1978). *Elliott Wave Principle—Key to Market Behavior*. Gainesville, GA: New Classics Library.

Prechter, Robert Rougelot. (1999). *The Wave Principle of Human Social Behavior and the New Science of Socionomics*. Gainesville, GA: New Classics Library.

Prechter, Robert Rougelot. (1982, October 6 and November 8). *The Elliott Wave Theorist*.

Chapter 4

Prechter, Robert Rougelot. (2001, September 11). "Elliott Waves and Social Reality." *The Elliott Wave Theorist*.

Chapter 5

Elliott, Ralph Nelson. (1946). *Nature's law*. Republished: (1994) R.N. *Elliott's Masterworks—The Definitive Collection*, Prechter, Jr., Robert Rougelot. (Ed.) Gainesville, GA: New Classics Library.

Jasen, Georgette. (1994, May 13). "Darts Beat Pros but Losses Are the Rule." *The Wall Street Journal*.

Jasen, Georgette. (1996, July 10). "Pros Lose Out to Chance, Industrials." *The Wall Street Journal*.

Jasen, Georgette. (1997, February 11). "Investment Pros Defeat Darts, but Can't Top Surging Market." *The Wall Street Journal*.

Jasen, Georgette. (1997, April 9). "Pros Beat Darts, but in a Losing Contest." *The Wall Street Journal*.

Jasen, Georgette. (1998, May 13). "Pros Beat Darts, but Picks Trail Dow Jones Industrials." *The Wall Street Journal*.

Jasen, Georgette. (1998, November 5). "Darts Draw Blood as Pro Losses Far Exceed Those of Industrials." *The Wall Street Journal*.

Prechter, Robert Rougelot. (1983, August 18). "The Superbull Market of the '80s—Has the Last Wild Ride Really Begun?" *The Elliott Wave Theorist.*

Kendall, Peter Mark. (1998, September 16.) "Wave V Fundamentals and Their Implications." *The Elliott Wave Theorist.*

Chapter 6

Prechter, Robert Rougelot, editor. (2002). *Market Analysis for the New Millennium.* Gainesville, GA: New Classics Library.

Glassman, James K. and Kevin A. Hassett. (1999, March 17). "Stock Prices Are Still Far Too Low." *The Wall Street Journal.*

Birger, Jon. (2002, March). "Faith Stocks." *Money.*

Chapter 7

Siegel, Jeremy J. (1999, April 19). "Manager's Journal: Are Internet Stocks Overvalued? Are They Ever." *The Wall Street Journal.*

Siegel, Jeremy J. (2000, March 14). "Big-Cap Tech Stocks Are a Sucker Bet." *The Wall Street Journal.*

Glassman, James K. and Kevin A. Hassett. (1998, March 30). "Are Stocks Overvalued? Not a Chance." *The Wall Street Journal.*

Dornbusch, Rudi. (1998, July 30). "Growth Forever." *The Wall Street Journal.*

Angell, Wayne D. (1999, February 3). "The Bubble Won't Burst." *The Wall Street Journal.*

Glassman, James K. and Kevin A. Hassett. (1999, March 17). "Stock Prices Are Still Far Too Low." *The Wall Street Journal.*

Ip, Greg. (1999, August 30). " Does Tech 'Explosion' Alter Market's Nature?" *The Wall Street Journal.*

Ip, Greg. (1999, September 13). "New Paradigm View for Stocks is Bolstered." *The Wall Street Journal.*

Gilder, George. (1999, December 31). "The Faith of a Futurist." *The Wall Street Journal.*

Kadlec, Charles W. (2000, April 18). "Market Mayhem. Don't Worry, the Great Prosperity Still Coming." *The Wall Street Journal.*

Ford, Constance Mitchell. (2000, January 3). "Economists Are Euphoric About the Prospect for 2000—Nearly All Surveyed Believe Expansion Will Become Longest on Record." *The Wall Street Journal.*

Ford, Constance Mitchell. (2001, January 2). "Euphoria Dominating Last Year Turns to Prudence in 2001." *The Wall Street Journal.*

Hilsenrath, Jon E. (2002, January 4). "Economic Forecasters Expect Moderate Recovery in 2002." *The Wall Street Journal.*

Hughes, Siobhan. (2002, February 22). "Economists Optimistic. Survey Says Recession Likely Is Already Over." *The Atlanta Journal-Constitution.*

Hager, George. (2002, February 28). "Recessionette' Might Be at an End." *USA Today.*

Fox, Justin. (2002, March 18). "The Profitless Recovery." *Fortune.*

Barnes, Angela. (2002, January 10). "Managers Bullish on Equity Markets. Expect Double-Digit Return, Survey Finds." *The Globe and Mail* (Toronto).

Prechter, Robert Rougelot. (1995). *At the Crest of the Tidal Wave.* Gainesville, GA: New Classics Library.

Leonhardt, David. (2002, March 12). "After Sept. 11, Diverging Attitudes about the Market." *The New York Times.*

Prechter, Robert Rougelot. (2001, September 11). "Elliott Waves and Social Reality." *The Elliott Wave Theorist.*

Altman, Daniel. (2001, December 29). "Positive Reports Hint at Swift Recovery." *The New York Times.*

Meyers, Mike. (2002, January 6). "Better Times Coming." *Star* (Minneapolis).

Torres, Carlos. (2001, December 29). "Hope Soars in U.S." *Rocky Mountain News.*

Sommar, Jessica (2002, March 1). "Recovery at Last." *New York Post.*

Hagenbaugh, Barbara and George Hager (2002, March 8). "Fed Chief Declares Recession at an End." USA Today.

Pethokoukis, James. (2002, January 14). "Business Bounces Back. How to Cash in. That Old Blue-Sky Feeling." *U.S. News & World Report.*

Curl, Joseph. (2002, January 1). "Bush Predicts 2002 Will Be 'a Great Year'." *Washington Times.*

Chapter 9
Bolton, A. Hamilton. (1957, February 11). Personal letter to Charles Collins.

Chapter 11
Federal Reserve System. (2001, December 31). "Flow of Funds Accounts of the United States." Washington, D.C: Board of Governors of the Federal Reserve System.

The Federal Reserve Bank of St. Louis. "FRED, an Economic Time Series Database." http://www.stls.frb.org/fred/.

Chapter 12
Prechter, Robert Rougelot. (1979, November 18). "Commodities, Interest Rates and Inflation: A Major Top?" *The Elliott Wave Theorist.*

Kondratieff, Nikolai. (1926). "The Long Waves in Economic Life." Republished: (1935, November). *Review of Economic Statistics.*

Chapter 13

Norton, Rob. (1997, September 8). "Why not to Worry about Deflation." *Fortune.*

Wiseman, Paul. (1991, January 17). "Deflation? Not Yet. Some Prices Are Tumbling but Not All." USA Today.

Reisman, George and Robert Klein. (1999, November 15). "No Inflation? Look Again." *Barron's.*

American Institute for Economic Research. (2002, February 25). "Deflation?" *Research Reports.*

Luskin, Donald L. (2001, November 19). "Deflation: The Basics." *The Luskin Report.*

Quinn, Jane Bryant. (1998, February 16). "In Praise of Deflation." *Newsweek.*

Shilling, A. Gary. (1998, August 26). "Deflation Is Nothing to Fear." *The Wall Street Journal.*

Nevallier, Louis. (1998, August 27). Interview CNBC.

Kanell Michael E. (2001, November 17). "Sliding Oil Prices a Break for Drivers." *The Atlanta Journal-Constitution.*

Cooper, James C. and Kathleen Madigan. (2001, November 16). " That's not Deflation Ahead, Just Slower Inflation." *BusinessWeek.*

Miller, Karen Lowry. (2001, December 10). "Beware the Bugaboo. What's Worse Than Inflation? Its Opposite." *Newsweek.*

Blackstone, Brian. (2001, April 16). "Fed's Parry: US Economy Growing at Slight Positive Rate." *Dow Jones Newswires.*

Miller, Rich. (1998, January 7). "Prices under Pressure. Deflation Could Slam Brakes on Economies." *USA Today.*

Birger, Jon. (2002, January). "Can Washington Save Wall Street?" *Money.*

Abelson, Alan. (1999, August 30). "Werner Visits Wall Street." *Barron's.*

Chapter 16

Birger, Jon (2001, December). "The Rock." *Money.*

Chapter 19

Van Dusen, Christine (2001, December 29). "Despite Woes, Banks Well-Capitalized." *The Atlanta Journal-Constitution.*

Weiss, Martin. (2002). *Ultimate safe money guide.* New York: John Wiley & Sons.

Chapter 20

The Dick Davis Digest. (2000, January 31 and 2001, January 15). "Top Stock Pick Special." Fort Lauderdale, FL: Dick Davis Publishing.

Chapter 22

Roosevelt, Franklin D. (1933, April 5). "Executive Order 6260." *Federal Register.*

Chapter 26

Prechter, Robert Rougelot. (2001, August). "On the Cresting Wave—a Q&A with Robert Prechter." *The Elliott Wave Theorist.*

Chapter 27

Lambert, Michael J. and Kristin D. Stanton. (2001, September). "Opportunities and Challenges of the U.S. Dollar as an Increasingly Global Currency: a Federal Reserve perspective." *Federal Reserve Bulletin.*

New York Times. Article unavailable.

UPDATE FOR *2014* EDITION

Special Update for 2014

Government, the Fed, and the Nation's Money: 100 Years of Theft and Failure; 50 Years of Economic Regression

The Government's Disastrous Reign over U.S. Money

Very few people know that the United States did not create a monetary unit pegged to "buy" some amount of metal, as if the dollar were some kind of money independent of metal. In 1792, Congress passed the U.S. Coinage Act, which defined a dollar as a coin containing 371.25 grains of silver and 44.75 grains of alloy. Congress did not say a dollar was *worth* that amount of metal; it *was* that amount of metal. A *dollar*, then, was a unit of weight, like a *gram*, *ounce* or *pound*. Since the alloy portion of the coin was nearly worthless, a dollar was essentially defined as 371.25 grains—equal to 24.057 grams, or 0.7734 Troy oz.—of pure silver. In a nutshell, a dollar was equal to a bit more than 3/4 of an ounce of silver; or, in reverse, an ounce of silver was equal to $1.293.

The same act declared that a new coin, called an Eagle, would consist of 247.5 grains of gold and 22.5 grains of alloy. It valued this coin by law at ten dollars, meaning 3712.5 grains of silver. In other words, Congress, rather than allowing gold and silver to trade freely against each other, established an "official" value for gold so that 247.5 grains of gold = 3712.5 grains of silver. This is an exchange ratio of 15:1. A dollar was 0.7734 ounces of silver, and Congress was declaring that a dollar would buy 0.0515625 ounces of gold, so gold was valued at **$19.39/oz.**

This attempt at creating an artificial parity drove gold coins out of circulation, because the market had determined that an ounce of gold was in fact worth more than 15 ounces of silver. Still trying to establish a workable parity, Congress in 1834 passed another coinage act, changing the value of a ten-dollar gold piece from 247.5 to 232 grains of gold (plus 26 grains of alloy), thereby tweaking the gold/silver ratio closer to 16:1. Now gold was pegged at 23.2 grains per dollar, which is equal to 0.04833 ounces, so gold was now valued at **$20.69** per ounce.

This was no remedy, because after gold was discovered in California the market quickly valued silver higher than gold, thus driving *silver* out of circulation. Neither Congress nor, as we will soon see, the Fed, can repeal the laws of economics and succeed at forcing a particular value on anything.

The Mint Act of 1837 tweaked the purity ratio of gold and silver U.S. coins, making it 90%. This change edged the gold content of an Eagle to 232.2 grains, meaning that one dollar would buy 23.22 grains of gold, so gold was now valued at **$20.67** per ounce. A *dollar*, however, was still 0.7734 oz. of pure silver.

The silver standard ended in 1873, when a new Coinage Act scrapped the definition of a dollar as a certain weight of silver and adopted a new standard based on the weight of gold, maintaining the formula of $1 = 1/20.67 ounce of gold. The Gold Standard Act of 1900 declared that gold would remain the only standard for valuing a dollar and confirmed that a dollar was 1/20.67 ounces of gold.

In 1913, Congress passed the Federal Reserve Act. This act gave a special new banking corporation the monopoly power to issue dollar-denominated banknotes backed by bonds issued by the Treasury. In other words, it gave the Fed the power, in a roundabout way, to use government debt as backing to counterfeit dollars to benefit the government. It was counterfeiting because the Fed issued its notes on dollars (gold) it never had, and it would never find itself obligated to liquidate its store of Treasury bonds.

The Fed's counterfeiting diluted the supply of dollar-denominated debt, which naturally led to gold's being worth more per dollar than the notes. In January 1934, Congress passed the Gold Reserve Act, under which the government seized Americans' gold, canceled all business contracts in gold, outlawed citizens' possession of gold and reduced the amount of gold that would define a dollar. President Roosevelt personally dreamed up a new value for the dollar, which he pronounced to be 1/35 of an ounce of gold, thus making the "price" of gold $35.00 per ounce. In one stroke, then, he stole 41% of the value of everyone's dollars in a single moment, to the benefit of the government.

Because the Act prohibited U.S. citizens from trading in gold, this new, lower value of a dollar was thereafter applied only to international transactions. To maintain a domestic monetary standard, Congress simultaneously gave the Treasury the privilege of issuing paper dollars redeemable in silver at the rate of $1.29/oz., which was its statutory value as established in 1792. With the silver price still depressed from the Great Depression, this was, for a brief time, a "fair" price. Congress passed the Silver Purchase Act of 1934 to acquire silver to back the notes.

This scheme didn't even last three decades. With the government's continued borrowing and the Fed's monetization of much of it, smart people began redeeming the government's paper IOUs for silver, and the Treasury's silver stocks began to dwindle. In 1960, President Kennedy ordered the Treasury to stop printing silver certificates above $1 in value, the aim being to make it nearly impossible for citizens to gather up enough notes to make redeeming them worthwhile. In 1961, the government's silver stock plummeted 80% as smart people redeemed their large-denomination bills. That year, Kennedy issued an

Executive Order to halt the redemption of silver certificates and urged Congress to let the Fed take over the nation's currency. In 1963, Congress obliged by passing Public Law 88-36, which revoked the Silver Purchase Act and authorized the Federal Reserve to issue banknotes unbacked by money. The U.S. mint continued to make silver coins through 1964 with what silver it had left. By 1965, the Fed had issued enough Federal Reserve notes to overrun the circulation of silver-backed U.S. Treasury notes. That year, on July 23, Congress passed the Coinage Act of 1965, which declared that commonly used U.S. coins would henceforth contain no silver. The half-dollar coin was reduced to 40% silver. For three more years, the government paid out silver to the few people who brought in silver certificates for redemption, but it ceased doing so in June 1968, reneging on the promise printed on its notes. The last year that 40%-silver half-dollar coins were minted for circulation was 1969.

The year 1965, then, is the key year marking the official end of metal-backed money in America. The Fed's notes, and even the government's old money-backed notes, became currency un-redeemable in anything. The dollar became merely an accounting unit. Americans were forced to use the Fed's accounting units and the Treasury's tokens for transactions or go to jail. In other words, it became illegal to circumvent the government's now-legal program of stealing value from citizens' savings accounts through the process of issuing debt and having the Fed turn it into checking accounts.

Meanwhile, gold was on its own road to complete de-mon-etization. In 1944, the U.S. had joined a group of other political price-fixers via the Bretton Woods monetary agreement, which allowed foreign governments—but not U.S. citizens—to redeem dollars for gold at the U.S. Treasury at the rate of $35/oz. This agreement gave the U.S. government the economic advantage of issuing the world's "reserve currency."

It took just fifteen years before foreigners began to figure out that the government and the Fed's legal counterfeiting factory was persistently reducing the value of Federal Reserve notes, thereby raising the value of gold in relation to them. They began quietly turning in the Fed's dollar-denominated IOUs to the Treasury and demanding gold in payment at the rate of 1/35 of an ounce of gold per dollar. Just as silver had flowed out of the Treasury in the early 1960s, gold began flowing out of the Treasury as well. For a dozen years, Congress allowed foreigners (and, according to conspiracy theorists, secretly connected individuals) to raid the U.S. Treasury, leaving Fed-note holders with increasingly devalued currency and foreigners and insiders with most of the government's gold.

In 1968, President Nixon issued an Executive Order reducing the official value of a Fed-owed dollar to 1/38 of an ounce of gold, thereby raising the "price" of gold to **$38.00** per ounce. This feeble attempt to stem the tide lasted only three years.

Finally the government had to admit that its monetary ruse had failed. In 1971, Nixon issued Executive Order 11615, which reneged on the government's obligation to pay out gold to foreign holders of the Fed's IOUs. Speaking on television on August 15, the President explained, "The effect of this action…will be to stabilize the dollar." What it really did was complete the eight-year transition during which the term *dollar* was transformed from indicating a specific amount of money to indicating nothing but an accounting unit. In 1972, the official value of a Fed-owed dollar was again lowered by statute, this time to 1/42.22 of an ounce of gold, making the gold "price" **$42.22** per ounce. This price was a fiction at the time and still is, but it remains on the books to this day.

In 1972, central banks announced that they would no longer pretend to equate their accounting units to any statutory amount of money but allow them to trade at whatever the market said they were worth. This announcement set the government and the Fed completely free to create and spend new accounting units at their pleasure. The Fed's banknotes were still written against Treasury bonds, but no longer would the Treasury's IOUs be paid in gold, silver or anything else.

The United States dollar had *been* approximately a twentieth of an ounce of gold or had been *redeemable* for that amount of gold for *142 years*. Following the government's theft of citizens' gold in 1934, the dollar was again redeemable in the original amount of silver but was newly valued at only a thirty-fifth of an ounce of gold. The original dollar, therefore, essentially managed to maintain parity to 0.7734 Troy oz. of silver for *173 years*. Then, from 1963 to 1971, Congress through a series of new laws ceased exercising its Constitutional "power to coin money, and regulate [*make regular*] the value thereof." Instead it outlawed money and replaced it with an elastic (non-regular) unit of account.

The only reason people use the Fed's money-substitute is that the government prohibits all forms of real and alternative money. It requires that all transactions, including the payment of taxes, be denominated in the Fed's accounting units, which, although no longer dollars, are still called dollars.

Section 19 of the original 1792 Coinage Act made the following declaration: "...if any of the gold or silver coins which shall be struck or coined at the said mint shall be debased or made worse as to the proportion of the fine gold or fine silver therein contained [by act of] any of the officers or persons who shall be employed at the said mint...every such officer or person...shall be deemed guilty of felony, *and shall suffer death*." All members of Congress since 1963—for passing and then failing to repeal Public Law 88-36—are *de facto* guilty of having "debased" and "made worse" the dollar, but they have hidden behind technicalities in cleverly crafted laws, which shroud the effect of their acts.

A primary source for this review is http://nesara.org/articles/nine_tenths_pure.htm.

Has the Fed Produced Any Benefits?

People speak of the Fed "buying" assets; but it can't buy assets, because it produces nothing of value with which to trade. Congress conferred upon it a monopoly privilege to manufacture new banknotes and swap them for the debts of others (primarily the U.S. government). By this method, the Fed stealthily transfers stored effort from savers' accounts to the issuer of the bonds for which it swaps its new credits, primarily the *government*. In conjunction with the FDIC, it has also benefitted profligate *bankers* in the short run by enabling them to make profits on dubious loans. It has also bailed out reckless speculators, allowing them to avoid accountability. But in doing so it has sucked value out of savers' accounts and burdened the American economy.

The Era of Money vs. the Era of Unbacked Accounting Units

The change wrought by fake money is far, far worse than you might think. Let's look at the timing of the government's abandonment of money.

For 173 years, as detailed above, the United States was on a *money* standard. Congress shifted the basis of the money standard between silver and gold twice during that period. In the fateful year of 1965, shortly after authorizing the Federal Reserve to issue notes as currency, Congress abandoned money altogether and authorized the Fed to provide the nation's currency and the Treasury to issue tokens in place of money, *all without any standard at all*. Dollars became accounting units anchored to nothing. Officials still call the new unit of account a "dollar" and "money," but they are lying on both counts. Or, one might say, they merely "re-defined" these terms; but they did so without telling anybody plainly what the change meant.

Although a few nuances attend U.S. monetary history, broadly speaking we may delineate the key periods as follows:

1792-1873: silver money standard
1873-1934: gold money standard
1934-1965: silver money standard
1965-present: Federal Reserve Accounting Units (no standard).

The year 1965 is not just any old year. It is the year that we have long recognized as the orthodox end of the great bull market in the Dow/gold ratio in Elliott wave terms. Figure A-1 shows this wave labeling, which we first posted in early 2001, and Figure A-2 brings the wave pattern up to date. Thus, the *true bull market* provided conditions under which the country would prosper, the most important of those conditions being a *money standard*. When the bear market started after 1965, conditions shifted to reflect the negative psychology of a bear market, the most important of those conditions being the *absence* of a money standard.

Figure A-3 is a chart you have never seen elsewhere. It shows the breathtaking rise in U.S. corporate worth during the bull market period and exposes the stunning net destruction of U.S. corporate worth since the bear market started. The year of the bull market top is when the government shifted the foundation of value for the nation's accounting unit from money to the whims of politicians and central bankers. The difference in result is stunning: From 1792, when a money standard was first made official, to 1965, when Congress abandoned the money standard, the U.S. stock market rose from being worth .09 ounces of gold to being worth 27.59 ounces, a difference of **+30,556%**. Since 1965, when the government abandoned the money standard, the U.S. stock market has *fallen* in value from 27.59 ounces of gold to 13.74 ounces, a difference of **-50%**.

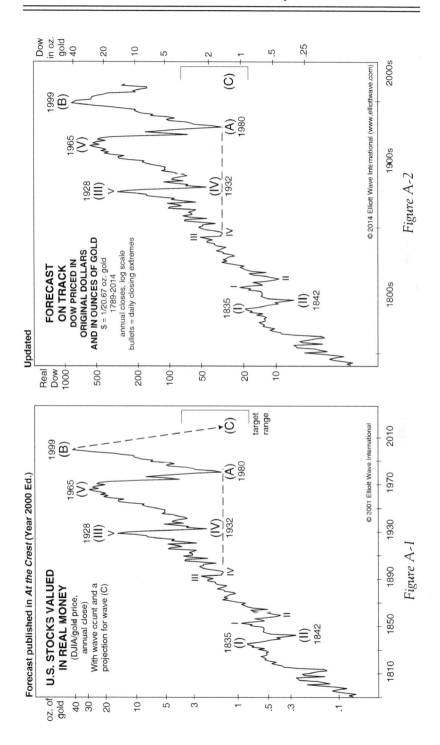

Forecast published in *At the Crest* (Year 2000 Ed.)

U.S. STOCKS VALUED IN REAL MONEY
(DJIA/gold price, annual close)
With wave count and a projection for wave (C)

© 2001 Elliott Wave International

Figure A-1

Updated

FORECAST ON TRACK
DOW PRICED IN ORIGINAL DOLLARS AND IN OUNCES OF GOLD
$ = 1/20.67 oz. gold
1789-2014
annual closes, log scale
bullets = daily closing extremes

© 2014 Elliott Wave International (www.elliottwave.com)

Figure A-2

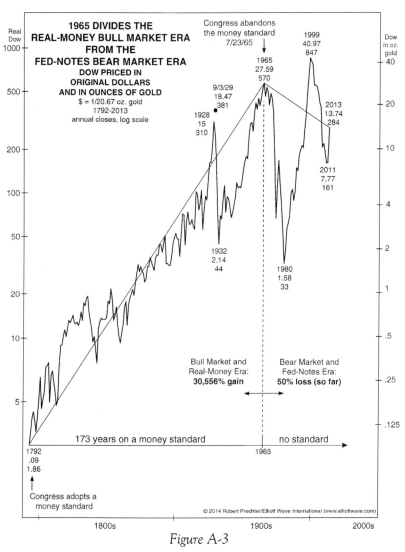

Figure A-3

Had the old trend continued at its preceding average pace, the Dow at the end of 2013 would be up 390% since 1965 instead of down by half; and since 1792 it would be up 150,009% instead of only 15,167%. Of course, social mood is in charge of these values, so we do not believe that the Dow *would* be worth that much; it would be worth just what it is today in gold-money terms. But the difference does reveal the power of a bear market to prompt destructive decisions among the political class.

The only reason people do not know the country's true stock market history and its current real worth is that the massive inflating of accounting-unit dollars has caused an attendant reduction in the value of the accounting unit, which in turn has masked the devastation of U.S. stock values. But Figure A-3 tells the truth: The bull market ended in 1965; the bear market has been raging ever since; and the accounting-unit monopoly engineered by the government and the Fed has been an intimate factor in the trend toward the financial and economic destruction of what was formerly the most prosperous country on earth.

Despite our delineation of the money era from the Fed-note era, the Fed deserves only part of the institutional blame for the monetary and economic effects of the bear market. Congress is primarily responsible for bloating credit and for ruining the economy, by means of its *debt engines* (FHLBs, FNM, FMAC, GNMA, student loans), *speculation guarantees* (FDIC, FSLIC, bank and corporate bailouts), *regulations* (OSHA, EPA, EEOC, etc.), *taxes* (income tax, social security tax, inheritance tax, gift tax, capital gains tax, excise tax, gas tax, medical tax, etc.) and *criminalization of enterprise* (via thousands of state and local laws prohibiting free enterprise). But the Fed has helped finance it all.

Has the Fed produced any benefits? No.

Has the Fed contributed to prosperity? No.

On the contrary, the Fed, by providing an inflatable accounting unit, has made it easier for the government and its friends to extract purchasing power from dollar-holders with very few being the wiser. This activity has paralleled the dramatic shift of trend in 1965, from 173 years of mostly rising corporate worth to 49 years of net stagnation and decline.

True Stock Values

So, why does everyone seem to think that the country is prosperous? The Dow is at 16,500! The S&P is at 1880! But, of course, they're not. In less than a century, government through its debt-creating engines and the Fed through its monetary policies managed to reduce the value of the original dollar by almost exactly 99%. From the dollar's original value of **1/19.39** of an ounce of gold in 1792-1834, it slid all the way to **1/1921.5** of an ounce in 2011. With the dollar's recent gain against gold (i.e., the fall in dollar price), the reduction from original value to date is about 98.5%. So everything today is dollar-priced about 67 times where it would be had the dollar remained worth approximately 1/20 of an ounce of gold.

As you can see in Figure A-3, the true price of the Dow at year-end 2013 was not 16,500 but 245. This is not a made-up figure. This is the Dow's *true price*. That's the price you would be reading in the paper had the dollar maintained its purchasing power in terms of gold. The Dow at year-end 2013 is worth less than it was at year-end 1928, 85 years ago. The government and the Fed have succeeded in one thing: hiding true values and keeping people complacent, even giddy, over their "gains" while they are secretly being robbed.

The Dow's Seemingly Low Real Price Does Not Portend More Gains Ahead

One might look at Figure A-3 and think that the Dow is now so cheap in real terms that it has nowhere to go but up. But thinking so would be to underestimate mightily the destruction that the government has wreaked on the U.S. economy.

Incredibly, the year-end-2013 price of the Dow—11.86 ounces of gold, or 245 original dollars (normalized to 1837-1933's 1/20.67 oz.)—is ridiculously expensive for what you get: a lousy 2.1% annualized dividend yield, even *lower* than it was at top

tick in 1929; a P/E ratio in the high end of the range for the
past century and three times what it was at major bear market
bottoms of the 20th century; and a 4.7 price-to-book-value ratio
(adjusted to the pre-2004 data series) for the S&P, which is two
to four times its range from year-ends 1929 through 1987. In other
words, the Dow is not cheap; it's absurdly overpriced. At the
same time, stock-market optimism is as extreme as it was at the
Dow's all-time record overvaluation in 2000 (see Section D). The
miserable value shown at December 2013 in Figure A-3 comes
from a snapshot of the Dow at its second-greatest overvaluation
in history. This condition virtually assures that the worst of the
devastation of U.S. corporate worth still lies ahead.

Is the Fed Run by Heroes?

It's amazing that the dilution of the nation's accounting
unit—by making the stock averages appear to be at new highs—
has fashioned a distorted lens through which people interpret
their ruination as their salvation. It's quite a trick.

We know how the trick works. Even John Maynard Keynes,
the economist whose ideas, ironically, have provided justifica-
tion for the government and the Fed's destructive actions, knew
about it. Early in his career, in an essay titled "Consequences of
the Peace" (1919), he wrote as follows:

> Lenin is said to have declared that the best way to destroy the
> capitalist system was to debauch the currency. By a continuing
> process of inflation, governments can confiscate, secretly and
> unobserved, an important part of the wealth of their citizens.
> By this method they not only confiscate, but they confiscate
> arbitrarily; and, while the process impoverishes many, it actu-
> ally enriches some. The sight of this arbitrary rearrangement
> of riches strikes not only at security but [also] at confidence in
> the equity of the existing distribution of wealth.

Those to whom the system brings windfalls, beyond their deserts and even beyond their expectations or desires, become "profiteers," who are the object of the hatred of the bourgeoisie, whom the inflationism has impoverished, not less than of the proletariat. As the inflation proceeds and the real value of the currency fluctuates wildly from month to month, all permanent relations between debtors and creditors, which form the ultimate foundation of capitalism, become so utterly disordered as to be almost meaningless; and the process of wealth-getting degenerates into a gamble and a lottery.

Lenin was certainly right. There is no subtler, no surer means of overturning the existing basis of society than to debauch the currency. The process engages all the hidden forces of economic law on the side of destruction, and does it in a manner which not one man in a million is able to diagnose.

The reality, then, per Keynes' description, is that the government, while claiming to do good works, has conspired with the Fed to loot the country.

Reality, however, does not determine most people's assessment of the Fed; social mood does. As we have long chronicled, people judge Fed chairmen as heroes when social mood is extremely positive and the stock market is near a major top; and they judge them as goats when social mood is negative and the stock market is near a major bottom.

As Figure A-4 shows, the Fed's chairman was revered at the tops in 1998-2000 and again in 2006-2007. At the bottoms in 2002-2003 and 2008-2009, the Fed was criticized. Over the past two years, during a period of extremely elevated stock values, Fed chairmen have been persistently adored.

But the elevation of mood of recent years has been taking place within a larger bear market. The next intermediate-term turn toward negative social mood will drive the stock market lower in real terms and almost surely cause the debt structure to

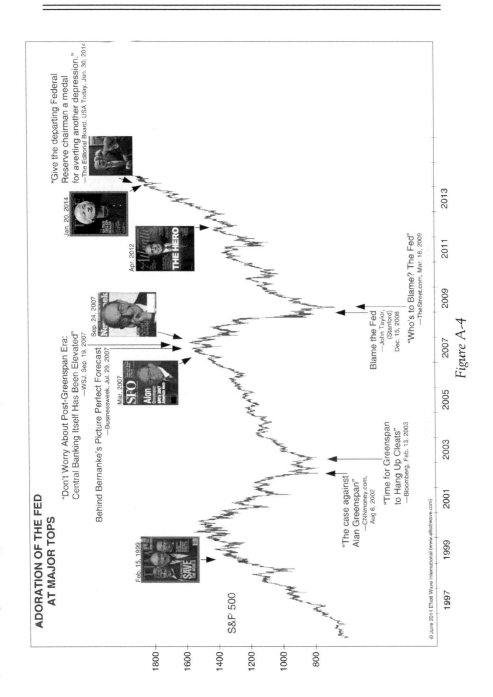

ADORATION OF THE FED
AT MAJOR TOPS

S&P 500

"Don't Worry About Post-Greenspan Era:
Central Banking Itself Has Been Elevated"
—WSJ, Sep. 19, 2007

Behind Bernanke's Picture Perfect Forecast
—Businessweek, Jul. 29, 2007

Sep. 24, 2007

Mar. 2007

Jan. 20, 2014

Apr. 2012

Feb. 15, 1999

"Give the departing Federal
Reserve chairman a medal
for averting another depression."
—The Editorial Board, USA Today, Jan. 30, 2014

"Who's to Blame? The Fed"
—TheStreet.com, Mar. 16, 2009

Blame the Fed
—John Taylor,
(Stanford)
Dec. 15, 2008

"The case against
Alan Greenspan"
—CNNmoney.com,
Aug 6, 2002

"Time for Greenspan
to Hang Up Cleats"
—Bloomberg, Feb. 13, 2003

© June 2014 Elliott Wave International (www.elliottwave.com)

1997 1999 2001 2003 2005 2007 2009 2011 2013

1800 1600 1400 1200 1000 800

Figure A-4

collapse, which in turn will drive the stock market lower even in nominal terms. These events will finally unmask the hidden financial and economic destruction of the U.S. economy and change the media's treatment of the Fed from adoration to vilification. It will be a horrible day and a glorious day at the same time.

Why the Government Wants All That Money

Figure A-5 confirms that the era of Big Government began precisely at the passages of the Federal Reserve Act in 1913 and the Income Tax in 1916. From that time forward, the United States ceased being a peaceful, prosperous country and became a nation of taxation, inflation, debt and foreign wars, activities that reward the political class.

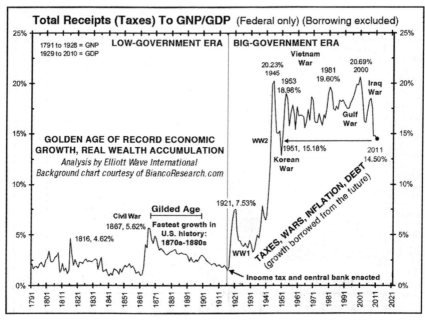

Figure A-5

Deflation Ahead

The next big monetary event will not be more inflation but *deflation*, as the huge quantity of accounting-unit indebtedness, built on a foundation of accounting-unit indebtedness, becomes unpayable and contracts. Most people believe such an outcome is impossible. But *Conquer the Crash* makes our case.

After the deflation runs its course, either reform will follow or the government will engage in hyperinflation. But first we have to go through the valley.

Section B

Major Turn in Gold Portends a Deflationary Crash

Here is excerpted commentary from *The Elliott Wave Theorist* and *The Elliott Wave Financial Forecast* in the month of the high in gold, which peaked on September 5/6 (close/intraday), 2011. Immediately thereafter is an update of our outlook.

The Elliott Wave Financial Forecast, September 2, 2011

Last month EWFF discussed the propensity of central banks to *sell* gold near the end of long price declines and *buy* gold near the end of long price rises. Just last week, Venezuelan strongman Hugo Chavez took the politicization of rising gold prices a step further by nationalizing Venezuela's gold mining industry and moving to repatriate more than 200 tons of gold held in foreign countries, thereby ordering one of the biggest physical-gold transfers in history. A Bloomberg story reveals that central banks are buying with no intention of ever selling, no matter how badly they need the money. "Central banks, net buyers of gold for the first time in a generation, are likely to retain their holdings even if they need to raise cash to counter an escalating debt crisis, according to Morgan Stanley." The story quotes the firm's chief metals' economist as saying, "Once they've sold, that's it. Buying back would be extremely expensive." Gold experts, naturally, are convinced this cannot happen. Perhaps the strongest sign of a gold top is a recent Gallup poll (below) showing Americans now consider gold to be the best long term investment. Gallup parsed the survey by gender, age, income level and political affiliation and in every single subset, gold won out. It took ten straight years of annual price gains, but now *everyone* is onboard gold's uptrend. It is surely a sign of exhaustion.

Americans' Ratings of the Best Long-Term Investment
Which of the following do you think is the best long-term investment?

GALLUP	Gold	Real estate	Stocks/ Mutual Funds	Savings accounts/CDs	Bonds
Aug. 11-14	34%	19	17	14	10

Gold's wave structure is consistent with a terminating rise. As Figure B-1 shows, prices exceeded the upper line of the channel formed by the rally from the 1999 low in what Elliott termed a throw-over (see *Elliott Wave Principle*, p.71). A throw-over occurs at the end of a fifth wave and represents a final burst of buying, as the last sub-waves of a rally conclude. The pattern is confirmed as complete once prices close back beneath the upper line, which currently crosses $1650.

While gold's rise has garnered the financial media's attention, silver's failure to confirm gold's rally goes largely unreported. In our view, this gigantic divergence is critical. Last month we showed silver's five-wave decline from the $49.91 high and subsequent three-wave rally. Silver made one more near-term pop to $44.28 on August 23 to complete wave (2) up. The next significant move should be a resumption of the larger decline that started at the April peak. A decline well into the $20s is a minimum expectation.

—End of EWFF, September 2, 2011

Figure B-1

The Elliott Wave Theorist, September 16, 2011

The recent reading of 98% bulls among futures traders, as reported by trade-futures.com, is not the only indication of the extreme level of bullish consensus on gold. Last November, the president of the World Bank opined that governments should reconsider the role of gold in their monetary systems. Governments thrive on counterfeiting money and hiding that fact. The notion of paying respect to gold, in this context, is a radical idea, indicating how deeply the bullish consensus on gold has influenced people's thinking. Gold's downturn is either already in place or really close.

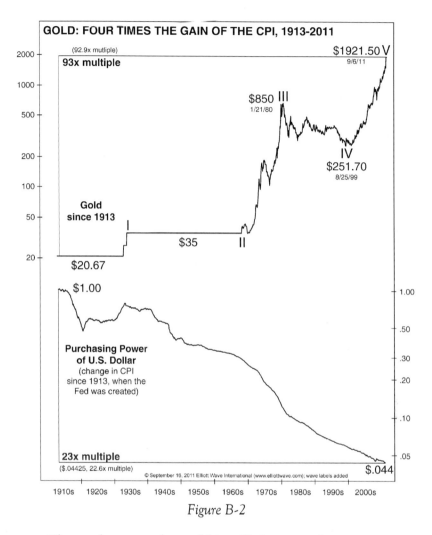

Figure B-2

Those who argue that gold is still cheap might want to consider Figure B-2, which shows that since 1913, when the Fed was created, gold has achieved four times the gain of the Consumer Price Index. To match the gain in the CPI, gold would have to fall below $500/oz. Granted, the CPI is a manipulated index, so it might understate the true gain in consumer prices. But there is still a notable disparity.

—End of EWT, September 16, 2011

The Elliott Wave Financial Forecast, October 7, 2011

Gold declined 20% in just three weeks in September. But probably the most important feature of the decline from the $1921.50 high basis spot on September 6 is the close beneath the upper line of its long-term channel. Last month EWFF said such a close would complete a throw-over and announce the end of the five-wave rally from the August 1999 low. Gold's final push was historic, because it ran through multiple sentiment stop signs, as the chart on the next page shows. Gold investors assumed these increasingly bearish signals were irrelevant, since prices pushed aside all but the last cluster on their way to September's top. But

Figure B-3

A FINAL BULLISH FLOURISH FOR GOLD

"Gold Fever Sweeps Criminal Underworld"
Societe Generale: "Fair Value at $10,000"
Venezuela Nationalizes Gold Industry

98% Bullish (DSI)
Gallup Poll Ranks Gold Best Long-Term Investment
SPDR Gold ETF Surpasses S&P 500 ETF

"Central Banks Pour Into Gold"
—World Gold Council

Radio Ads Forecast $5,000 Gold

"World Bitten by Gold Bug"
—WSJ

"Not owning gold is a form of insanity."
—Wall Street Strategist

First U.S. Gold ATM

98% Bullish (DSI)

Gold
weekly

© October 2011 Elliott Wave International
(www.elliottwave.com)

Figure B-4

gold's persistent rise constitutes a stretched emotional extreme, which will result in an opposite downside extreme, similar to what occurred in stocks after their 2007 peak. The decline that started last month will eventually correct the entire 10-year long rally, so it should be significant in size and scope.

September also ripped holes in the prevailing belief that silver was a precious metal that would rise as stocks fell. The active futures contract closed the month down 28%, falling in conjunction with stocks and commodities. Prices declined $6.47 on one day alone, September 23, which was silver's second largest daily point decline in modern history. The only decline larger was a $10 drop on January 22, 1980, the day after silver's all-time high. When the precious metals move, they *move*, and the recent decline should carry silver to the next target range in the "low $20s."

—*End of EWFF, October 7, 2011*

Update for *Conquer the Crash*

An article in a major financial magazine dated a year ago tried to make sense of the metals' plunge in terms of economic causality but was unable to do so:

April 20, 2013
**It is hard to find an economic explanation
for gold's sharp fall**
GOLD suffered its biggest two-day fall in 30 years on April 12th and 15th. When an asset falls so sharply in price, it is tempting to believe that significant economic changes must be afoot. But an examination of the background to bullion's decline <u>simply produces puzzlement</u>. In short, it is hard to find a rationale in the current economic outlook that would simultaneously send gold and bond yields down, and stock markets up.

Even when no external cause can be identified, socionomic causality is mystifying to most people. It seems unnatural that a major market rise or decline need have no economic explanation. But financial pricing is determined by unconscious herding impulses and regulated by Elliott waves, so mass psychology pushes markets up and down without needing to make economic sense. Nevertheless, we do believe that significant economic changes in fact are afoot, namely a turn to deflation at Grand Supercycle degree and a resumption of the trend toward economic depression. When those trends develop further, gold's recent action will start making sense to observers.

Successful market analysis is rooted in irony and paradox. Our gold and silver analysis at the peak in 2011 relied heavily on the converses of five arguments offered everywhere else we looked. Here are two of them, to give you the idea:

1) Central-Bank Buying

An article published on April 19, 2013 quoted a report issued by one of the world's most famous money managers. It reads, "We believe that ongoing central bank purchases and strong gold demand from China and India will help support the gold price in the near term." At Elliott Wave International, we have used the very same fact of central bank interest in gold to come to precisely the opposite conclusion on the month of the all-time high in gold.

2) Fed Inflating

Since mid-2008, the Fed has been inflating the supply of dollars (the "base money supply") at the unprecedented rate of 33% per year. In 2012, it accelerated its policy by inaugurating a program to monetize government-guaranteed mortgages and Treasury bonds at the rate of a trillion dollars' worth per year, with no time limit. Precious metals bulls seized upon these facts as guarantees that gold and silver would soar to stratospheric heights. This style of argument would be useful if financial markets obeyed the rules of mechanics, but they don't. As The Economist put it, "Many of the most enthusiastic buyers of gold believed that QE would ultimately lead to rapid consumer inflation. So far that has not come to pass."

Here at Elliott Wave International, we again made the opposite argument. Figure B-5 was published in the December 30, 2012 issue of *The Elliott Wave Theorist*. Our headline read, "*Biggest Inflationary Fed Commitment in History Provides another Selling Opportunity in the Metals*." Who else in the world would write such a headline?

Figure B-5

Here is the commentary from that issue:

> Speaking of paradox, gold and silver peaked on Fed day, December 12, at a lower high. I haven't seen any commentary about that amazing event. This wasn't any old Fed day, either. It was the day the Fed promised to inflate the money supply indefinitely at the rate of over $1 trillion per year, the most aggressively inflationary policy—by many multiples—in its 99-year history.

> Figure 12 [reproduced here as Figure B-5] shows gold and silver prices for the past year along with the dates of the Fed's unprecedented announcements. Both times, metals bulls got everything they feared and hoped for. Yet both markets peaked shortly after the first announcement, and they fell hard from a lower peak starting the very hour that Ben Bernanke confirmed the start of his program to more than double his inflating from an already unprecedented rate.

> During that hour on December 12, from 1:30 to 2:30, as Bernanke was making his announcement and holding his press conference, I was on the phone doing an interview with GoldSeek radio. (Thanks, Chris Waltzek!) If you would like to hear what I had to say during those heady minutes when the world was sure that gold and silver could only go straight up, go to www.elliottwave.com/wave/goldseek-1212.

> If the historic "Fed day" of December 12 was truly a trap for the bulls, gold and silver prices should not exceed their peak levels on that date. (See the rightmost arrows in Figure B-5.)

At the time of the Fed's first announcement (QE3), gold was trading at $1770 and silver at $35. The metals edged higher for another three weeks and then began to retreat. At the time of the second announcement (QE4), gold was at $1720 and silver at $33.60. Since then, gold has traded below $1200 and silver below $20, meeting our initial target (see Figure B-6.) Those are drops of 38.6% and 63.6%, respectively.

Figure B-6

Shown in October 2011 EWFF:

Figure B-7

The *Elliott Wave Financial Forecast* showed the first part of Figure B-7 in October 2011. The Elliott wave labeling shown that month on that chart indicated the end of the bull market at both Cycle and Supercycle degree. The last chance to sell (not buy) coincided with the Fed's launching of its trillion-dollar-a-year bond and mortgage-buying program.

The *Elliott Wave Financial Forecast* also showed the first part of Figure B-8 at that time. With gold now down by 1/3, optimism has waned substantially. But investors have not reached the level of pessimism toward gold that existed on February 12, 2001, when a major article was sub-headed, "*Nobody expects gold prices to turn up soon,*" and one of the typical comments recorded was, "*There doesn't seem to be anything on the horizon that will make gold prices go up.*" Gold at the time was days from its low at $253/oz. When gold reaches its next major bottom, we'll see articles with similar comments and quotes.

Shown in October 2011 EWFF:

Figure B-8

Major Turn in Interest Rates Portends a Deflationary Crash

Economists' opinions tend to lag Cycle and Supercycle-degree waves by five to ten years. Once they agree on a direction, they don't change their minds for a long time.

To understand how exquisitely a financial consensus can crystallize in the wrong direction at a market's turning point, read the following interest-rate analysis from the July 11, 1984 issue of *The Elliott Wave Theorist*:

The background of investor psychology is very suggestive of an important bond market low. In fact, if this were the only measure I followed, it would appear that bonds are the buy of a lifetime.

The news media, which all but ignored the rise in interest rates until May 1984, has been flooding the pages of the press with "higher interest rate" stories. Most of these came out, in typical fashion, *after* the May low, which was tested in June. During second waves, investors typically re-live the fears which existed at the actual bottom, while the *market* demonstrates an understanding, by holding above the previous low, that the worst has passed. The last five weeks have demonstrated this phenomenon vividly.

On June 11, the WSJ headline read, "Fed Move to Tighten
Credit is Expected during the Summer by Many Economists."
On June 18, two full articles, including a front page feature,
focused on the prospects for higher interest rates: "Cooler
Economy Seen Failing to Stem Further Rise in Interest Rates
This Year" and "Interest Rates Begin to Damp Economy; Many
Analysts See Further Increases." On June 22, the WSJ featured
an incredible *five-page* in-depth report entitled "World Debt in
Crisis," complete with a picture of falling dominoes and quotes
such as these: from a Congressman, "I don't think we're going to make it to the 1990's"; from a V.P. at Citicorp, "Let's be
clear—nobody's debts are going to be repaid"; and from a former
assistant secretary of state for economic affairs, "We are living
on borrowed time and borrowed money." On July 2, the WSJ
reported, without saying so, that economists have panicked.
Their forecasts for higher rates now extend halfway into next
year! The headline reads, "Higher Interest Rates Are Predicted
for Rest of Year and Further Rises Are Seen for 1985's First 6
Months." Says the article, "Some say it would take a miracle
for rates to fall." The WSJ is not alone in taking the pulse of
economists. Financial World magazine's June 27 poll listed
the forecasts of 24 economists against their beginning-of-year
predictions. *Every single one of them* has raised his forecast, in
a linear-logic reaction to the rise in rates which has already
occurred. They are using the same type of thinking that led
them to a "lower interest rates ahead" conclusion a year ago,
at the bottom.

This overwhelming consensus based on fundamental analysis
is no guarantee that rates have peaked, but history shows that
this type of analysis will rarely result in market profits. I prefer
to bet on an overlooked theory which recognizes that market
patterns repeat themselves over and over again because people
are people.

—*The Elliott Wave Theorist, July 11, 1984*

Figure C-1 is a long term chart of U.S. interest rates showing where this intense consensus took place. You can see that economists' conviction in June-July 1984 that interest rates would rise (and bond prices would fall) derived from the persistent trend that had been in force since the 1940s. That trend had already ended in 1981, but their memory for the old trend was so strong that when rates tested their highs in 1984 the only direction that felt right to them was up.

Figure C-1

A consensus pretty much requires exogenous-cause thinking and then agreement on the "fundamental factors" that will drive prices higher or lower. The more convincing the arguments seem, the surer one can be that a consensus is signaling a turn in the opposite direction.

It seems unnecessary to take space to argue why economists' thinking in this case was in fact rationalization of a powerful herding impulse. The chart says it *must* have been, as their reasoning and logic were *strikingly* erroneous. Just look at the crash in interest rates over precisely the twelve-month period that they predicted rates would rise. Herding is a good explanation—and a respectful one—for an error that large and perfectly timed.

Any individual can be wrong about markets. In the past when I have been wrong I realized in retrospect that either I was a member of a herd or I bet too early against one. But the fact remains that when representatives across an entire profession of exogenous-cause thinkers agree on the future trend of a market, it's a signal. An alert analyst can learn to recognize these times and use them to advantage.

Consensus had the same implication of pending reversal at the *low* in rates two years ago. Here is the long term analysis my colleagues and I published in June 2012:

June 6, 2012
Special Report

MAJOR TOP IN THE BOND MARKET:
Bond Yields are Poised to Begin Rising
on the Way to Deflationary Credit Crisis

U.S. Treasury Bonds

Our long term outlook for interest rates on U.S. Treasury securities has been a contrary opinion for many years. Most commentators have been expecting either economic expansion or Fed-induced inflation to push bond yields higher. Figure 12-2 of

Conquer the Crash predicted that long term rates on AAA-rated bonds would fall much further as the monetary environment shifted from lessening inflation to outright deflation. Figure C-2 updates that chart.

With updated prices:

Figure C-2

In line with our outlook, the interest rate on the Treasury's 10-year note has just plunged to the *lowest level in U.S. history*. The decline from 1981 to the present is a stunning 91%. Figure C-3 shows a close-up of the entire move.

Those predicting economic expansion or hyperinflation have been unable to explain this persistent plunge. Yet each of these camps got exactly the "fundamentals" they expected: *record* monetization by the Fed (advocated by the monetarists) and *record* spending by government (advocated by the Keynesians). Rates ignored these events and continued to fall.

Under the Elliott wave model, five-wave patterns occur in the direction of the main trend, and countertrend moves trace out three-wave patterns. Interest rates do not follow the Elliott

wave model as well as stock averages, which are more responsive
to overall social mood. Rates are the price of just one thing:
money. But it is still interesting to see how many five-wave patterns unfolded in the same direction as the long decline over the
past 31 years, as labeled in Figure C-3.

Figure C-3

In the Great Depression, interest rates on low-grade bonds trended lower until 1930, and those on high-grade bonds continued lower until 1931. *Then they soared, on fears of default.* (See Figures 15-1 and 15-2 in *Conquer the Crash.*)

Interest rates finally peaked, and bond prices bottomed, in June 1932; stocks bottomed in July; and silver bottomed in December. Following expectations under socionomic theory, the economy bottomed afterward, in the first quarter of 1933. If the same sequence occurs at the next major bottom, rates should peak (and bonds should bottom) first, stock prices should bottom next, and individual commodities should make lows throughout the period, with some of them bottoming last. Finally the economy will hit bottom.

Investor psychology should work like this: As positive social mood initially retreats, investors looking for a haven buy bonds that they perceive to be safe. But as social mood continues to trend toward the negative, fear increases, deflation accelerates, the incomes of businesses and governments decline, and bond investors begin to worry about losing their principal due to bankruptcy and default by bond issuers. That's when they start selling bonds, and rates begin to rise. Rates on the weakest issues rise first, but eventually fear spreads to holders even of formerly presumed safe paper. Finally, the economy contracts so severely that it reaches *depression*, wiping out many debtors and, in the process, many creditors as well.

In the current cycle, low-grade bond yields have yet to begin climbing. As shown in Figure C-4, yields for the Baa group have been moving lower right along with those for Treasuries. Commentators are saying that investors' persistent move into bonds is a sign of fear. But in line with continued predictions of a "sustained but slow economic recovery," bond buyers have reached a state of epic complacency in the belief that all of these bonds are safe. At this point, we still cannot place "peak" arrows on Figure C-4. But we should be able to do so soon.

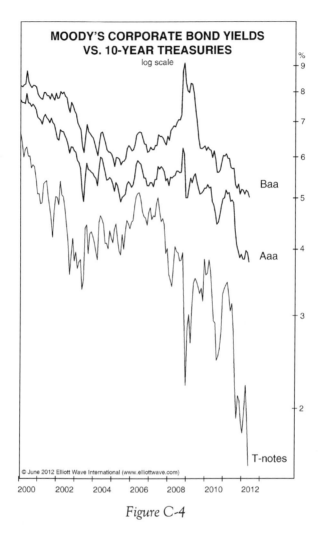

MOODY'S CORPORATE BOND YIELDS
VS. 10-YEAR TREASURIES
log scale

Baa

Aaa

T-notes

© June 2012 Elliott Wave International (www.elliottwave.com)

2000   2002   2004   2006   2008   2010   2012

Figure C-4

Figure 15-2 in *Conquer the Crash* shows the history of the Bond Buyer index of 40 corporate bonds during the Great Depression. Figure C-5 shows the history of its modern equivalent, the Bond Buyer 20-bond index. Bond prices today seem poised to do what their predecessors did: plunge.

In early 1932, prices on these bonds fell *below*—and rates rose above—those registered at the preceding peak rate of inflation

Figure C-5

in 1920. This is a good reason to expect interest rates on these bonds in coming years to rise *above those of 1981*, i.e. above 16%.

The question is, when will rates begin rising in this cycle? We think the answer is "now." Evidence is rapidly mounting that the trend in interest rates on high-grade debt is poised to reverse:

1. As shown in Figure C-3, the latest drop in rates has traced out five waves to a new low, and bond futures have hit a new all-time high of 152½. This plunge in rates should mark at least *a* bottom and probably *the* bottom.

Figure C-6

2. The *public* has been buying a lot of U.S. government bonds
   since 2002, as shown in Figure C-6. Investors stayed en-
   amored of government bond funds in 2011 while selling
   into the stock rally. The public loved *real estate* at the top;
   it loved *stocks* at the top; it loved *commodities* at the top; it
   loved *silver* at the top; and it loved *gold* at the top. What do
   you think it means now that the public is heavily invested
   in U.S. government bonds?

3. The Commitment of Traders report shows that Large Speculators have become heavily invested in T-bond futures (see
   Figure C-7). Large Specs are not always wrong, but they

Figure C-7

are usually wrong when they *follow a trend*. The asterisks in Figure C-7 show times when their buying or selling was in concert with the trend, and in those cases the market was approaching a reversal.

4. According to the Daily Sentiment Index (courtesy trade-futures.com), there were 97% *bulls* among futures traders on Friday [June 2, 2012]. This is the third-highest reading on record. (It reached 99% in December 2008, at the spike high in T-bonds following the Fed's pledge to buy them.) The DSI reached 90% bulls in June 2011, and except for a brief period in January-March it has been near the 90% level for much of the past year. This is both an extreme level and a lengthy period of bullish sentiment.

5. T-bonds have enjoyed their longest and biggest bull market on record. There are no guarantees in life or investing, but we are pretty sure that buying an extended market after three decades of rise is not a good idea. Regardless of whether our monetary and economic expectations turn out right, the bull market in bonds is aged and ripe for reversal.

If rates do begin to rise as we expect, most observers will probably be fooled. Bulls on the economy may take the new trend as a sign of economic expansion. Those betting on hyperinflation may take it as a sign that inflation is ready to soar. But the real reason for the coming rise in rates will be that investors will be selling bonds and demanding higher rates due to *fear of default.* We have seen this development already in the debt paper of Greece and other weak debtors. It should soon seep over to the IOUs of stronger debtors.

The coming fear of default will not be misplaced. With a turn of Grand Supercycle degree behind us, the unfolding depression will be deeper than that of the early 1930s. Most debtors around the world *will* default.

The Coming Yield-Spread Explosion

The recent spike in high-yield mutual fund inflows (per the bottom graph in Figure C-8) shows that investors have continued to reach for yield. Ownership of junk bonds is at an all-time record by a huge margin. The impending downturn in junk bond prices will be bigger than any of the declines over the last 30 years. In the not-too-distant future, junk will finally live up to its name.

Figure C-8

What To Do

Generally speaking, if you are invested in long-term debt, sell it. Avoid high-yield bonds like the plague. Stay away from most municipal, corporate, government agency and now even Treasury bonds. If you wish to hold any unhedged debt, make it *short term debt.* T-bill rates have been stuck near zero, but if rates overall begin to rise, bondholders will *lose money* while bill holders will benefit by rolling continually into higher and higher yields. At the end, the U.S. government might default, so do not consider T-bills a permanent solution. It's only a last debt-based strategy until the ultimate crisis. We have already recommended substantial holdings of outright cash. At some point, it will be time to convert even the safest debt instruments to cash and/or gold.

—*End of June 2012 Special Report*

Update for *Conquer the Crash*

We made our case for the end of the 31-year bull market in bonds just before Fed Chairman Ben Bernanke assured investors that the Fed's program to buy bonds would keep long term interest rates down and bond prices up for the indefinite future. Most economists and investors take such pronouncements at face value; we recognize them as evidence of the extreme psychology typical of market turns. Figure C-9 shows the progress of Treasury bond prices since that time.

The New York Times reported that, as with the major downturn in gold, many observers have remained confused even after the reversal. Here are key excerpts from an article from last summer:

Figure C-9

The New York Times
June 7, 2013
A Bond Market Plunge that Baffles the Experts
by James B. Stewart [excerpt]

The month of May, and this first week of June, were terrible for many fixed-income investors who have spent the last few years reaching for higher yields.

Consider the damage: mutual funds that invest in long-term United States Treasury bonds lost an average 6.8 percent in May, according to Morningstar, with the loss in principal wiping out years of interest payments. But that's not the worst-hit sector. Higher-yielding bonds and fixed-income securities, to which investors have turned in droves in recent years, have suffered even more, especially mortgage-backed securities and emerging market debt, as well as just about anything that uses borrowing to increase returns.

Many individual securities and funds were hit much harder than the averages. Vanguard's Extended Duration Treasury Index fund was down more than 6 percent in the last month. In the mortgage area, Annaly Capital Management, a popular real estate investment trust that invests in mortgages, fell 8.7 percent, and an iShares mortgage exchange-traded fund lost 10.4 percent. Pimco's Corporate Opportunity Fund, which is managed by the star analyst Bill Gross and which invests in a mix of corporate bonds and mortgage-backed securities and uses some borrowing, lost nearly 13.4 percent. Annualized, such declines are off the charts. "There are many closed-end bond funds and mortgage funds that were just annihilated in May," said Anthony Baruffi, a senior portfolio manager at SNW Asset Management in Seattle, which specializes in fixed-income assets.

Fixed-income funds are where investors have traditionally looked for safety and low volatility, unlike stocks, and such precipitous moves are rare.

The sudden recent moves in the markets have left many experts scratching their heads, because, on the face of things, not much has changed in the overall economic outlook. This week's employment number—American employers added 175,000 new jobs in May—was the average rate for the last year, suggesting slow but steady growth in the economy. Other measures released in May, like consumer confidence, consumer spending, and personal income, were generally positive, but nothing to suggest any imminent surge in economic growth.

"Last week's sell-off was very indiscriminate," said Jonathan A. Beinner, chief investment officer for global fixed income and liquidity at Goldman Sachs Asset Management. Added Mr. Baruffi, "I was surprised at how severe the market reaction was." "The magnitude of the moves was extreme in some cases," Mr. Beinner said. "It wasn't based on fundamentals, and may have been a liquidity-driven event, with hedge funds" selling when prices fell to target levels.

Whether or not the current sell-off continues, <u>the plunge has startled investors who may not have realized how much risk was embedded in their portfolios</u>.

One of the little-appreciated results of rising interest rates will be to curtail dramatically the use of borrowed money for speculation. In the past three years, hedge funds and investment companies have invested billions of nearly costless dollar credits to buy stock and real estate. As rates go higher and borrowing becomes expensive, all that buying will stop.

What will it mean when stocks, bonds, precious metals and commodities are *all weak?* According to rotation theory, it's not supposed to happen. It is indeed a rare event, but it does reliably occur in times of *severe debt deflation.* Eventually investors will realize that all these market sectors are no longer competing with each other but with *cash.*

Section D

Major Top in Stocks Portends a Deflationary Crash

In 1982 and 1983, when the majority of investors were afraid of stocks and hiding in money-market funds, the Elliott wave position of the market gave us a unique and valuable perspective. *The Elliott Wave Theorist* recognized that a bull market akin to that of the Roaring 'Twenties had started. In April 1983, *The Elliott Wave Theorist* made this prediction: "In wave V, investor mass psychology should reach manic proportion, with elements of 1929, 1968 and 1973 all operating together and, in the end, to an even greater extreme." As radical as that statement was, I didn't anticipate that we would eventually see each of these extremes, *in a row.* Over the past 14 years, we have seen not just one stock market top combining the craziest peaks of the 20th century but *one after another*: 1929 on steroids, followed by 1968 on steroids, now followed by 1973 on steroids. Never before have there been three consecutive stock manias of such intensity in so short a time. Within that span there have also been sister manias for real estate, commodities, precious metals, bonds and even bitcoins, every one constituting a multi-century rarity in its own right. The extent of this manic behavior went far beyond the radically bullish description we issued 31 years ago. Despite what amounted to foreknowledge about an approaching era of nearly unprecedented optimism, I underestimated the extent of every mania that has occurred. I truly wonder if the extremes of this period indicate something even larger than a Grand Supercycle peak in optimism.

Throughout, my colleagues and I have understood that each market was simply enjoying its turn in the rotation, each one expressing at least a Grand-Supercycle-degree extreme in positive social mood and therefore in financial optimism. One thing that has been crystal clear to us each time is that payback for succumbing to the enticing lure of these investment sirens would be vicious. The real estate market is in the deepest shambles, but investors who believed the "Peak Oil" scenario or "$200 silver" are paying the price, too.

We patiently look forward to the time when Elliott waves, sentiment readings, valuation and momentum indicators finally depict a major bottom in *anything*. But that time remains in the future. Not a single investment market—be it stocks, bonds, real estate, commodities or precious metals—stands anywhere near a major bottom today. Every one of them continues to show characteristics of being on the left or right side of a historic top of sentiment so extreme as to occur on average only once in centuries.

Real vs. Fake New Highs

The top graph in Figure D-1 shows the S&P that everyone is watching. New bull market, right? Wrong. The middle graph shows the real S&P, which has been in a bear market since the first quarter of 2000. The Fed's liquidity has re-fattened the banks, and bankers in turn are lending the new money to wealthy institutional speculators, who use it as collateral to buy stocks on margin. This is not a bull market but a hyped-up bear market rally. As *Elliott Wave Principle* (p.81) said 36 years ago, "If the analyst can easily say to himself, 'There is something wrong with this market,' chances are it's a B wave [a bear market rally]." There is something wrong about a market that has been making new all-time highs for a full year on the subterfuge of a purposely debased measuring unit.

The lower graph on the chart confirms our interpretation. Main Street senses that the recovery is phony, and its assessments of the economy are in lock-step with the real S&P, not the phony one. The depression is ongoing, and issuing new fiat-money credits can't stop it.

Figure D-1

Psychological Indicators

The Elliott Wave Theorist and *The Elliott Wave Financial Fore-cast* have shown thirty charts of sentiment indicators at or near all-time expressions of optimism. I will show six of them here, just to give you the flavor.

Optimism prompts investors to employ leverage. At the end of March, margin debt reached an all-time record level of $466 billion dollars, up 116 times since the stock market low of 1974 (see Figure D-2).

Figure D-2

You might think that the Fed's monetization justifies the rise shown in Figure D-2. But if we normalize this indicator to GDP, as shown in Figure D-3, margin debt as a percentage of annual GDP is still *11 times* the 1974 level. So, people are willing to be indebted, relative to production, eleven times as much as they were in 1974, to own their shares of stock. The current margin debt/GDP ratio is also more than 3 *times* what it was at previ-

Figure D-3

ous *major tops* in the stock market in the 20th century. This is
not a sustainable amount, much less a sustainable trend, because
the amount of available money and credit already committed is
also at an all-time high. Figure D-4 shows that individual investors with brokerage accounts are so leveraged that margin debt
exceeds cash and available credit in cash and margin accounts
by a record $178 billion. The previous (lower) high was set in
2000. Brokerage clients' unprecedented willingness to borrow is
yet another measure indicating historically extreme optimism.

Figure D-4

According to Bloomberg, hedge funds are the most levered on record, with data going back to 2004, which means they are the most levered ever. Gross leverage is 153% in the week ended January 4. We don't have figures since then, but no doubt they'll be higher than that given action in the stock market recently. If the Fed's new dollars have gone anywhere, they seem to have gone through banks to institutional stock market speculators.

A bubble is an overpriced financial market that has been pumped up with credit. The stock market today qualifies as a bubble.

The Rydex family-of-funds data afford good sentiment indicators. Recent stock buying has created a lopsided investment ratio among fund sectors. Figure D-5 shows a *record low percentage of investment* in conservative money-market funds, meaning nearly all of Rydex's customers are invested in stocks and bonds.

Figure D-5

At the same time, the ratio of money in bullish stock funds vs. bearish stock funds is over 5:1, and per sentimenTrader.com the ratio of money in *leveraged* bull vs. bear funds (see Figure D-6) is 10:1! This reading leaves past extremes in the dust. Once this epic complacency melts, we will not see such a ratio again in our lifetimes.

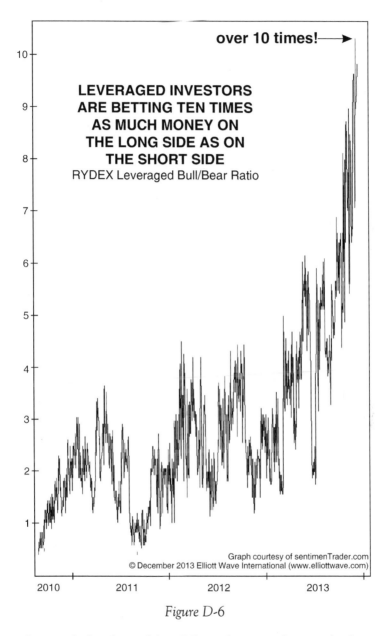

Figure D-6

So much for the public. What about professional advisors? Figure D-7 shows that newsletter advisors polled by Investors Intelligence have just reached the lowest percentage of bears since

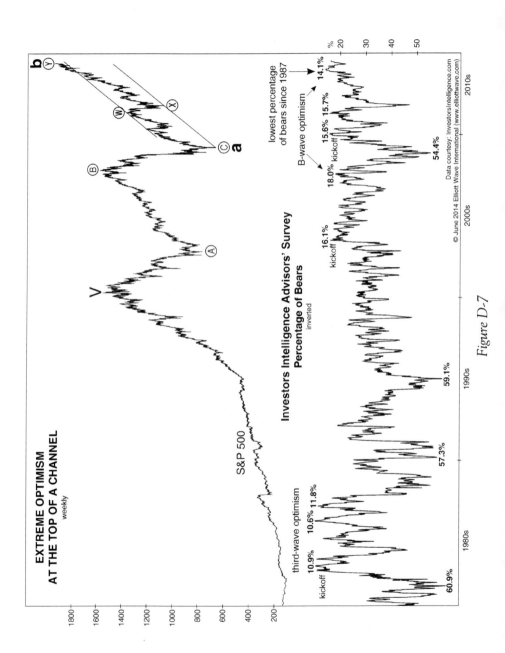

Figure D-7

1987, over a quarter century ago! The reading today is lower than at the stock market peak of 2007, lower than at the peak of 2000, and just one-quarter of the percentage of bears typically recorded near major stock market lows. In addition, the Daily Sentiment Index recently recorded 93% bulls among S&P futures traders.

What about economists? They are euphoric, too. Here is a sample of their recent thinking:

> For six months, the Federal Reserve has struggled to engineer a pullback of its bond-buying program without unhinging financial markets. <u>Yesterday, the Fed did it</u>. [P]olicy makers have tried to convince investors that tapering quantitative easing isn't tightening policy. <u>They succeeded yesterday</u> by coupling a $10 billion reduction in monthly asset buying with a stronger commitment to keep interest rates at record lows, according to [the] chief financial economist at [a brokerage firm] in New York. "The Fed is trying to get policy back in the direction of normal without causing setbacks in the economy and too much distress in financial markets," said [the] former Fed economist, who predicted the Fed would taper. "Based on the initial reaction, *they found a magic elixir*."
>
> —Bloomberg, Dec. 19, 2013

What about the media? Recent articles offer many pages of optimistic commentary. For this book, I am trimming it substantially but you will still get a taste of the mood. These articles express today's heightened optimism among the media and the people reporters choose to interview.

Even the few remaining bears are caving into the bullish psychology. The idea that the stock market will end its rally with a near-vertical advance—a "melt-up"—is appearing in articles, interviews, newsletters, web posts and emails to EWI, even from super-bears who have long recognized that the market is extended and overpriced.

This Bull Market Could Last Another
15 Years   —Yahoo Finance, February 26, 2014

Retirement Investors Flock Back To Stocks

The average workplace retirement-plan participant at Vanguard Group, the biggest U.S. mutual-fund company by assets, had 72% allocated to stocks in 2013, up from a low of 65% in 2008 and four percentage points higher than 2007, according to the Valley Forge, Pa., firm.

—The Wall Street Journal, May 1, 2014

▮▮▮▮▮▮▮: My Fears Have Been 'Alleviated'

the ECB on Thursday reduced interest rates, pushing the deposit rate into negative territory, and announced a series of other measures designed to boost bank lending and keep ultralow inflation from gaining traction.

▮▮▮▮▮▮, the hedge-fund manager who spooked some investors last month when he said he was "nervous" about the markets, said many of his concerns have been "alleviated" thanks to the ECB's unorthodox moves.

—Bloomberg News, June 6, 2014

5 Reasons The Stock Market Is Glowing Again

—USA Today, June 9, 2014

Blast From the Past: Could Stocks Melt Up?

Reuters —Even after small declines last week, the major stock indexes remain near records. Money managers and analysts are beginning to talk about an idea that dates from the roaring '90s: a rapid stock gain known as a melt-up.

—WSJ.com, Jun 15, 2014

Few want to risk taking profits, missing gains

Sitting out isn't an option. Moves by central banks around the world make it costly to not be involved in stocks, says ▮▮▮▮▮ of ▮▮▮▮ Investment Group. With interest rates low and an uptick in inflation possible, holding cash appears to be a loser. "Investors recognize the penalty from sitting on the sidelines," ▮▮▮▮ says.

—USA Today, June 23, 2014

Bull Has Legs to Run Another 10 Years If ███ 's Math Is Right
— June 23 (Bloomberg)

Why Dow 44,000 Is Coming

No matter what you read in financial media, no bull market has ever died of old age. It makes for an interesting data-mining experiment to compare the duration of historic bull markets, but it's simply not an actionable piece of information.

For those of you who think otherwise, it's going to be a long ten years, at least as far as ███ is concerned.

—Yahoo Finance, June 24, 2014

U.S. optimism highest since '08

Associated Press

WASHINGTON — U.S. consumers are more confident about the economy than they have been in more than six years.

The Conference Board's confidence index rose to 85.2 this month from a revised 82.2 in May, the private research group said Tuesday. The June figure is the highest since January 2008, a month after the Great Recession officially began.
—AJC June 25, 2014

By Time You Know Stocks Are in Correction, It'll Almost Be Over
—June 27, 2014 (Bloomberg)

Nothing Threatens This Stocks Bull Market
Jun 27, 2014
By: Money_Morning

I believe the conditions now in place could foster a bull market that could last 18 to 20 years.

If you want to improve your net worth and plan for an exciting, enriched retirement, you absolutely have to do two things:

First, make sure you are invested in the U.S. stock market.

Second, invest that money in the technology companies that will send the market zooming upward for the next generation.

The Great Obama Bull Market will roar till 2016
Historic market up 250%, aims for a 300% gain by election

Yes, it's time to celebrate. We're in a historic bull market. GOP conservatives keep fighting the wrong war, against the Obama economy. Meanwhile, the Obama bull market keeps roaring ahead! And the long term looks even better:

So what can we expect from the stock market by 2016 and the election of the next American president? More! Fabulous 250% gains so far. And bigger gains possible coming in the next couple years till we elect a new president. Maybe over 300%. Gains likely to favor a Democrat.

Get it? GOP conservatives may have been successful in slowing America's economic recovery. But the bull market keeps roaring and roaring. Get it? As the war against all-things-Obama accelerates, as the economic recovery slows, as the GOP fights infrastructure funding, as they fail to pass jobs stimulus programs ... the stock market gets stronger, roars bullishly ahead.

—MarketWatch, July 5, 2014

Bullish pundits predict stocks will continue climbing into the 2016 presidential election.

Check out these predictions: "Expect a 30% gain before the bull market ends," is the headline prediction of Decision Economics CEO ▇▇▇ in Bottomline Personal. He sees 18,500 on the Dow in 2014. And ahead we don't even "need a robust 4%-to-5% GDP to keep the bull market going," echoing the bullish forecasts of other forecasters, like ▇▇▇ and Merrill Lynch strategist ▇▇▇ who also see a roaring bull till 2017.

And in "Best Guesses for the Next Two Years," one of America's more accurate market forecasters, ▇▇▇ strategist and founder of the $117 billion GMO money team writes: "This year should continue to be difficult." But after October "the market is likely to be strong, especially through April and by then or in the following 18 months up to the next election (or, horrible possibility, even longer) will have rallied past 2,250, perhaps by a decent margin."

Yes, folks, you are seeing a rare historical event, two bulls back-to-back, end-on-end with no real bear market in between. Celebrate the birth of our great nation ... a bull run till 2016 ... the Dow roaring to 22,000!

—MarketWatch, July 5, 2014

The problem with this idea is that the Dow and S&P have never accelerated upward at a market top. The stock market often accelerates off bottoms, and it always accelerates in the center of a third wave; *but it has always lost momentum in a fifth wave relative to the third wave.* Predictions for a blow-off defy history.

Commodities are the exception, as pointed out in Chapter 6 of *Elliott Wave Principle* (1978). In fifth waves of Primary and higher degree, commodities often accelerate upward before reversing. Recent examples include oil in 2008 and silver in 2011 (see Section E). The reason for the difference is that commodities peak on fear, whereas stocks peak on complacency.

Some people are arguing that the stock market has become "commoditized," and that's why it's about to go into a parabolic rise. While we cannot say such an event is outright impossible, it's never happened. One thing that does happen repeatedly near a top in the stock market is that investors *raise their upside forecasts dramatically.* In 1999-2000, at the market's true peak, books came out calling for Dow 36,000, Dow 40,000 and Dow 100,000. Today's calls for a melt-up, then, are probably capitulation to the bullish imperative, a rationalization of unconscious optimism. By this means, long term bears have switched from predicting a collapse to predicting *soaring prices.* In other words, "Sure, it's a bubble; but it's not topping *now.* In fact, it's going to start going up *faster!*" These melt-up predictions are yet another indicator that positive social mood has reached an extreme and therefore that the market is close to a peak in the biggest B wave in recorded history.

Meanwhile, the stock market has been losing upside momentum for a full year. This is how market tops have always formed, not with a rocket blast but with a subtly slowing ascent. Even in 1929 the market did not blow off; the rise that year was slower and narrower than the market's rise in the second half of 1928. *Is this time different?* Well, so far it's exactly the same in that people are saying it's different.

The strongest reason bulls give for believing that stock prices will continue to rise is the Fed's unprecedented inflation of the base money supply through its QE policy. It might be useful simply to point out two counter-indicative precedents: "Endless Fed inflating" is the reason precious metals bulls offered in 2011 for why gold and silver couldn't go down. How well is that working out? "Endless Fed buying" is the argument bond bulls offered in 2012 for why long-term interest rates couldn't go up. Today, rates are near a two-year high.

What matters most in each of these cases is not the reasoned argument for bullish conviction but the *fact* of bullish conviction. At the metals top in 2011 and the bond market top in 2012, the majority of investors believed that Fed policy made a reversal impossible. That's what we have today in the stock market, and that's what matters.

Can you imagine investors, advisors, economists, the media and even "bears" showing this much confidence and unanimity at a *truly* good buying opportunity? In March 2009, the Daily Sentiment Index (trade-futures.com) recorded an all-time *low* of 2% *bulls*, meaning that 98% of S&P traders thought the market would go lower. Money managers who are bullish today will tell you that March 2009 was an "obvious" buying opportunity. But most of them never got out at the previous top so they *could* put cash to work, and when the time arrived they were cautious if not scared stiff. Now they are devoid of fear. They won't raise cash at this top, either. One thing we can count on is that all of the sentiment extremes we have observed here will lead to their opposite.

Elliott Wave Position

Figure D-8 is from Chapter 2 of *Elliott Wave Principle*. It displays a typical progression of prices and psychology in a bear market. We can apply this picture to the stock market from 2000.

Idealized Corrective Wave

TOP
Large degrees: prosperity and peace appear guaranteed forever. Arrogant complacency reigns.
Intermediate degrees: economic improvement, good feeling.
Minor degrees: often accompanied by "good news."

NARROW, EMOTIONAL ADVANCE
Technically weak, selective.
Results in non-confirmations.
Fundamentals weaken subtly.
Aggressive euphoria and denial.

TECHNICAL BREAKDOWN
Trendlines broken.
Viewed as buying opportunity.

wave A

wave B

wave C

WORST OF BEAR MARKET
Strength. Breadth.
Prices decline relentlessly.
Fundamentals ultimately collapse in response.

Figure D-8

Since then, the stock market has been in an "expanded flat" pattern of Supercycle degree. Wave B of this pattern carries prices to a new high *within* the correction, as occurred in the S&P in 1968, 1973, 2007 and now.

It takes powerful optimism to propel a bear market rally to a new high. At such times, some indicators of investor sentiment reach more extreme levels than they recorded at the preceding orthodox top. There has never been an expanded flat pattern as large as Supercycle degree in recorded stock market history, going back 300 years. It's a first. So, we are getting commensurate expressions of stupendous optimism, which will prove worthy of the record books.

As shown in Figure D-9, the orthodox top (wave V) for the Dow and S&P occurred in 2000. That's when the five-wave bull market ended. This is not just semantics. Elliott wave forms tell

Figure D-9

you which stock market advances are part of a true bull market
and which aren't. The rallies since 2000 are *not* bull markets but
bear market rallies.

The year 2000 is also when the all-time high was recorded
in the major averages' valuation as measured by annual dividend
yield, price to book value, and the corporate bond/stock yield

spread. Indicators such as Gallup's poll of Economic Confidence peaked then, too, by a wide margin (see Figure D-1). That was the end of the one-way good times.

From there, wave **a** was a complex pattern that ended in 2009. The rally since 2009 is wave **b**, a rally in a bear market, as shown in Figures D-7 and D-9.

Figure D-1 shows that wave **b** has *not* carried to a new high in real terms. In other words, the Dow and S&P today buy fewer goods and services than they did in 2000. This sad condition fits this description from *Elliott Wave Principle*:

> B waves are phonies. They are sucker plays, bull traps, specu- lators' paradise, orgies of odd-lotter mentality or expressions of dumb institutional complacency (or both). They are rarely technically strong, and are virtually always doomed to complete retracement by wave C.

This wave **b** has about run its course. Wave **c** down is next. To anticipate the ultimate resolution of this ongoing bear market, read this description, also from *Elliott Wave Principle*, regarding what to expect in the final wave of decline:

> Declining C waves are usually devastating in their destruc- tion. They are third waves and have most of the properties of third waves. It is during these declines that there is virtually no place to hide except cash. The illusions held throughout waves A and B tend to evaporate, and fear takes over. C waves are persistent and broad.

Despite widespread belief that the economy, interest rates and the money supply are under the Fed's firm control, my opinion is that the Fed can do nothing to stop the approaching crash. Worldwide debt is on the verge of a swift, stunning, deflationary implosion.

The models for the coming collapse are British stock prices in 1720-1722 and American stock prices in 1929-1932, except this one should be bigger. As at those times, the market should undergo a few years of persistent melt-down, and wave c will be done.

A Once-in-a-Century Deflationary Setup

Consider these confluences: In the summer of 1929, stocks were rising to a new all-time high, bonds had peaked a year earlier, real estate had peaked four years earlier, and commodities were trading at lower prices after having topped out several years before. As you can see in Figure D-10, the setup today is nearly identical. Everything is bigger and has lasted longer this time around, but the progression of events is nearly the same.

The outcome of today's progression should be the same as that in 1929. The primary difference is that the waves are of larger degree under the Elliott wave model, so the percentage crashes will be bigger.

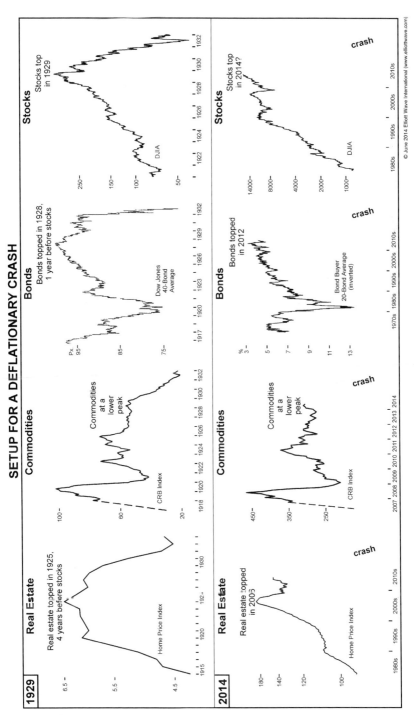

Figure D-10

Section E

Stalled Prices for Physical Goods Portend a Deflationary Crash

The main reason investors are expecting runaway inflation is illustrated in Figure E-1, which shows the value of assets held at the Federal Reserve. The Fed has been inflating the supply of

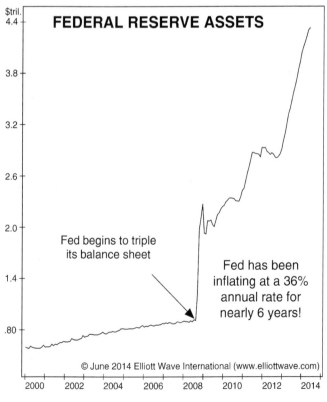

Figure E-1

dollars at a stunning 36% *annual rate* over the past six years. It has kept open the possibility that it will do so indefinitely. With this dramatic a rise, it's no wonder investors expect overall inflation and have aggressively positioned for it. Look elsewhere, however, and you will see subtle evidence of deflationary pressures.

Producer and Consumer Prices

Given knowledge of the Fed's inflating, many people would expect the Producer and Consumer Price Indexes to be rising at a rate of 33% annually. But, as you can see in Figure E-2, the PPI's annual rate of change is stuck at zero and the CPI has been rising at only a 2% rate.

Figure E-2

Commodities

The CRB index of commodities has been losing ground for more than two years, as shown in Figure E-3. Notice the four short arrows on the chart. Based on their positions, you might think they would mark the timing of accurate sell signals generated by a secret indicator. But there's no secret indicator. These happen to be the times at which the Fed launched its inflationary "quantitative easing" (QE) programs!

Investors almost universally take news at face value rather than paradoxically as they should. So they believed the Fed's QE actions would be bullish for commodities. But—ironically yet naturally—every launch of a new QE program provided an opportunity to sell commodities near a high. The first time the Fed bought a slew of new assets (QE0) was in 2008, and commodities went straight down during the entire buying spree. QE1 was just a swapping of assets, not new buying, so it wasn't inflationary; ironically, commodities rose during this time. Commodities rose a little bit after the inflationary QE2 started but ultimately went lower. Since QE3 and QE4—the two most aggressive programs of inflating the Fed has ever initiated—commodity prices have been trending lower as well.

Figure E-3

Are commodities just late in responding and poised to soar? I don't think so. Figure E-4 shows a chart of the CRB index published in *The Elliott Wave Theorist* back in May 2011. It shows a

As shown in May 2011 EWT

Figure E-4

Figure E-5

three-step, countertrend rally...inside of a parallel trend channel...at a 62% retracement...thus giving three reasons to expect
a peak at that time. Figure E-5 shows that the CRB index has
trended moderately but persistently lower since then.

Key Commodities also Hint at Deflation

Crude Oil

Crude oil is a major component of the CRB index. In 2008
(see Figure E-6), oil crashed by 78% in just five months. Under
the Elliott wave model, that decline is wave **a** of an unfinished
bear market. From that low, a three-wave, countertrend rally

Figure E-6

took place, just as in the CRB index. That rally, wave **b**, seems to have ended in 2011.

Bearish fundamentals usually start falling into place during C waves. That's what's been happening with respect to oil. There's an oil boom in the Dakotas, companies are drilling new wells in the Caribbean, and the Japanese have discovered methane hydrate under the sea. There is more carbon energy available in this form than in all other carbon-based fuels combined. A few years from now, at the final bottom in price, articles will feature these and other reasons why you shouldn't invest in oil.

The long term wave pattern supports this interpretation. Figure E-7 shows crude oil's bull market going back a hundred years. The structure is clearly five waves up within a parallel trend channel. Wave V ended in what Elliott called a "throw-over". A throw-over is a move above the upper channel line and then

Figure E-7

a fall back below it, indicating exhaustion of the trend (see *Elliott Wave Principle*, p.73). Look carefully and you'll notice that the 2011 peak—the one labeled wave **b**—precisely touched the upper channel line. Wave **c** should carry the price of oil below the 2008 low.

So, both the long term and near term Elliott wave patterns make a case that the hundred-year rise in oil prices is over. Since oil's price rise is almost entirely a reflection of the decline in the value of the dollar, I think this chart tells us that the century-long era of inflation is over, too.

Silver

Silver is an interesting case. As Figure E-8 shows, it has been falling for three years. Its decline of over 60% has surprised precious metals advocates. From 2010 through 2012, we heard calls for $200 silver. Instead it's selling for $20. There is no evidence of inflation in this chart. For a discussion of gold, see Section B.

Figure E-8

Copper

Figure E-9 is an interesting chart. Copper participated in three different manias. It first topped in 2006 along with housing. That confluence makes sense, because copper is an important component of house construction. It topped again in 2008 with the commodities market. That confluence makes sense, too, since copper is a commodity. Then it went up a third time, peaking in 2011 along with the precious metals. This makes sense, too, as copper is the poor sister of the precious metals complex. Back in 1979-80, as the precious metals boom of the 1970s came to a close, people began melting down pennies.

So, copper has participated in three manias in just five years. I don't think it's going to embark on another one all on its own. It's begun a secular bear market. The long washout coming in copper should be a sight to see.

Figure E-9

Real Estate

Real estate prices are also down substantially from their all-time highs, as shown in Figure E-10. They are lower than when the Fed began its first debt-buying spree, in 2008. Since 2012, property prices have come back a bit, but there is no indication in this sector of inflation running wild, either. One reason

Figure E-10

is that for decades real estate buyers employed more leverage than anyone. The debt they incurred is a ball and chain around the market's neck. I don't think we're going to see inflation reflected here anytime soon, either. According to reports, most institutional buyers of real estate these days are buying for cash, since borrowers and lenders are both reluctant to get back in the game. Remember this chart, because given the use of substantial leverage in the stock market today, the charts of stock averages should eventually look like this chart of real estate.

Countless people this year are saying that the Fed's inflating is showing up in the stock market. While that may be true, it's a selective argument, because effects of inflation are certainly not showing up in the PPI, the CPI, commodities, precious metals or real estate.

Debt Levels and a Sluggish Economy Portend a Deflationary Crash

Deflation nearly always manifests as a contraction in the amount of outstanding debt. Let's look at where we are in terms of debt in Europe and the United States.

Figure F-1 shows the total amount of debt in the European Union. The top line shows total loans, and the lower line shows total bonds outstanding. In 2012, both lines turned down.

Figure F-2 combines the two types of debt and plots the rate of change. The peak rate of change occurred in 2008. By the 2012 peak in debt issuance, the rate of change had slowed considerably, as you can see by the two arrows. A couple of months after Mario Draghi, head of the European Central Bank, told the world he would do "whatever it takes" to preserve the euro, the rate of change in total credit growth in the EU crossed the zero line into negative territory. Deflation is now a reality in Europe.

The U.S. is different. Figure F-3 does show a weak profile in the private debt market. It peaked in 2008, fell hard, and has barely recovered since.

But Figure F-4 shows that government has increased its indebtedness by a tremendous amount while private debt was shrinking. When you put them together, as we have in Figure F-5, you can see that total dollar-denominated debt has been creeping higher.

EU Total Credit

Figure F-1

EU Rate of Total Credit Growth

Figure F-2

Figure F-3

Figure F-4

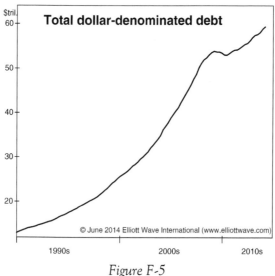

Figure F-5

One of the things keeping total private debt from falling further is the tremendous increase in student loans, as you can see in Figure F-6. Total student debt has reached $1.08 trillion. Although this is private debt held by individuals, it is promoted and backed by the government, the same conditions that jacked up real estate debt.

Figure F-6

If borrowing continues forever, then deflation won't happen. Is student-loan borrowing going to continue? Not likely. Students who owe money are in extreme trouble, and the failure rate is rising. A depression will wipe out these debts, which will be deflationary.

Business debt is also reaching new extremes. The total debt incurred by non-financial—i.e., manufacturing and service— businesses has just reached a new all-time high of $13.5 trillion. This is *not* self-liquidating debt, the kind spent on plant and equipment. Far from it. It is being used to finance LBOs, stock dividends, mergers, acquisitions and stock buybacks. In other words, even non-financial companies have become financially oriented, and they are playing the game by borrowing.

Aggressive speculation is a hallmark of fifth waves, and this trend, too, appears to be near a terminal point. Figure F-7 shows that from a low in the 1940s the rise in debt carried by nonfinancial businesses is tracing out a five-wave advance, and

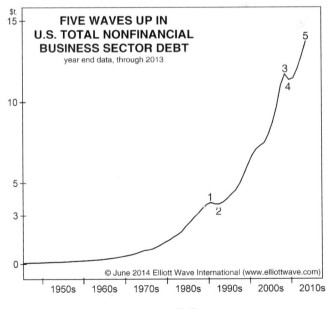

Figure F-7

it's nearing the end. No matter how we analyze it, the amount of debt incurred for the purpose of speculation is extreme and precarious.

Another debt implosion is looming in real estate. Since 2006, government agencies took up the slack when banks stopped lending on real estate. But now even the feds are running dry. The FHA is incurring portfolio losses. Its power to expand housing credit is shrinking. Entities of all kinds, then, have begun to have problems trying to expand debt.

Central bank lending and government borrowing are failing to generate economic growth

The economy is sluggish despite record inflating by central banks and the record spending by governments all over the world. Economic stagnation affects debtors' ability to repay.

Japan had one of the strongest economies in the entire world, growing at a 9% rate for 20 years up to 1973, and then a pretty strong rate of about 4½% through 1994. From there, it's averaged about 1% (see Figure F-8).

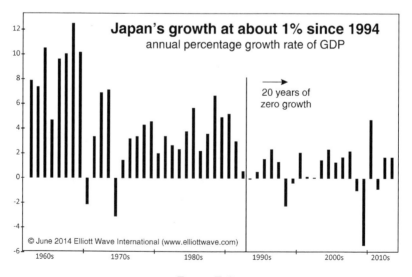

Figure F-8

The reason Japan is in trouble was expressed in a November 1, 2012 headline from *MarketWatch*: "Japan Is in Worse Than a Deflationary Trap." But it's not worse than a deflationary trap. It's just a deflationary trap. Here's what the article says: "Policy makers have spectacularly failed. Brutal deflation persists. Japanese officials tried monetary stimulus, including zero interest rates and quantitative easing." *Does that sound familiar?* And here: "Past fiscal stimulus has ballooned the national debt to 200% of GDP." *Does that sound familiar, too?* And finally, "The most troubling aspect of Japan's malaise may be psychological." That's the key to the whole thing. Psychology changes with social mood from ebullience to conservatism. That's what shifts a trend of expanding credit into a new trend of declining credit and therefore inflation into deflation.

The United States is starting to look like Japan. The U.S. is in its weakest economic recovery on record. It is dramatically weak relative to the amount of central-bank inflating. Now GDP is hovering just above zero, as you can see in Figure F-9. It seems,

Figure F-9

then, that the trend in the U.S. is just behind that in Europe. There is no indication as yet of a super strong recovery, despite what economists keep expecting.

We read a few months ago that housing starts were the best in five years. Well, that's true, but let's put this report in perspective. Figure F-10 shows the 50-year history. The big jump in housing starts brought them back to the level of *old recessionary lows*. The same is true of total new one-family homes sold, as shown in Figure F-11. If these lines had gone straight down to present levels from the top in 2006, people would say it's a terrible situation.

Figure F-10

Where has this recovery, miserable as it is, come from? Figure F-12 is an important chart, published by economist John Hussman, showing the net amount of savings among individuals and

Figure F-11

Figure F-12

the government. It's gone extremely negative because people are spending most of the money they're making and even delving into savings, while government in the meantime is borrowing like crazy. So this recovery is being financed by people using up their savings and by entities borrowing against the future. This trend will not continue for very long. When it reverses, the change is going to be violent.

The global economy is weak, too. The Baltic Dry Index (Figure F-13) is a measure of the cost of shipping goods across the oceans worldwide. Shipping rates double-topped in 2007 and 2008, the peaks coinciding with the peaks in stocks and commodities, respectively, in those years. Shipping costs, and by implication shipping activity, plunged from that point. For the past few years there has been what we call a dead-cat bounce. To put it bluntly, governments and central banks are failing to increase trade activity *even in an environment of extreme optimism.* When pessimism returns, the economy will contract from an already-weak background, and debtors will be unable to service or repay their obligations, and the credit supply will deflate.

Figure F-13

Erroneous Faith in the Fed Prompts Epic Complacency about Deflation

Four Myths of Central Banking

To understand some of the reasons why I'm not snowed by the power of central bankers, I will present what I believe to be five myths of central banking.

Number 1: "The Fed will drop money from helicopters."

Former Chairman Ben Bernanke himself told us he would do this. But what did he mean, really? Fed employees are not physically going to climb into helicopters and disperse money like so many leaflets. He presumably meant they would buy up all the bad debts in the world. *But they haven't been doing that.*

In August 2007, at a stock market high, before the latest crisis, I outlined the way I thought the Fed would behave:

In the early 1930s, the Fed offered loans only on the most pristine debt. Its standards have fallen a bit, but not by much. Today it will still lend only on highly reliable IOUs, not junk. One might imagine various schemes by which the government would guarantee some mortgages, but if it did, the mortgages would in effect become Treasury bonds.

During the initial buying spree in 2008 (QE0), the Fed did buy almost anything to try to save the system. But it immediately went back to its usual way. As noted in Figure G-1, QE1 was a period where the Fed began exchanging all its newly acquired weak assets for government-guaranteed mortgages, which are, in effect, Treasury bonds. For QE2 it purchased more Treasury bonds. For QE3 it purchased more government-guaranteed mortgages. For QE4 it was more Treasury bonds.

What the Fed has always done, and is still doing, is to buy U.S. Treasury bonds, which are among the safest assets in the world. It's not going around to banks teetering on the brink of failure to assure them, "We'll take all your bad stuff." The Fed doesn't want to own bad mortgages or business loans. In fact, it has been buying government-guaranteed mortgages *of only the most recent vintages*, meaning they're post-crisis mortgages, which have better collateral and a much better chance of being paid off. The Fed's members are bankers; they don't want their bank to fail.

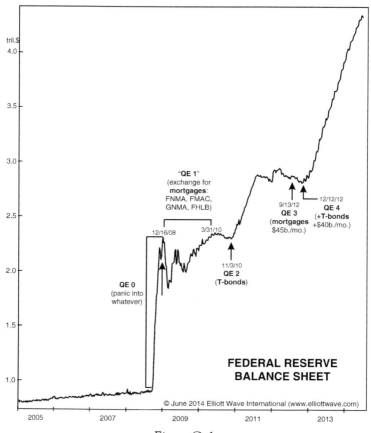

Figure G-1

Number 2: "Central banks will just print money."

This is a nearly universal belief, especially among people who expect hyperinflation. But tell this fable to the people who live in Cyprus. Losses in Cypriot banks in 2013 were estimated to be as high as 60%. That's a systemic banking failure. Were depositors rescued? Read this news report from 2013: "A weekend agreement between Cyprus and its European partners called for the government to *raid bank accounts*." To grab the money, authorities shut down Cyprus' second-largest bank, "imposing steep losses on deposits with more than 100,000 euros." The lenders in this case were the Eurozone, the IMF and the European Central Bank. They are supposed to be the saviors, the bailers-out. But the ECB did not print money to save these depositors. European officials said, "We lent you money. We want it back. Now you pay *us*." They called the seizure a "tax" on depositors. But it was nothing more than a banking failure. The creditors forced to pay were not the big institutional lenders but those hapless souls known as depositors. To trap people, authorities imposed "strict controls on money transfers in and out of the economy." At air and seaports, officials were confiscating amounts over 10,000 euros. See how it works? No helicopters.

Number 3: "Central banks stand ready to be lenders of last resort."

Founders of central banks always make this promise. But in Europe we found out something very different. According to a March 25, 2013 article in *The Telegraph*, "Savings accounts in Spain, Italy and other European countries *will be raided* if needed to preserve Europe's single currency by propping up failing banks, a senior Eurozone official has announced." But raiding accounts is not "propping up failing banks"; it's just structuring the failures. The Dutch chairman of the Eurozone said—listen to this—"Look, where *you* take on risks, *you* must deal with them, and if *you* can't deal with them, then *you* shouldn't have taken them on." Notice it's not *us* but *you*.

He then said, "Banks should basically be able to *save them-selves.*" Wait a minute! Didn't they used to call this policy "wildcat banking," whereby a bank was responsible for its own health and depositors paid for failures? It seems we're back to square one! But we're not; we're way worse off. In the old days, when one bank failed, one bank failed. Under central banking, debt is socialized, so failures must be systemic.

Surprise: There's no free lunch. Not only did central bankers not ride to the rescue but they also decided on "mothballing the 700 billion Euro bailout fund, the European Stability Mechanism (ESM)." Of course they did. Infinite credit works only in theory.

Consider the psychology of these lenders. They abandoned the expansionary attitudes they held for over a decade. Instead, they worried, "Maybe we won't get paid later; we'd better get paid today." By acting to protect themselves, they were thinking in a deflationary manner, just like the average person.

Number 4: "Inflation is determined by the expansion of base money."

Figure G-1 depicted the expansion of base money. Many people have been saying it guarantees hyperinflation. But infla-tion, as I've long argued, is a net expansion of money *and credit.* Usually an episode of deflation is a swift contraction in credit, not base money. With that understanding, let's look at the potential for credit deflation (see Figure G-2).

Base money, produced by the Fed, has risen to $4 trillion. That is a tremendous amount of money. But relative to the amount of dollars owed, it's still pretty small. Dollar denominated debt is $59 trillion. U.S. bank deposits amount to $10 trillion. These are all IOUs; most of the money's not there; it's been lent. Federal unfunded liabilities amount to $84 trillion. That's a total of about $157 trillion worth of IOUs. The base of $4 trillion doesn't look so big when compared to that number.

Inflation is the net expansion of money + **credit**

Base money: **$4t.**

Dollar denominated debt: **$59t.**
U.S. bank deposits: **$10t.**
Federal unfunded liabilities: **$84t.**
                    total: **$157t.**

Total global debt: **$223t.***
Global unfunded liabilities: **$150t.**?
                    total: **$373t.**

Dollar-based derivatives: **$693t. - 1.3 quadrillion**

Total: **$1.07 quadrillion****

> *Only $4t. of global debt (2%) is rated AAA
> **only 0.4% of the total is base money

Figure G-2

Globally, there is about $223 trillion worth of debt. Total unfunded liabilities, I'm guessing, amount to around $150 trillion, for a total of $373 trillion.

This figure doesn't take into account global financial derivatives. The lowest estimate I have seen is $693 trillion. I call derivatives "IOU-if's." They're not IOUs now, but if certain events were to happen they would *turn into* IOUs. That's a lot of potential new debt. So total debt plus potential debt is somewhere north of a quadrillion dollars' worth, making $4 trillion not seem like a whole lot. In fact, it is less than 0.4% of the total.

Moreover, consider that only $4 trillion worth of total global debt is AAA. That's only 2%; 98% of the debt is graded lower.

Number 5: "The Fed's Inflating Will Change People's Psychology"

The Fed's actions cannot change people's psychology. On the contrary, people's psychology prompts actions by the Fed.

Figure G-3 shows very clearly that deflationary psychology is hindering the Fed's drive to inflate. Money velocity—the rate at which money is changing hands—tends to rise when social mood is trending positively and economic activity is expanding, and fall when mood is negative and the economy is contracting. As you can see in Figure G-3, money velocity in the U.S. peaked in the third quarter of 1997 and has been falling ever since. The only significant bounce along the way is the one that accompanied the final three years of the real-estate mania from 2003 into the second quarter of 2006. From there, money velocity plunged along with financial markets into the second quarter of 2009, when the economy bottomed. All of this is normal behavior. But then, following an even weaker bounce, *money velocity has been making new lows quarter after quarter* since Q3 2010. Changes in money velocity are a psychological phenomenon, not a mechanical one.

Figure G-3

Sliding velocity is a big reason why the Fed has been inflating. The Fed chairmen think inflation will force velocity to turn back up. So far, it hasn't. Rather, its persistent fall is occurring amidst the Fed's most aggressive inflationary monetary policy ever.

Conquer the Crash predicted that hubristic macro-directors would be unable to fend off the tides of social mood, which derive from the unconscious workings of human nature. So far, the two combatants are at a standstill. But a winner will emerge. When social mood turns toward the negative again, velocity will fall even further, credit will shrink, the stock market will fall, and the economy will contract. Induced inflation will prove inadequate to the task of reversing these trends.

Today's Precarious Conditions

Today, we're in an amazing situation far worse than that of 1929. People have gorged on investments. They own debt in the forms of junk bonds, muni bonds, corporates, Treasuries and mortgages. They have invested in real estate and are praying for a turnaround. They own stocks at record prices. They own precious metals. And they've got bank accounts, which are IOUs backed by IOUs. There is a widespread, unstated conviction that you have to *own something*, that whatever you do, *don't hold cash,* because cash is trash.

Tell that to the people who live in Cyprus. When access to credit was curtailed, there was a soaring demand for cash—the one thing nobody had. A March 26, 2013 article in *The Financial Times* reported, "The most immediate problem confronting businesses was a scarcity of cash." A businessman in Cyprus said, "The market is operating on a cash basis—everybody wants cash." That was the immediate result of deflation in Cyprus. When you look at the huge quantity of low-quality of debt that U.S. investors are buying, it is not hard to imagine something similar happening in the United States.

A Quiz

Here is a test I conducted a year ago for a presentation to the annual conference of the Market Technicians Association:

> You can type just about anything into Google and find it on the web. If you put your query in quotes, Google tells you the number of times that someone somewhere entered onto the Internet the exact phrase you typed in. First I tested "The world is coming to an end." There was a lot of talk in 2012 about the Mayan calendar, so I figured we'd get quite a few postings of this statement. A friend of mine suggested a couple of phrases one would not expect to find, such as "Dinosaurs love to dance." Would anybody ever type that in? Or how about "Plus equals minus," which is a contradiction?

> Figure G-4 shows the results. "The world is coming to an end" got 4.5 million results. A lot of people were talking about the world coming to an end. Believe it or not, 1710 times somebody typed into the Internet, "Dinosaurs love to dance." I didn't read these entries, so I don't know the contexts, but they're there. And "Plus equals minus"— I guess that gives you one reason why the world is in trouble—produced 48,700 results.

Google Search (3/13/13)	
"the world is coming to an end":	**4,510,000** results
"dinosaurs love to dance":	**1,710** results
"plus equals minus":	**48,700** results

Figure G-4

I am showing you this list of results so we have benchmarks for comparison.

Now we're going to get to the point. When I typed "Inflation for 2013," there were 47,700 results. On March 13th, when I put this slide together, I also typed in "Deflation for 2013." How many results do you think I got? Remember, there were 48,000 results for "Inflation for 2013," 49,000 results for "Plus equals minus" and 1700 for "Dinosaurs love to dance."

Ready? Here we go.

Take a look at Figure G-5. The answer is **5**.

```
Google Search (3/13/13)
"Inflation for 2013":  47,700 results
"Deflation for 2013":        5 results
```

Figure G-5

That's right. Only five times over the entire global Internet did somebody type in "Deflation for 2013." The ratio is nearly 10,000 to 1.

Maybe a quote about deflation is too much to ask. Let's make it easier to get a big number.

First let's type in "Inflation will rise in 2013." This entry produces **50,200** results. On the contrasting side, we will *not* search for a matching quote about deflation. Instead, we will search just on the clause, "Inflation will fall in 2013." Certainly there must be a fair number of people at least talking about the *possibility of a moderation of inflation*, right? Any guesses on that one?

Take a look at Figure G-6. The answer is **7**.

That's right. The ratio is **50,200** to **7**. These results show how one-sidedly the global crowd is thinking.

```
Google Search (3/13/13)
"Inflation will rise in 2013":  50,200 results
"Inflation will fall in 2013":        7 results
```

Figure G-6

I conducted one last test. I typed in "The world is coming to an end in 2013." It got 9 results. "Inflation will fall in 2013," remember, got 7 results (see Figure G-7). Apparently more people think the world is coming to an end *this year* than that inflation could possibly moderate.

```
Google Search (3/13/13)
"The world is coming to an end in 2013":  9 results
"Inflation will fall in 2013":        7 results
```

Figure G-7

Expecting deflation, to put it mildly, is a contrary opinion.

I conducted that test when the impossibility of deflation was essentially unanimous. And why not? The Fed was inflating at a record rate, the government had bailed out the biggest debtors, and the stock market was zooming. But since then, despite new highs in U.S. stock averages, the deflation developing in Europe has begun to make news. I re-ran the test today (April 25, 2014) and found some significant changes. Figure G-4 has about the same results. But in Figure G-5, the query "Deflation for 2014" brought up 202 results, a significant rise from 5. Still, that number is a lot less than the 55,200 results for "Inflation for 2014." The biggest change was in Figure G-6, where the query "Inflation will fall in 2014" got 7760 results, a huge jump from 7. Even then, the number is only 1/6 of the 45,300 results for "Inflation will rise in 2014." I am confident that within a few years, there will be a historical "first": more Google results for the deflation queries than for the inflation queries.

This just in: On April 29, 2014, Bloomberg reported that the famous manager of a $24b. hedge fund said in a letter to clients, "Either scenario...asteroids hitting the earth or a major solar storm that could bring down the power grid...is more likely to happen than...deflation...."

We'll see about that.

More Social Forecasts

Modern monetary theorists don't talk about the psychology of human beings. Yet this is the very factor that ruins their neat models. They think governments and central banks need only to pull on levers to make things happen. But when people suddenly get angry, fearful and conservative, the entire situation changes. The neat lab becomes a circus. Only socionomists understand the primacy of social mood to all things financial.

In 1929, the party was on, and no one could envision how dramatically things would change. Just three years later, banks were failing across the country and unemployment was pushing 25% in the deepest depression since the late 1700s.

In 1937, people were celebrating the economic recovery and dancing to Benny Goodman. No one had a clue as to how different the world would soon become. In just three years, Hitler's tanks were raging through Europe, people were being rounded up for shipment to concentration camps, Japan joined the Axis, and World War II was raging.

Had an Elliott wave analyst/socionomist been on hand at the highs of 1929 and 1937, there might have been a prayer of anticipating some of the devastating changes to come. Certainly such a person would have understood the *character* and the *degree* of looming changes, even if specifics were elusive.

Conversely, in 1942, the market had sunk to its cheapest P/E ever, Japan had wiped out U.S. naval ships at Pearl Harbor, and Germany was winning the war in Europe. That's when R.N. Elliott published a chart predicting 70 years of rising stock prices. He was right, and prosperity and peace followed.

Today, the market is at an extreme in the other direction, and a record-breaking bear market looms. What will be its social results?

We can get a hint from recent events: The bear market of 2000-2003 led to a mild recession and the 9/11 terrorist attack, the first successful foreign assault on the U.S. mainland since 1812. The bear market of 2007-2009 led to the deepest economic contraction since 1933, the biggest fall in housing prices in U.S. history, the first-ever quarter of negative earnings for the S&P and the near meltdown of the global financial system.

Each of these sets of events was the result of a negative trend in social mood at fairly high degree. Observe that the second of these manifestations was more financially destructive than the first. The Elliott wave structure today (see Figure D-9) indicates a stock market top of *one larger degree* than that of 1929, which in turn portends a commensurately sizeable reversal in social mood. So, this third peak will lead to an even greater change toward negative social mood and therefore even more severe social results.

As shown in Section D, financial optimism is back at early 2000 levels. The widespread bullish forecasts for 2014 among economists are based on *linear* projection. Our forecasts are based on *fractal* projection.

Many of our forecasts prompted by the orthodox top in 2000 have already come to pass. The U.S. got mired in the longest war in its history. Corporate heroism has been replaced by corporate scandal. There was financial and economic turmoil in 2008-2009.

Values for all but the rarest collector coins have shrunk. And interest rates fell to zero. In 2003 we wrote, "The U.S. space program will be shut down." Per Wikipedia, "The Space Shuttle program formally ended on August 31, 2011." In 2003 we wrote, "Eventually, possession and sale of recreational drugs will be decriminalized." This is already happening with marijuana. In 2003 we wrote, "Entertainment media will feature fewer heroes and more anti-heroes." Last month an article observed, "There are no purely good guys left on TV." In 2003 we wrote, "The occupation of Iraq by the U.S. will progress from a quagmire to a financial, political and public relations disaster." This has been the ongoing trend. In 2003 we wrote, "People will rate 'the future' as increasingly less promising." Over the past fourteen years, both the peaks and troughs in the consumer sentiment polls have trended lower. In 2003 we wrote, "Debt packages made of mortgage-backed bonds, auto loans and credit card debt will become viewed as unworthy investments." That's already happened. In 2003 we wrote, "'The rich' will be vilified, and their property will be increasingly taxed and seized." That's already happening, in Obamacare's skewed taxes and the IRS's draconian penalties for overseas non-reporting. In 2003, we wrote, "Fannie Mae and Freddie Mac will shut down." They haven't been shut down (yet), but they did go broke. In 2003 we wrote, "The U.S. will increase restrictions on immigration." After years of lax policies, several states recently passed draconian anti-immigrant laws. In 2003 we wrote, "Financial news networks will change formats or go off the air." That hasn't happened yet, but the trend is in place as the leading financial network's viewership is half what it was at its peak. In 2003 we wrote, "Wave (a) of the bear market in social mood will bedevil more than one president." George W. Bush left office with one of the lowest popularity ratings ever. Barack Obama's popularity is already slipping, even though the stock averages are at an all-time high. In 2003 we wrote, "The U.S. will accelerate its trend toward socialism. Opposition to that trend will be vigorous." Obamacare and the vigorous opposition to it are just the start of these trends. In 2003 we wrote, "Terrible secret activities that we could not even imagine will take place, some to be revealed only years or decades later." Despite the sideways trend of the bear market to date, we have already discovered that the U.S. military tortured prisoners at Guantanamo Bay, that the government has set up secret courts, and that the NSA secretly constructed a vast network to spy on Americans. The latter is no surprise, since we also said in 2003, "Openness and transparency will give way to secrecy. Spies and exclusive social organizations will have increased standing and power."

Social mood affects all areas of social life. When positive mood arises, the stock market turns up, the economy improves and society becomes productive and safe. When negative mood arises, the stock market turns down, the economy deteriorates and society becomes destructive and dangerous.

The stock market has gone sideways for fourteen years, indicating a negative long term trend in social mood, which has led to some of the events described above. Within that sideways trend, it has been rising for the past five years. It appears to be on the cusp of its largest downward reversal yet. If so, the social changes will be commensurately extreme.

Chapter 14 of *The Wave Principle of Human Social Behavior* presented a list of emotional and behavioral aspects of society that express positive vs. negative social mood. These words provide a guide to predicting social actions. Simply stated, over the next few years, we should see a *dramatic* change in social expressions toward the *right-hand* words among the pairings below.

With the S&P 500 making a new all-time high this month amidst entrenched optimism about the future, it seems the right time to anticipate changes we expect to see in just a few years.

Positive mood/Negative mood

acceptance/rejection
accommodation/obstruction
adventurousness/protectionism
agreeableness/antagonism
alignment/opposition
allowance/restriction
benevolence/malevolence
centrism/radicalism
certainty/uncertainty
clarity/fuzziness
concord/discord
confidence/fear
constructiveness/destructiveness
convergence/polarization
daring/defensiveness
desiring power over nature/desiring power over people
ebullience/depression
embrace of effort/avoidance of effort
feelings of safety/feelings of vulnerability
forbearance/anger

friskiness/somberness
frivolity/seriousness
happiness/unhappiness
homogeneity/heterogeneity
hopefulness/despair
inclusion/exclusion
interest in love/interest in sex
optimism/pessimism
practical thinking/magical thinking
romanticism/cynicism
search for joy/search for pleasure
self-assurance/anxiety
self providence/self deprivation
sharpness of focus/dullness of focus
supportiveness/opposition
sympathy/meanness
tendency to excuse/tendency to accuse
tendency to praise/tendency to criticize
togetherness/separatism
trust/suspicion

Social Predictions For Wave c And Its Immediate Aftermath

The events described below are likely to happen only if social mood prompts wave c down in stocks. If wave c doesn't occur, these events won't happen.

Accuracy in *specific* forecasts is impossible. In 1982, we were super-bullish, but at that time who would have predicted the iPhone? No one has a crystal ball.

I nevertheless venture into the unknown. If a third of these potential events occurs in coming years, we will judge the exercise as having been worthwhile.

Finance

- U.S. stock indexes will drop more than 90 percent.

- Real estate values will resume their descent and ultimately fall more than they did in the 1930s-1940s.

- States, counties, cities, corporations and nations will default on bonds in record amounts.

- Throughout the process, rating services will be late in downgrading most or all of the debts they cover.

- Rating services will also fail to upgrade surviving issues at their price bottoms.

- Many, if not most, pension plans will fall in value and be unable to provide the promised benefits.

- Prices for collectibles will fall a long way.

- More U.S. banks will fail than failed in the 1930s.

- The total amount of credit outstanding worldwide will decline substantially.

- The Chairman of the Fed will be labeled at least partly if not largely responsible for the collapse.

- Popular media will make fun of the Fed.

- The Federal Reserve System will be discredited if not abolished.

- Currencies will be reformed and/or retired.

- "The rich" will be further vilified, and their property will be increasingly taxed and seized.

- Hedge funds, mutual funds, money-market funds, managed accounts and brokerage accounts will go out of favor, and many will go out of existence.

- Regulatory and legislative reforms will limit, curtail or ban a number of structures facilitating speculation.

- Government will further restrict banking activities with new regulations.
- Government will raise banks' capital requirements.
- Fannie Mae and Freddie Mac will shut down.
- Financial news networks will change formats or go off the air.
- Commodities will continue to decline in value.
- The world price of oil will continue to decline. (An exception may occur if production facilities are destroyed or shipping halted during wartime.)
- Earnings for the S&P will have a larger negative quarter than in 4Q 2008.
- IPOs will contract to zero.
- Merges and acquisitions will nearly cease.
- Margin debt will contract by 80% or more.
- Stock market sentiment indicators will reflect record levels of pessimism.
- Corporate dividends will be cut, a lot.
- Investing in stocks will be considered foolhardy.
- "Buy and hold" will be denounced as a flawed approach to investing in the stock market.
- Market timing will come to be viewed as the best approach to investing.
- Many of the financial corporations bailed out by the Fed and the U.S. government will fail again, along with new ones.
- Money-market funds will implode.
- The FDIC will fail as an independent agency.
- The Fed and U.S. government will bail out a few more companies and nationalize others.

- Eventually the Fed and U.S. government will stop bank and other corporate bailouts.
- The IMF will become unfunded.
- The World Bank will become unfunded.
- Interest rates on most corporate bonds, now historically low, will exceed 20%.
- Most existing high-yield "junk" bonds will fall to zero, and their issuers will default.
- Junk bonds will no longer be considered a sensible investment.
- Issuers of junk bonds will become few to none.
- Government will outlaw various types of financial derivatives.
- The student loan program will fail.
- There will be a period of derisive and negative popular allusions to the stock market.
- Eventually, references to stocks in non-financial settings will become rare to non-existent.
- Investment clubs will go away.
- The financial system will fail more spectacularly than in 2008-9.
- Employment in finance will decline dramatically.
- Bearish speculators will make a lot of money if they cash out before their creditors fail.
- Safety-minded investors will see their purchasing power rise.
- In response to (not in anticipation of) events, the government will issue tardy and ineffective financial reforms.

The Economy

- The economy will fall into a deeper depression than in 1933.

- The true unemployment rate in the U.S. and in most countries around the world will rise and eventually exceed 25 percent, probably peaking in the 33%-50% range.

- A record number of manufacturing companies in the U.S. will fail.

- Governments will adopt trade restrictions.

- Governments will impose tariffs on imported goods.

- Consumer confidence will fall to record low levels.

- Many insurance companies will fail.

- The number of new skyscrapers being designed and built will decline dramatically.

- There will be a trend of family members moving in with each other.

- Homelessness will increase.

- Trans-oceanic shipping will contract severely if not come to a halt.

Politics

- The president's popularity ratings will reach all-time lows, exceeding the lowest numbers for Harry Truman, Richard Nixon and George W. Bush.

- Voters in 2016 will be angry.

- The U.S. elections of 2016 (if they occur) will be tumultuous.

- The public will come to believe the U.S.'s military adventures abroad cause more harm than good.

- Isolation will be debated as a legitimate foreign policy and possibly adopted.

- Terrorists or a government or governments will attack the U.S. and inflict more damage than occurred on 9/11/01.

- There will be increasing calls in the media for impeachment, resignations and/or prosecutions of politicians.

- There will be increasing calls in the media for the subdividing of states, the reformation of governmental charters (such as a constitutional convention) and/or the dissolution of political entities.

- Some U.S. states will split into smaller ones.

- Movements to secede from the U.S. will become popular.

- One or more new nations will form on the North American continent.

- Separatist movements will become popular in other parts of the world.

- Politics will become more polarized, splintered and radical.

- Many states and municipalities will go bankrupt.

- Government buildings will become objects of violent assault.

- Social Security in its current form will fail.

- Medicaid in its current form will fail.

- Obamacare will fail.

- The United Nations will be temporarily suspended and/or permanently shut down.

- The government will either increase its military attacks abroad, retreat substantially from foreign engagement, or both, in succession.

- More countries will oppose U.S. interests.

- The U.S. will require internal travel papers.

- Anti-government sentiment will grow into powerful emotional forces.

- Openness and transparency in government will continue to give way to secrecy.

- The U.S. will continue to accelerate its trend toward socialism.

- Governments will seize and destroy wealth through higher taxes, fines, penalties, seizures, "forfeitures" and other means of confiscation.

- Government will destroy certain goods in order to try to keep their prices from falling.

- Opposition to socialism will become more vigorous.

- The Right will rise in power and become more extreme.

- Libertarianism will expand in influence and popularity.

- Nations will tend away from liberal, representative governments and toward dictatorships.

- Possession and sale of recreational drugs will be further decriminalized.

- Government will ration goods and services in which it is, or has become, involved (such as gasoline, vaccines, medical care, electricity, water, food, etc.).

- International travel will be restricted, whether by statute or dangerous conditions.

- The U.S. and state governments will finish their takeover and demolition of the medical industry.

- If I'm wrong about that, the medical industry will be freed (a smaller chance).

- Government will reduce its programs for free food, free medicine, free cell phones, housing subsidies, education subsidies, corporate subsidies, retirement benefits, etc.

- One or more third parties will gain political clout and win local elections and perhaps a state election or two.

- At least one of the two major parties will disappear or re-form.

- Cyber attacks will become major tools of terror and/or war.

- Security will become a primary concern of people and governments.

- People will blame government more than business for the downturn.

- Governments of currently democratic countries will turn their militaries against their own citizens.

Other Social Trends

- Social groups, including ethnic, racial, economic, political, religious, gender and class, will polarize, both internally and with respect to opposing groups.

- Suspicion and hatred of foreigners will increase around the globe.

- Public demonstrations will increase in frequency.

- Public demonstrations will increase in size.

- Some public demonstrations will be violent.

- Governments will clash violently with citizens.

- The birth rate will continue to fall in the U.S. and Europe until after the bear market ends.

- Belief in magic will increase.

- Science will be turned to malevolent purposes.

- Epidemics will increase in number and severity.

- Films will break new ground in horror.

- Disney's family-fare feature cartoons will fall in popularity, and the studio will stop making them.

- Professional baseball will suffer a major setback in attendance, viewership, income and salaries.

- Professional basketball will suffer a major setback in attendance, viewership, income and salaries.

- Professional sports leagues will split, restructure and/or encounter new competitors.

- New record performances in sports by individuals will become rarer during the bear market.
- No team will have a "dynasty" during the bear market.
- New brutal, violent sports will be introduced and gain popularity.
- Physical fitness ("working out") will go out of style.
- Conspiracy theories will become more plentiful, and more people will believe them.
- People will rate "the future" as unhopeful.
- The suicide rate will go up.
- Hemlines will fall.
- Music sales will slump.
- Popular music will become somber, atonal, noisy and/or angry.
- Hedonism will flourish.
- Pornography will become more bizarre.
- Mainstream behavior will become more conservative.
- New religious sects will form.
- Current religious denominations will splinter.
- College attendance will fall off.
- College tuitions will fall, a lot.
- Popular self-help books will change focus from wealth and self-improvement to surviving hard times and beating adversaries.
- Escapist communities will be established.
- Food scares will increase.
- There will be shortages of necessities.
- The number of Broadway shows will fall dramatically.
- Interest in producing the plays of Shakespeare will wane.

- Anti-gay, racist and/or xenophobic entities will organize and openly pursue their agendas.
- Areas of cities will become dangerous places in which street gangs "rule" some neighborhoods.
- Luxury will go out of fashion.
- Well-off people will adopt fashions that conceal rather than accentuate their wealth.
- Lines on automobile bodies will become rounder and less angular.
- Black, brown and grey will replace bright colors in clothing, cars and art.
- Entertainment media will feature nastier, uglier and more horrible characters and story lines.
- The Olympic Games will be cancelled at least once if not terminated altogether.
- Many amusement parks will close.
- The number of coffee shops in the United States will decline substantially.
- Per capita consumption of alcohol and other depressants will increase.
- Public art, such as sculptures and murals, will become ponderous and ugly.
- One or more of the sciences will go through a "paradigm shift."
- Terrible secret activities will take place, some to be revealed only years or decades later.

With crisis comes opportunity. When you see many of these expectations manifested, it will be time to buy financial assets again. If you've implemented the strategies in this book, you'll be one of the few who can do so.

UPDATED LISTS FOR SERVICES DESIGNED TO HELP YOU SURVIVE AND PROSPER IN THE DEFLATIONARY DEPRESSION

Suitability and Risk

Many of the services listed in this book are suitable for all investors. Some are suited only for those of a certain level of expertise, wealth and/or income. In pursuing your chain of inquiries, you may occasionally discover some financial services that are unavailable to certain investors who fail to meet legal and financial criteria required by their nations' Accredited, Qualified and/or Professional Investor rules. These rules may prohibit your access to services that authorities deem to be unsuitable for you. Entities that need to comply with such rules should be able to explain which rules, if any, pertain to you. As you explore and judge various courses of action, please forgive any entities that refuse to fulfill your desires because they are following legal requirements. I have endeavored to provide enough avenues of inquiry in this book so that readers at all strata of wealth — small to large — will find methods for protecting their capital in times of deflation and depression.

We have positive information and impressions about the service providers listed in this book and believe them to have integrity. Nevertheless, I cannot endorse or guarantee other people's products or services. Therefore, it is imperative that each reader do his own proper investigation regarding suitability. I have experience with many of these service providers or know their principals personally. You will probably get even better service if you mention that you read about them in this book.

Changes to Recommended Services

Some aspects of our recommended services have changed since 2002:

Chapter 19 of *Conquer the Crash* recommended only three financial rating services. The second edition added a fourth. Observe that the biggest, best-known and most widely followed rating services, which had long been sanctioned by government regulators, are *not* among them. The ratings posted by these firms blew up in 2008-2009, crushing the finances of the people who relied on them. Generally speaking, it pays to deal with independent judges who have no obligation to those they judge and no special privileges granted by government.

Federated Investors, Inc. has bought the Prudent Bear Fund. Whether the fund will continue to behave as it did in the past is uncertain. I have kept it on our Recommended Services list, but do your own due diligence.

Asset Allocation Consultants, listed in the original edition, now provides services to Access Fund Management, a discussion of whose services appeared in Chapter 20 of a later printing of the book and is maintained in this edition. Although I think this service is well thought out, I now decline to include it in our Recommended Services list due to the myriad systemic risks that could affect a structure involving multiple managers, brokers, banks and an insurer to boot, all based in the U.S., especially now that we face the worst of the crisis.

The "beta slippage" described in Chapter 20 for the inverse ("bear") index funds—as with index-tracking inverse ETFs as well—has proved to be a bigger issue than most people, including the fund managers themselves, expected. These funds track the market exceptionally well day by day but not over the long term, especially in choppy and volatile markets. They are therefore unsuited for long term investors. At the same time, the index funds impose difficult time constraints on short-term traders, who would have far more flexibility using futures contracts. Sometimes inverse index funds offer the only available option, for example if one's retirement plan prohibits short sales. But this is why in Chapter 23 I recommended getting out of controlled structures. I have omitted these inverse index funds from the Recommended Services list, but the information remains in Chapter 20. For a good explanation of the slippage problem, see http://www.altenergystocks.com/archives/2009/02/ultrapromises_fall_short.html.

I have also added GoldMoney to the recommended list. GoldMoney stores customers' gold, silver, platinum and palladium in fully insured vaults in London, Zurich, Hong Kong, Singapore and Toronto. External auditors ensure that the company has the metal that it credits to you. GoldMoney never lends, which means that, unlike a bank, it can never become a participant in a credit bubble and thereby subject to a bust. An account with GoldMoney is not the same as having physical metal in your hands. But that is both a drawback and an advantage. If you have to leave your jurisdiction someday due to political unrest, you won't have to figure out how to get your gold out, too. All you have to do is remember your account number. And if you do wish to hold physical gold, GoldMoney will ship your gold in bar form to virtually any requested location.

GoldMoney advertises with EWI, and when I told the firm that I was going to recommend their services, they decided to arrange a special deal for you. If you open an account, you can receive six months of free gold storage to kick off your relationship with them. This offer may end or change; go to www.elliottwave. com/GoldMoneyCTC to learn more. Be aware that, as for all institutions, adverse events such as political aggression could endanger the company or its holdings. Make sure you satisfy yourself that opening a holding is the right thing to do. For more information about GoldMoney, see the contact information in the Recommended Services list.

For this edition, I have omitted the list of active money managers added to the 2nd edition but kept the list of safety-minded money managers. In the coming environment, safety will dwarf all other concerns. I have also declined to update the lists of safest large banks and insurance companies. None of these banks qualifies for the highest safety rating, and absent bailouts they seem to be the most vulnerable to going bust. Also, in my judgment, there will be no safe insurance companies in wave c down.

Finally, it seems to be good idea to invest in something the government has only begun offering this year: 2-year U.S. Floating Rate Notes (FRNs). The interest rate paid on FRNs is pegged to the 13-week T-bill and adjusts quarterly to the auction rate. You can learn more about FRNs by going to the Treasury's website at www.TreasuryDirect.gov and typing "FRN" into the search window.

Naturally, anything pegged to T-bills is the last item on investors' buy list. In 1980-1982, T-bills were #1 on their buy list, and that's just when they should have held zero T-bills, because in fact it was time to own stocks and bonds. Now stocks and bonds are tops on investors' buy list, but they should be holding zero stocks and bonds, because it's time to own the safest investments available.

The main reason to hold short term bills instead of bonds is to escape the risk of losing principal and to increase the probability of a big gain. If interest rates soar, bond investors will lose a lot of money, and with long rates two years ago at their lowest levels in the history of the republic, the risk of getting killed in bonds is inordinately high. In contrast, if rates rise, yields on rolled-over short-term bills will follow rates upward, paying out more and more interest.

Rates on most corporate and municipal bonds will almost certainly rise in coming years due to fears of default. T-bills and FRNs, on the other hand, may be perceived as a refuge for safety, so their rates may or may not rise. With short rates essentially at zero, the lowest level ever, there seems little chance of losing principal in an FRN. Rates have never fallen below zero (although that could change), and if inflation rages—contrary to my expectations—rates should rise to compensate. That's a lot to like.

With FRNs, we avoid the hassle of rolling over T-bills. More important, there will probably be a shortage of T-bills when the panic hits, just as there was a shortage of Swiss Money Market

Claims in 2008. Investors were turned away, and their nearest option was Eurodollar debts, which were not nearly as safe. Owners of FRNs cannot be turned away during the two-year duration of the notes.

Like any other Treasury security, you can buy or sell these notes in the open market, so you don't have to wait until the next auction to buy or until they mature to cash out. Also, interest earned is untaxable at the state and local level. Your bank or broker can buy FRNs, or you can buy them through Treasury Direct.

Treasury-Only Money Market Funds
(updating the list from Chapter 18)

In 2008-2009, banks came under pressure of insolvency, just as *Conquer the Crash* predicted. Quite a few closed. In the next phase of the depression, bank runs and mass closings are highly probable. A better alternative for capital protection is money market funds that invest only in short-term Treasuries. You can even write checks against these accounts, which could be a handy service if banks close. For a review of how T-bill money-market funds work, see Chapter 18.

When I wrote *Conquer the Crash*, Vanguard's Treasury-only Admiral fund was the best bargain available. Now Vanguard accepts no new investors in either of its Treasury-only funds. As I warned in Chapter 19, you have to act while you can. Readers of the original book secured their accounts when they were available.

The update to Table 18-1 lists the two sizeable, still-available funds that hold no mortgages, asset-backed "securities," corporate debt, municipal bonds or anything aside from Treasuries. To the best of my knowledge, these are the only major money market funds that have committed to invest primarily in short-term Treasury debt and which still accept new depositors. New York Mellon Bank owns Dreyfus, which could prove problematic. American

STILL-AVAILABLE TREASURY-ONLY MONEY MARKET FUNDS WITH NO TRANSACTION CHARGES OR LIMITS		
Fund Name	**Toll-Free No.**	**Web Address**
American Century Capital Presv Fund I	(800) 345-2021	www.americancentury.com
Dreyfus 100% US Treasury MMF	(800) 782-6620	www.dreyfus.com

updating Table 18-1

Century is independent. Fund policies change over time, so be sure that you completely understand a fund's investment strategy and prospectus before committing any money.

Highest-Rated Banks in America by State, per Veribanc.com (updating the list from Chapter 19)

In 2002, *Conquer the Crash* noted that depositors would soon become concerned about bank risks and move their money from weak banks to strong banks, making the weak banks weaker and the strong banks stronger. This happened in 2008-9. A Washington Post article noted that one of the banks listed in CTC has received a windfall from migratory deposits. When the next wave of problems hits, the shift will be even more pronounced.

Nevertheless, do not assume that once you find a relatively safe bank you can simply move all of your funds to it and sleep soundly. The entire U.S. banking system faces problems. Many U.S. banks are at risk, some in ways that even the best ratings firms may be unable to recognize or track. To illustrate the problem, consider that Lehman Brothers Commercial Bank was rated B+ on a list dated 6/30/08 from one of our recommended rating services. Just a few months after that list was published, Lehman filed for bankruptcy.

Because of such uncertainty, banks in general are not the safest place to put the bulk of your money right now. Some smaller U.S. banks have been better at staying out of trouble, but the safest banks, by far, reside in Switzerland. Readers with substantial capital should place a comfortable amount of it in the safest institutions there, per the leads in Chapter 19. Those of lesser means who must bank in risky systems in their home territory should keep, even in relatively strong local banks, only enough money on deposit to cover living expenses and whatever additional funds you trust the bank to hold. Keep a comfortable amount of cash currency safely stored in case your bank shuts down. Also keep some non-numismatic gold and silver coins. Place a substantial portion of your liquid wealth in safe cash equivalents such as directly-held Floating-Rate Notes (FRNs), T-bills and Treasury-only money market funds on which you can write checks. Diversify into the currencies and short-term debt of the governments of Switzerland, Singapore and New Zealand, per our Stable Currency Index (stablecurrencyindex.com).

The longer a bank stays on the top-rated list, the more it implies a consistent policy of relative safety. I suggest you compare this list with that in Chapter 19 to see which banks have maintained a consistent safety rating over this time.

Quarterly ratings are reported with a four-month time lag. As with all the lists in this Section, the ratings reported in the update to Table 19-1 are the latest available. They carry through the first quarter of 2014, at a time when bank pressures are low. Although this list is a valuable resource, be advised that I cannot be held responsible for the ratings accuracy of an outside service. I encourage you to research financial firms carefully on your own before committing funds. The next wave down should be severe, so keep an eye on updated ratings from our recommended ratings firms.

Note: The following lists are updated with information available through March 2014. For periodic updates to these lists, visit www. conquerthecrash.com/readerspage. For more comprehensive reports, contact Veribanc.com.

THE TWO HIGHEST-RATED BANKS IN EACH STATE

Source: VERIBANC RATINGS for the Quarter Ending 03/31/2014. Ratings are effective 07/07/2014.

All banks listed are rated GREEN /***, VERIBANC's highest rating.

BB = The bank has been designated as a Blue Ribbon Bank continuously for at least eight consecutive quarters.

B = The bank has been designated as a Blue Ribbon Bank for 1 - 7 consecutive quarters.

Name	City	Assets $000	Blue Ribbon Rating
Alabama			
SERVISFIRST BK	BIRMINGHAM	3,572,232	B
BRYANT BK	TUSCALOOSA	1,224,859	BB
Alaska			
FIRST NB ALASKA	ANCHORAGE	3,204,443	BB
NORTHRIM BK	ANCHORAGE	1,189,429	BB
Arizona			
NATIONAL BK OF AZ	TUCSON	4,748,697	B
1ST BK YUMA	YUMA	223,287	B
Arkansas			
CENTENNIAL BK	CONWAY	6,779,811	B
BANK OF THE OZARKS	LITTLE ROCK	5,023,293	B
California			
BANK OF THE WEST	SAN FRANCISCO	67,725,004	B
CITY NB	BEVERLY HILLS	29,491,283	BB
Colorado			
FIRSTBANK	LAKEWOOD	13,979,963	BB
COBIZ BK	DENVER	2,818,763	BB
Connecticut			
WEBSTER BK NA	WATERBURY	21,152,991	BB
ROCKVILLE BK	ROCKVILLE	2,373,322	B
Delaware			
WILMINGTON SAVINGS FUND SOCIETY	WILMINGTON	4,541,673	BB
WILMINGTON TR NA	WILMINGTON	2,587,521	BB
District of Columbia			
NATIONAL CAPITAL BK OF WA	WASHINGTON	430,507	B
BK OF GEORGETOWN	WASHINGTON	983,475	
Florida			
BANKUNITED NA	MIAMI LAKES	15,602,915	BB
MERCANTIL COMMERCEBANK NA	CORAL GABLES	6,899,280	B
Georgia			
UNITED CMNTY BK	BLAIRSVILLE	7,376,836	B
COMMUNITY & SOUTHERN BK	ATLANTA	2,814,342	B
Hawaii			
FIRST HAWAIIAN BK	HONOLULU	17,252,217	BB
CENTRAL PACIFIC BK	HONOLULU	4,803,523	B
Idaho			
HOME FED BK	NAMPA	940,280	B
PANHANDLE ST BK	SANDPOINT	907,850	BB
Illinois			
PRIVATEBANK & TC	CHICAGO	14,277,119	B
MB FNCL BK NA	CHICAGO	9,418,572	B
Indiana			
OLD NB	EVANSVILLE	9,399,241	B
FIRST MRCH BK NA	MUNCIE	5,430,423	BB
Iowa			
BANKERS TC	DES MOINES	2,965,526	BB
HILLS B&TC	HILLS	2,234,279	B

updates Table 19-1

Kansas			
CAPITOL FEDERAL SAVINGS BANK	TOPEKA	9,131,895	BB
SUNFLOWER BK NA	SALINA	1,682,809	BB
Kentucky			
STOCK YARDS B&TC	LOUISVILLE	2,349,938	BB
BANK OF KY	CRESTVIEW HILLS	1,858,292	BB
Louisiana			
IBERIABANK	LAFAYETTE	13,492,033	BB
FIRST NBC BK	NEW ORLEANS	3,476,950	BB
Maine			
BANGOR SVG BK	BANGOR	3,040,957	B
CAMDEN NB	CAMDEN	2,618,958	B
Maryland			
SANDY SPRING BK	OLNEY	4,166,832	BB
COLUMBIA BK	COLUMBIA	1,995,535	BB
Massachusetts			
EASTERN BK	BOSTON	8,683,723	BB
BOSTON PRIVATE B&TC	BOSTON	6,526,268	BB
Michigan			
CHEMICAL BK	MIDLAND	6,329,777	B
ISABELLA BK	MOUNT PLEASANT	1,454,929	BB
Minnesota			
BREMER BK NA	SOUTH SAINT PAUL	2,863,486	BB
KLEINBANK	BIG LAKE	1,571,496	B
Mississippi			
BANCORPSOUTH BK	TUPELO	13,136,461	B
TRUSTMARK NB	JACKSON	12,053,867	BB
Missouri			
COMMERCE BK	KANSAS CITY	22,692,707	BB
NBH BK NA	KANSAS CITY	4,889,407	B
Montana			
GLACIER BK	KALISPELL	7,812,597	B
FIRST INTRST BK	BILLINGS	7,588,184	B
Nebraska			
PINNACLE BK	LINCOLN	3,846,364	B
CORNERSTONE BK	YORK	1,244,953	BB
Nevada			
NEVADA B&TC	CALIENTE	108,794	BB
FIRST NB	ELY	86,664	BB
New Hampshire			
BANK OF NH	LACONIA	1,180,448	BB
NORTHWAY BK	BERLIN	915,993	B
New Jersey			
COLUMBIA BANK	FAIR LAWN	4,567,449	B
FULTON BK OF NJ	MOUNT LAUREL	3,374,584	B
New Mexico			
VECTRA BK COLORADO NA	FARMINGTON	2,606,013	B
FIRST AMER BK	ARTESIA	883,624	BB
New York			
MANUFACTURERS & TRADERS TC	BUFFALO	87,754,113	BB
FIRST NIAGARA BK NA	BUFFALO	37,930,363	B
North Carolina			
FIRST-CITIZENS B&TC	RALEIGH	21,848,242	B
SQUARE 1 BK	DURHAM	2,467,574	BB
North Dakota			
BREMER BK NA	FARGO	1,649,577	BB
ALERUS FNCL NA	GRAND FORKS	1,364,396	BB

updates Table 19-1

Ohio			
HUNTINGTON NB	COLUMBUS	60,961,626	BB
FIRSTMERIT BK NA	AKRON	24,476,230	BB
Oklahoma			
BANCFIRST	OKLAHOMA CITY	6,355,002	BB
FIRST UNITED B&TC	DURANT	2,434,186	B
Oregon			
UMPQUA BK	ROSEBURG	11,830,061	BB
PACIFIC CONTINENTAL BK	EUGENE	1,472,171	BB
Pennsylvania			
CITIZENS BK OF PA	PHILADELPHIA	32,470,102	B
SUSQUEHANNA BK	LITITZ	18,350,567	BB
Puerto Rico			
BANCO POPULAR DE PR	SAN JUAN	27,400,000	
BANCO SANTANDER PR	SAN JUAN	6,373,084	
Rhode Island			
BANK RHODE ISLAND	PROVIDENCE	1,827,271	BB
CENTREVILLE SVG BK	WEST WARWICK	981,967	BB
South Carolina			
FIRST CITIZENS B&T CO	COLUMBIA	8,463,317	B
SCBT	COLUMBIA	7,994,908	B
South Dakota			
GREAT WESTERN BK	SIOUX FALLS	9,270,904	BB
DACOTAH BK	ABERDEEN	2,069,368	B
Tennessee			
PINNACLE BK	NASHVILLE	5,581,997	BB
FIRST BK	LEXINGTON	2,323,931	B
Texas			
COMERICA BK	DALLAS	65,686,755	BB
FROST BK	SAN ANTONIO	24,704,768	BB
Utah			
ZIONS FIRST NB	SALT LAKE CITY	18,789,115	B
BANK OF AMER FORK	AMERICAN FORK	1,048,546	B
Vermont			
MERCHANTS BK	SOUTH BURLINGTON	1,665,929	BB
NORTHFIELD SVG BK	NORTHFIELD	762,282	BB
Virginia			
UNITED BK	FAIRFAX	6,893,802	BB
CARTER BK & TR	MARTINSVILLE	4,626,690	BB
Washington			
STERLING SVG BK	SPOKANE	10,214,194	B
COLUMBIA ST BK	TACOMA	7,232,297	BB
West Virginia			
WESBANCO BK	WHEELING	6,226,713	BB
PUTNAM CTY BK	HURRICANE	635,158	B
Wisconsin			
JOHNSON BK	RACINE	3,894,516	B
BANK MUTUAL	MILWAUKEE	2,318,302	B
Wyoming			
PINNACLE BK WY	TORRINGTON	666,391	B
FIRST NB OF GILLETTE	GILLETTE	540,804	BB

updates Table 19-1

NOTE: *Contact information can change. If in doubt, check the web.*

RECOMMENDED SERVICES

Consultants on the World's Safest Banks and Storage Facilities

SafeWealth Consultants Ltd.
Email: clientservices@safewealthconsultants.com
Address: Service Center, Grand-Rue 114, 2nd Level East,
        CH-1820 Montreux, Switzerland
Phone: (U.S. dial 011) 41-21-966-7200
Fax: (U.S. dial 011) 41-21-966-7201
Contact: Sr. Vice President Cari Lima

SafeWealth Report: Complimentary upon request

Qualified institutions' typical minimums:
        Banks: 1m. CHF
        Gold acquisition and/or storage: $100,000
        Silver, platinum, palladium: $200,000
        Currency cash notes: 250,000 units
        External asset managers: 3m. CHF

Managed Bear Funds

Comstock Capital Value Fund
Website: www.comstockfunds.com
Email: info@comstockfunds.com
Address: 24 S Main Street, Yardley PA 19067
Phone: 215-493-7076
Fax: 215-493-8083
Minimum: $1000 or $250 in an IRA
Managers: Charles Minter and Martin Weiner

Federated Prudent Bear Fund
Website: www.federatedinvestors.com
Address: P.O. Box 8600, Boston, MA 02266
Phone: 800-245-4770
Minimum: $1500
Manager: Douglas Noland

GAMCO Mathers Fund
Website: www.gabelli.com
Address: One Corporate Center, Rye NY 10580
Phone: 800-422-3554
Minimum: $1000
Manager: Henry van der Eb

Money Managers with a Safety Orientation

Hillier Advisors, LLC
Email: jamie@hillieradvisors.com
Address: 6035 SW 54th Steet, Suite 101, Ocala, FL 34474
Phone: 352-694-3622
Fax: 352-687-2846
Minimum: $2 million
Contact: Jamie Zink

Lang Asset Management, Inc.
Website: www.langasset.com
Email: investments@langasset.com
Address: 5605 Glenridge Dr., Suite 1080
        Atlanta, GA 30342
Phone: 800-732-4171 and 404-256-4100
Fax 404-256-1473
Minimum: $200,000
CEO: Robert B. Lang

Newsletters for Staying Globally Informed

Casey's International Speculator
Website: www.caseyresearch.com
Email: info@caseyresearch.com
Address: P.O. Box 1427, Stowe, VT 05672
Phone: 888-512-2739/602-445-2736
Editor: Louis James

The Gloom, Boom & Doom Report
Website: www.gloomboomdoom.com
Email: info@gloomboomdoom.com
Address: Suite 801, The Workstation,
            43 Lyndhurst Terrace, Central, Hong Kong
Phone: (U.S. dial 011) 852-2-801-5410
Fax: 852-2-845-9192
Editor: Marc Faber

Grant's Interest Rate Observer
Website: www.grantspub.com
Email: webmaster@grantspub.com
Address: 2 Wall Street, Suite 603,
            New York, NY 10005
Phone: 212-809-7994
Fax: 212-809-8492
Editor: James Grant

Economic Winter
Website: www.longwavegroup.com
Email: info@longwavegroup.com
Longwave Group
Address: Long Wave Analytics
            202-15388 24th Ave, South Surrey, BC
            Canada V4A 2J2
Phone: 778-294-4286
Editor: Christopher Funston

Rosen Numismatic Advisory
Email: mauricerosen@aol.com
Numismatic Counseling, Inc.,
Address: P.O. Box 38, Plainview, NY 11803
Phone: 516-433-5800
Fax: 516-433-5801
President: Maurice Rosen

Safe Money
Website: www.moneyandmarkets.com
Address: Weiss Research Inc.
15430 Endeavor Drive, Jupiter, FL 33478
Phone: 800-291-8545 and 561-627-3300
Fax: 561-625-6685
Editor: Mike Larson
Contributing Editor: Dr. Martin D. Weiss

U.S. & World Early Warning Report
Website: www.chaostan.com
Email: service@earlywarningreport.com
Address: P.O. Box 84908, Phoenix, AZ 85701
Phone: 800-509-5400 and 602-870-9329
Fax: 602-943-2363
Editor: Richard Maybury

Physical Safety

This is a diverse field. See Chapters 26 and 28 for leads.

Real Money (Gold, Silver, Platinum) Account

GoldMoney
Website: www.goldmoney.com
Address: Net Transactions Limited, 1st Floor,
32 Commercial Street, St. Helier

Jersey, JE2 3RU, British Channel Islands
Phone: (U.S. & Canada) 855-583-4653
          (UK & International) 44-1543-633-900
Fax: (U.S. dial 011) 44-1534-633-901
Director: Geoff Turk

Safety Ratings for U.S. Banks and Insurance Companies

for institutions only:
Egan-Jones Ratings Company
Website: www.egan-jones.com
President: Sean J. Egan

IDC Financial Publishing, Inc.
Website: www.idcfp.com
Email: info@idcfp.com
Address: P.O. Box 140, Hartland, WI 53029
Phone: 800-525-5457 and 262-367-7231
Fax: 262-367-6497

Weiss Ratings, LLC
Website: www.weissratings.com
Address: 15430 Endeavour Dr., Jupiter FL 33478
Phone: 877-934-7778
Fax: 561-277-2576

Veribanc, Inc.
Website: www.veribanc.com
Email: service@veribanc.com
Address: P.O. Box 608, Greenville, RI 02828
Phone: 800-837-4226
Fax: 401-531-2290

U.S. Gold, Silver and Coin Dealers

American Federal Rare Coin & Bullion, Inc.
Website: www.americanfederal.com
Address: PO Box 5810, Carefree, AZ 85377-5810
Phone: 800-221-7694 or 480-553-5282
Fax: 480-553-5290
President: Nick Grovich

FideliTrade, Inc.
Website: www.fidelitrade.com
Email: info@fidelitrade.com
Address: 3601 North Market Street, Wilmington,
        DE 19802
Phone: 800-223-1080 and 302-762-6200
Fax: 302-762-2902
President/CEO: Jonathan Potts

Hancock & Harwell
Website: www.raregold.com
Address: Suite 310, 3155 Roswell Rd,
        Atlanta, GA 30305
Phone: 404-261-6565
Fax: 404-237-6500
President: Robert L. Harwell

Investment Rarities, Inc.
Website: www.investmentrarities.com
Email: contact@investmentrarities.com
Address: 7850 Metro Parkway,
        Bloomington, MN 55425
Phone: 952-853-0700
President: James R. Cook

Miles Franklin Ltd.
Website: www.milesfranklin.com
Email address: andy@milesfranklin.com

Address: 801 Twelve Oaks Center Drive, Ste 834
            Wayzata, MN 55391
Phone: 800-822-8080 and 952-929-7006
Fax: 952-476-7971
President: Andrew Schectman

Straight Talk Assets, Inc.
Website: www.coinmoney.com
Email: straighttalk@mindspring.com
Address: P.O. Box 1301, Gainesville, GA 30503
Phone: 800-944-9249 and 770-536-8045
Owner: Glenn R. Fried

Watching the Fed

Federal Reserve Board
Website: www.federalreserve.gov
Phone: 202-452-3000

Ludwig von Mises Institute
Website: www.mises.org
Email: contact@mises.org
Address: 518 West Magnolia Avenue,
            Auburn, AL 36832
Phone: 334-321-2100
Fax: 334-321-2119
Book catalog: www.mises.org/store/Books-C1.aspx

The Money Market Observer
Website: www.wrightson.com
Email: sales@wrightson.com
Wrightson ICAP, LLC
Address: Harborside Financial Center, Plaza V
            Jersey City, NJ 07311
Phone: 212-815-6540
Fax: 212-341-9103
Chief Economist: Lou Crandall

TrimTabs Investment Research
Website: www.trimtabs.com
Address: 2320 Marinship Way, Suite 120,
         Sausalito, CA 94965
Phone: 415-324-5873
Chairman/Portfolio Manager: Charles Biderman

Wave Analysis and Economic Forecasting

Elliott Wave International, Inc.
Website: www.elliottwave.com
Email: customercare@elliottwave.com
Address: P.O. Box 1618, Gainesville, GA 30503
Phone: 800-336-1618 and 770-536-0309
Fax: 770-536-2514
Paid services: Financial periodicals, global market
     coverage, opportunity alerts, intraday market
     forecasts, books, online courses
Free services: EWI Independent, Weekly Select,
     Club EWI
Free for readers of this book: Special offers and free
     updates on services designed to protect you and
     your finances: www.conquerthecrash.com/readerspage
Related websites:
     www.robertprechter.com
     www.socionomics.net
CEO: Robert R. Prechter, Jr.

48251787R00233

Made in the USA
Charleston, SC
30 October 2015